Caring for Infants and Toddlers

A Supervised, Self-Instructional Training Program

Volume II

Diane Trister Dodge
Amy Laura Dombro
Derry Gosselin Koralek

Teaching Strategies, Inc.
Washington, DC

Updates to Module 13 (Professionalism) © 2003

Teaching Strategies, Inc.
P.O. Box 42243
Washington, DC 20015
ISBN 1-879537-02-8
LCCN 91-65115

Teaching Strategies and *The Creative Curriculum* names and logos are registered
trademarks of Teaching Strategies, Inc., Washington, DC.

Printed and bound in the United States of America
Sixth Printing: 2003

Contents

Module 7
Creative

What Is Creativity and Why Is It Important?

Creativity is a way of experiencing the world. Creative people are innovative and resourceful. They can take an idea, a plan, or an object and adapt it to make something new. Although some people are more creative than others, everyone has creative abilities that they use on the job and at home. Artists, musicians, architects, and writers are all creative people—but so are cooks, secretaries, lawyers, plumbers, and caregivers. You don't have to be able to paint a picture or write a book to be creative. Thinking of new ways to help children learn self-help skills, making up a song to sing when you are changing an infant, or rearranging your room to create a cozy reading area are all examples of creativity. Being creative is really an attitude, a state of mind.

Children are eager learners, naturally imaginative and creative. They learn by doing as they interact with people and things in their environment. Children are curious about how things work and why things happen as they do. They naturally see more than one possibility for how a toy can be explored or an art material used. In a supportive environment they feel good about their efforts and accomplishments.

Infants learn about the world primarily through their senses. Everything is new to them, and they want to explore everything around them. Martha (5 months) reaches for a mobile because she sees it hanging over her crib. Her exploration leads her to discover that when she hits the mobile, it moves. This exploration is the beginning of creativity. By providing infants with many opportunities to use their senses and explore the world, caregivers can promote creativity.

As toddlers develop their motor and language skills, they can play with a wider variety of materials than they could when they were infants. They begin learning how to play with each other, and they make use of materials in many inventive ways. When caregivers encourage toddlers to be creative thinkers and offer them an interesting and stimulating environment, their creativity continues to grow. Their ideas may not always work and their answers may not always be "right," but when toddlers feel that their ideas and plans are appreciated and valued, they feel good about themselves and their abilities.

The relationships between children and caregivers set the stage for creativity. When young children develop a sense of trust and feel secure with their caregivers, they feel free to express themselves and to explore. Caregivers can support the creativity of infants and toddlers as they plan the day and set up the environment. A schedule that allows children plenty of time to explore and play at their own pace, and an environment that includes interesting materials and activities, are both effective means of supporting children's creativity.

Caregivers promote infants' and toddlers' creativity by:

- arranging the learning environment to support creativity;

- offering a variety of activities and experiences to promote creativity; and

- interacting with infants and toddlers in ways that encourage creative expression.

Listed below are examples of how caregivers demonstrate their competence in promoting children's creativity.

Arranging the Learning Environment to Support Creativity

Here are some examples of what caregivers can do.

- Make changes in the learning environment to highlight sensory experiences. "William, crawling on that butcher paper makes such a lovely noise. It makes me laugh. Oh, it makes you laugh, too, doesn't it?"

- Encourage young children's exploration of sounds. "I hear that gurgling you're making in your throat, Stephanie. It makes me think of a little bird song."

- Arrange the indoor and outdoor environment so children can move freely, work alone, or work in small groups. "Marybeth and Tyesha, would you like to use the funnels at the water play table? It's such a beautiful day, we could set up the table outside."

- Hang interesting and beautiful pictures and objects at a child's height on the wall. Invite children, beginning in infancy, to explore and enjoy the world around them. "Lamont, I put a new picture of a cow on the wall. Would you like to come over and see it?"

- Introduce a variety of materials and props, including some from the children's own cultures. "Sari, your mom brought us some magazines from India, where she was born. We can use them to make a picture book."

Offering a Variety of Activities and Experiences to Promote Creativity

Here are some examples of what caregivers can do.

- Include a variety of music activities in the daily schedule. "Kim, shall we sing a song to your baby to help her fall asleep?"

- Play make-believe games with children. "Thank you, grocery shoppers, for bringing me an apple. You must have known I was getting hungry."

- Use descriptive language as you talk with even the youngest infants. "Close your eyes. I'm going to pull your green fluffy sweater over your head now."

- Call attention to sensory aspects of daily routines. "See how the soapsuds squish between your fingers while you wash your hands?"

- Include movement and dance activities in the daily schedule. "Let's curl up as small as we can. Now, let's stretch as big as we can."

- Provide materials that children can use in their own ways, such as blocks, finger paint, dough, clay, or water. "Jacci, you are poking the playdough with your finger. Colin, you are squeezing the dough in your hand."

Interacting with Infants and Toddlers in Ways That Encourage Creative Expression

Here are some examples of what caregivers can do.

- Share your interest in and appreciation of infants' sensory explorations. "Anna, it sounds like you're making music when you slap the floor like that." "Leslie, the way you're playing with your cereal makes me think you're ready to finger paint."

- Accept and value each child's creative expression. "Maya, would you like me to take a picture of your dress-up outfit so your whole family can see what you looked like?"

- With an infant in your arms, sing a song, smile, and make eye contact, encouraging the infant to join in with her sounds. "Fa, la, la, la, la...Cheryl, some day you may be singing in the choir!"

- Give children positive feedback about their creative thinking. "Al, you made a great hat out of that bowl."

- Ask questions that encourage creative thinking. "Raoul, what can you do to get the ball out from under the bushes?"

- Share your enjoyment of language. Introduce children to fun and interesting words. "Betty, would you like to help me water our chrysanthemum?"

- Model creative thinking. "I'm thinking about what we should make for snack today. What do you think, Jamal?"

- Show your respect for children's creativity by not interrupting them. "Ms. Gonzalez, Henry is busy crawling back and forth through the tunnel. I'll wait until he is finished before changing his diaper."

Promoting Children's Creativity

In the following situations, caregivers are promoting children's creativity. As you read, think about what the caregivers are doing and why. Then answer the questions that follow.

Arranging the Learning Environment to Support Creativity

Ms. Bates has made a new mobile for the infant room. It has a set of spoons attached to a brightly colored ribbon. She hangs the mobile from a cubby so that the infants lying on their backs can bat it with their hands. Ms. Bates watches Jenny (6 months) hit the mobile. "Listen, Jenny, the spoons rattle when you touch them," she says. Jenny smiles and hits the mobile again. Later, Ms. Bates positions the mobile so the infants can hit it with their feet. At the same time she places a toy made from another set of spoons attached to ribbons on the floor for David (8 months) to explore. "See the spoons?" she says to David. "Da, da," says David as he bangs the spoons on the floor. "The spoons make music, David," says Ms. Bates.

1. How did Ms. Bates arrange the environment to promote creativity?

_____

_____

_____

_____

2. What do you think the infants will do with the spoons on the floor?

_____

_____

_____

_____

Offering a Variety of Activities and Experiences to Promote Creativity

Mr. Jones is making playdough with a small group of toddlers. Emily (32 months) picks up some flour and rubs it on her hands. "How does that flour feel?" he asks. "Soft," she says as she smiles proudly and pours the flour in the bowl. Maggie (30 months) adds the water. "Woosh," she says, imitating its sound. Tomas (34 months) spills the salt as he begins to pour it. There is a look of concern on his face. "Don't worry," says Mr. Jones. "I have an idea. I'll hold the bowl and you can sweep the salt into it." As they stir the ingredients together, Maggie and Emily use a spoon. Tomas says, "I can stir with my hands." "There are many ways to stir," says Mr. Jones. "I think our playdough is ready."

1. Why are cooking activities such as making playdough good opportunities to promote creativity?

_____

_____

_____

_____

2. How did Mr. Jones support creative thinking?

_____

_____

_____

_____

Interacting with Infants and Toddlers in Ways That Encourage Creative Expression

Ms. Gonzalez notices that Tara (12 months) needs to have her diaper changed. She picks up Tara and carries her to the changing table. On the way, Ms. Gonzalez sways back and forth, singing a song. "Tara needs her diaper changed, diaper changed, diaper changed." Tara laughs. She likes to hear her name and sway back and forth as Ms. Gonzalez sings the "Tara" song. When they get to the changing table, Ms. Gonzalez tells Tara that she is going to lay her down. Tara wiggles and kicks her legs. Ms. Gonzalez sings her song again, adding new verses. "First we pull the pants down, pants down, pants down." She gives Tara the clean diaper to play with. Tara stops wiggling and listens to the song, waving the diaper. Ms. Gonzalez says, "Look, the diaper is dancing."

1. What did Ms. Gonzalez teach Tara about creative expression?

_____

_____

_____

_____

2. How did Ms. Gonzalez encourage Tara's creative expression?

_____

_____

_____

_____

Compare your answers with those on the answer sheet at the end of this module. If your answers are different, discuss them with your trainer. There can be more than one good answer.

Your Own Creativity

As adults, we sometimes confuse creativity with talent. It is important to remember that creativity is a way of thinking—an attitude that helps us explore new ways to do something, solve a problem, or achieve a goal. You don't have to be an artist to plan activities for children that encourage creativity. Understanding your own creativity and how you approach problems and new situations will help you become sensitive to creativity in young children. Recognizing how you feel when you are being creative will help you support children's efforts at trying out new ideas.

Think about the satisfaction you feel when you solve a problem while cooking, gardening, using a new appliance, visiting a new city, or helping a child master a new skill. That feeling is similar to the pride that children feel when they have figured out something for themselves.

Here are some exercises you can do to help stimulate your own creative thinking.

1. **How do you get to work each day? Can you think of an alternative route to work or mode of transportation?**

   _____

   _____

   _____

   _____

   _____

2. **Think of some unusual ways to use a common object—for example, an egg carton, a newspaper, a pencil, or a suitcase.**

   _____

   _____

   _____

   _____

   _____

3. **Think of three ways to make a sandwich without using bread.**

   a. _____

   _____

   b. _____

   _____

   c. _____

   _____

4. Write a new ending for a favorite story, movie, or book.

_____

_____

_____

_____

_____

5. Describe something you did with children that was very creative.

_____

_____

_____

_____

_____

These questions or similar ones can help you think of new ways to approach a problem. They can also be useful in helping children develop their creativity. Supporting children's creativity is part of being a caregiver. It is a role that gives much satisfaction in return, as you watch children gain in self-confidence and enthusiastically explore their world.

When you have finished this overview section, you should complete the pre-training assessment. Refer to the glossary at the end of the module if you need definitions of the terms that are used.

Pre-Training Assessment

Listed below are the skills that caregivers use to promote infants' and toddlers' creativity. Think about whether you do these things regularly, sometimes, or not enough. Place a check in one of the columns on the right for each skill listed. Then discuss your answers with your trainer.

SKILL	I DO THIS REGULARLY	I DO THIS SOMETIMES	I DON'T DO THIS ENOUGH
ARRANGING THE LEARNING ENVIRONMENT TO SUPPORT CREATIVITY 1. Arranging the indoor and outdoor environment so that children can move freely and safely.			
2. Setting up the environment so that children can easily select and replace toys and other materials without assistance.			
3. Hanging interesting pictures and other objects at children's height for them to explore and enjoy.			
4. Providing toys and materials that infants and toddlers can use in different ways.			
5. Providing materials that encourage creative expression through music and movement, art, sand, water, dramatic play, and so on.			
OFFERING A VARIETY OF ACTIVITIES AND EXPERIENCES TO PROMOTE CREATIVITY 6. Including a variety of music and movement experiences, both planned and spontaneous, throughout the day.			

SKILL	I DO THIS REGULARLY	I DO THIS SOMETIMES	I DON'T DO THIS ENOUGH
7. Providing sensory experiences to stimulate young children's imagination and creative expression.			
8. Providing simple props and playing make-believe games with children.			
9. Providing opportunities for infants to explore simple materials such as fabric squares in creative ways.			
10. Including sand play in the daily schedule.			
11. Including water play in the daily schedule.			
12. Encouraging infants and toddlers to solve problems and do things for themselves.			
13. Implementing simple, open-ended art activities using a variety of media.			
14. Providing opportunities for infants and toddlers to explore cause and effect.			
INTERACTING WITH INFANTS AND TODDLERS IN WAYS THAT ENCOURAGE CREATIVE EXPRESSION 15. Asking young children open-ended questions that encourage creative thinking.			

SKILL	I DO THIS REGULARLY	I DO THIS SOMETIMES	I DON'T DO THIS ENOUGH
16. Showing that you value children's ability to concentrate on a task.			
17. Establishing a secure and trusting relationship with each infant and toddler.			
18. Responding to infants and toddlers when they communicate their needs.			
19. Allowing young children the space and time they need to explore, use their imaginations, and learn by doing.			
20. Encouraging young children's creative use of language by sharing your pleasure in the sounds of words.			

Review your responses, then list three to five skills you would like to improve or topics you would like to learn more about. When you finish this module, you will list examples of your new or improved knowledge and skills.

_____

_____

_____

_____

_____

Now begin the learning activities for Module 7, Creative.

I. Using Your Knowledge of Infant and Toddler Development to Promote Creativity

In this activity you will learn:

- to recognize some typical behaviors of infants and toddlers; and

- to use what you know about infants and toddlers to promote their creativity.

Infants are naturally curious. They have an amazing ability to concentrate. Infants learn about their world through exploration. They use all their senses—touch, sight, hearing, taste, and smell—to play with objects and observe what is happening around them. But this can happen only if infants feel safe and secure. When infants have a trusting, caring relationship with a special caregiver, they are more likely to discover things on their own and enjoy interacting with other children and with adults.

Caregivers need to keep infants safe, but to promote creativity, they also need to give infants freedom to move, explore, and do things for themselves. As infants begin to roll over, crawl, and walk, they gradually realize that they can make things happen. When they touch musical toys, the toys make a sound. When they roll over, infants can get from one place to the next.

Infants quickly learn that what they do attracts the attention of adults. When their cries are answered, they begin to realize that they can have an effect on their world; they can make things happen. They are experiencing cause and effect: I'm hungry so I cry, and my caregiver brings my bottle. When infants realize they can make things happen, they are eager to try again to bring about a change or a desired result. This sense of strength and effectiveness sets the stage for creativity in later childhood.

Toddlers experience tremendous changes in the period from 18 months to 3 years. They are no longer infants, but they are not yet preschoolers; and at times they act like both. Their back-and-forth behavior and striving for independence can puzzle and often exhaust the best-intentioned adults. Caregivers need to understand who toddlers are and what they need from adults so they can support their curiosity, creativity, and unique forms of self-expression.

During toddlerhood, make-believe play begins. Their new language skills enable toddlers to talk about their pretend play with caregivers and other toddlers.

Toddlers are eager to be independent, so they want to do more and more things for themselves. They now have the fine motor skills needed for holding paintbrushes, crayons, and pencils, and they can draw, "write," or paint on paper. They can poke, pound, roll, and squeeze playdough; use sieves to sift sand; and shake tambourines. Their rapidly developing gross motor skills enable them to run, climb, jump, and try out new ways of using their bodies. Caregivers need to provide time, patience, and lots of different materials to encourage each toddler's creative efforts.

The chart on the next page identifies some typical behaviors of infants and toddlers. Included are behaviors relevant to the development of creativity. The right-hand column asks you to identify ways that caregivers can use this information about child development to promote infants' and toddlers' creativity. As you work through the module, you will learn new strategies for encouraging children's creativity, and you can add them to the chart. You are not expected to think of all the examples at one time. If you need help getting started, turn to the completed chart at the end of the module. By the time you complete all the learning activities, you will find that you have learned many ways to foster young children's creativity.

Using Your Knowledge of Infant and Toddler Development to Promote Creativity

WHAT YOUNG INFANTS DO (0-8 MONTHS)	HOW CAREGIVERS CAN USE THIS INFORMATION TO PROMOTE CREATIVITY
They learn by using their senses.	
They develop motor skills.	
They learn through their interactions with others.	
They grow and change rapidly, each at his or her own rate.	
They can focus for a long time as they explore their world.	
WHAT MOBILE INFANTS DO (9-17 MONTHS)	
They want to do things for themselves.	

WHAT MOBILE INFANTS DO (9-17 MONTHS)	HOW CAREGIVERS CAN USE THIS INFORMATION TO PROMOTE CREATIVITY
They learn to communicate with language.	
They are curious about other children.	
They respond to stimulation in different ways.	
They enjoy playing games.	
WHAT TODDLERS DO (18-36 MONTHS)	
They become more independent and have their own ideas about how to use materials and toys.	
They have trouble sharing toys and materials that interest them.	

WHAT TODDLERS DO (18-36 MONTHS)	HOW CAREGIVERS CAN USE THIS INFORMATION TO PROMOTE CREATIVITY
They rely on familiar routines to organize their world.	
They begin to engage in dramatic play.	
They thrive on exploration and are intensely curious.	
They enjoy making their own music with instruments or by chanting or humming as they play.	
They like to dance and move to music.	
They are developing and refining their fine motor skills.	

WHAT TODDLERS DO (18-36 MONTHS)	HOW CAREGIVERS CAN USE THIS INFORMATION TO PROMOTE CREATIVITY
They are developing language and communication skills.	

When you have completed as much as you can do on the chart, discuss your answers with your trainer. As you proceed with the rest of the learning activities, you can refer back to the chart and add more examples of how caregivers promote creativity.

II. Setting the Stage for Creativity

In this activity you will learn:

- to interact with infants and toddlers in ways that promote creative thinking; and

- to establish an atmosphere in the room that encourages creativity.

A positive relationship between infant and caregiver is the key to encouraging an infant's creativity. When infants feel cared for and secure, they can turn their attention to explorations of their world. Creativity is encouraged by caregivers who talk with infants, respond to their attempts at communication, let them learn by discovering things independently, and provide a consistent base of security.

Toddlers' creativity is promoted when caregivers encourage learning by doing, respond to questions, and recognize a toddler's overriding need to "do it myself." Toddlers need many opportunities to learn firsthand through experimentation; they use their creativity as they begin to understand concepts such as in and out, up and down, and big and little.

Infants and toddlers need both space and time to be curious, to find out how things work, and to learn about what their bodies and muscles can do. Each of these experiences promotes creativity.

Interacting in Ways That Promote Creative Thinking

Infants learn to communicate their needs long before they can talk. Responding to infants' movements, cries, gestures, and babbling is extremely important in setting the stage for creative thinking. When caregivers respond to infants, they send the message that each child is valued as an individual. When infants see that adults respond to them and meet their needs, they develop a sense of trust and security. This encourages them to try new things.

Here are some suggestions for responding to infants in ways that encourage their creativity.

- **Learn to interpret their babbling and attempts to communicate.** Jorge (16 months) brings the toy radio to Ms. Gonzalez. "Ah, ah, ah," he says as he sways back and forth. "What do you want, Jorge?" says Ms. Gonzalez. Jorge gives the radio to Ms. Gonzalez. She responds, "Oh, you want me to wind up the radio so you can dance. Here it is."

- **Learn to recognize nonverbal cues.** Peter (10 months) is whimpering in the book corner. He lies down, puts his thumb in his mouth, and gets up again. He crawls to the crib area. He lies down again and sucks his thumb. Ms. Lewis says, "Peter, are you sleepy? It's early, but I think you're trying to tell me you need a nap. Let me put you in your crib."

- **Learn to watch and wait.** When Ms. Bates notices the look of concentration on Jian Guo's (5 months) face as he reaches for the mobile hanging over his crib, she waits to change his diaper. When he begins fretting, she goes over to him and says, "Are you finished with the mobile for now? How about if I change your diaper?"

Along with responding to their needs, talking with infants throughout the day encourages their creativity. Infants take pleasure in their growing communication skills. They feel good about being able to communicate with a trusted caregiver. Experiencing this pleasure regularly, they feel secure and thus free to explore and to learn from all their daily routines—feeding, diapering, napping, and playing.

Toddlers also learn to be creative thinkers through their interactions with caregivers. Here are some suggestions of what you can do to encourage the creativity of toddlers.

- **Acknowledge and support toddlers' many attempts to do things independently.** Provide many opportunities for toddlers to do things for themselves, even if they make mistakes. Recognize that each toddler will demonstrate the need for independence in different ways. When you observe toddlers' efforts to be independent, encourage them with your positive words. "Why Alison, you put on your sock all by yourself!" "It's okay if some juice spills, Craig. You are learning how to pour."

- **Provide many opportunities for toddlers to observe and experience cause and effect.** Provide toys and materials that toddlers can manipulate and experiment with. When you observe cause-and-effect relations in their play, help toddlers focus on what they are seeing. "Travis, your block tower was so high, it fell down." "Anita, look what happened when you pounded the playdough with your hand."

- **Encourage toddlers' developing language skills.** Toddlers' vocabulary increases rapidly, and they become increasingly able to express themselves with words. Take plenty of time each day to talk with toddlers about what they are doing. Share the pleasure and joy of language by telling stories about things the children do, reciting simple nursery rhymes, and having fun with sounds. "What kinds of noises does your truck make, Bruce? I hear it go vroom, vroom."

- **Realize that even though they want to be independent, toddlers still need help from adults.** Toddlers typically go back and forth in their moves toward independence. One day a child will refuse to let you help her eat, and the next day she may climb in your lap and ask to be fed. Toddlers move away from adults and try things on their own but come back periodically to be sure that help and support are still available if they need it. While this behavior can be confusing and tiring for caregivers, understanding toddlers' need for emotional reassurance will help. It also helps to verbalize this need for toddlers: "It's okay to need help sometimes, Peter. I will be here to help you." "Let me help you with your jacket, Sherrie, and you can put your hat on all by yourself." "Can you help me wipe the floor with the sponge, Joy? The mop looks too big for you."

Using Everyday Experiences to Encourage Creativity

Infants and toddlers are by nature curious. On their own they are constantly making discoveries as they investigate their world. Caregivers can encourage this natural process by giving children many varied opportunities to learn from ordinary experiences. Here are some suggestions.

- Place a new toy or interesting objects on the floor. Without saying anything, watch their reactions as children explore the objects on their own.

- As you prepare snack together, provide opportunities for children to explore with their senses. "How does that banana taste?" "Can you feel the soft fuzz on this peach?"

- Take advantage of how much children can learn as they help you with everyday chores. Give them the time they need to gain a sense of completion even if what they are doing isn't what you had planned. When Young Sim is helping you wipe the table after lunch, protect her from interruption as long as she looks interested in squeezing water from the sponge and wiping it up.

- Use diaper changing time as an opportunity to talk and sing with children. Help them become more aware of their bodies as you play "Where Are Your Toes?" or "Tickle Your Chin." Enjoy language together as you sing silly songs or say simple nursery rhymes.

- As children move around the room and the outdoor play area, talk with them about going around, under, over, through, in and out.

- When reading a picture book with children, ask open-ended questions to prompt their creative thinking: "Why is the little boy crying?" "I wonder where the bunny is going."

Providing Opportunities for Children to Make Choices

One important way to encourage children's creativity is to provide opportunities for them to make choices. Making their own decisions allows children to feel important and helps them see themselves as persons apart from parents and caregivers. When offering choices to infants and toddlers, you need to be sure that you will be comfortable with whatever choice the child makes. Also, all the options should be ones that children can safely and capably handle.

Here are some examples of choices you can offer to the infants and toddlers in your room.

- **Which toys to play with.** Even infants can decide if they would like to hold the blue rattle or the red one. You can hold both rattles within a child's reach and let the child reach for the preferred one. Arrange toys and materials on low shelves so mobile infants and toddlers can choose the ones they want without having to ask an adult. Offer children the chance to select colors of crayons, paint, and paper.

- **Which snacks to eat.** Learn the children's favorite snacks and whenever possible offer a choice between two nutritious and appropriate snacks: "Karl, would you like a graham cracker or a wheat cracker?" "Anna, do you want apple juice or water?"

- **How to accomplish a new task.** Infants and toddlers can often figure out how to do things for themselves without adult intervention. For example, children come up with many ways to accomplish the difficult task of using a spoon. Some beginners hold the spoon in one hand while picking up and eating food with the other hand. Some pick up food with their fingers and carefully place it on their spoons. Others may be able to scoop up food with their spoons but will then use their fingers to eat it. Try to be patient as children learn new skills, and recognize their creativity as each tries his or her own way of doing something new.

When offering choices to infants and toddlers, remember that they like consistency and develop trust from knowing that their needs will be met. Toddlers in particular like to have their routines remain the same, and they like to know what is going to happen next. For this reason, choices that involve changes in the daily routines or rituals are not recommended.

In this learning activity you will observe a caregiver's interactions with a child as he or she uses everyday experiences in the room to promote creativity. You might want to do this activity with another caregiver who is also working on this module. Keep notes while you are observing; then use the notes to answer the questions. Begin by reading the examples that follow.

Promoting Creativity
(Infant Example)

Child _Mark_ **Age** _14 months_ **Date** _November 12_

Setting _Play period_ **Caregiver** _Ms. Lewis_

Materials _Napkin rings_

What happened?

Before the children arrived, Ms. Lewis placed a set of brightly colored plastic napkin rings in a pile on the floor. When Mark arrived, he went straight to the pile. Ms. Lewis watched Mark as he played.

Mark put one of the rings in his mouth. Then he tried to put them on his fingers, but they fell off. Then he bit one. He pushed one around with his finger. Then he banged two together and laughed. He banged them together again.

What did the caregiver do to promote the child's creativity?

Ms. Lewis stepped back. She watched to see what Mark would do with the rings. When he banged them together she said, "What a funny sound that makes!" She didn't interrupt his exploration of the new objects.

Promoting Creativity
(Toddler Example)

Child _Kay_ **Age** _21 months_ **Date** _November 12_

Setting _Lunch_ **Caregiver** _Mr. Jones_

Materials _Butter knife, peanut butter, crackers_

What happened?

Today's snack was peanut butter on crackers. Mr. Jones asked, "Would you like a rice cake or a whole wheat cracker, Kay?" Kay chose a rice cake. She put a glob of peanut butter on the butter knife that she was using as a spreader. She picked up a cracker and licked the peanut butter off the knife. Then she ate the cracker. Mr. Jones watched without interrupting.

What did the caregiver do to promote the child's creativity?

He gave Kay the opportunity to choose what kind of cracker she wanted. He watched as she experimented with spreading. He didn't interrupt her exploration of a new skill. He let her do it her way.

Promoting Creativity

Child _____ Age _____ Date _____

Setting _____ Caregiver _____

Materials _____

What happened?

_____
_____
_____
_____
_____
_____

What did the caregiver do to promote the child's creativity?

_____
_____
_____
_____
_____

What else might you do to promote children's creativity?

_____
_____
_____
_____
_____

Discuss this learning activity with the caregiver you observed and with your trainer.

III. Using Music and Movement Experiences to Promote Creativity

In this activity you will learn:

- to recognize how music and movement experiences foster creativity in infants and toddlers; and

- to plan a variety of developmentally appropriate music and movement activities for infants and toddlers.

From birth, **infants** are aware of the many sounds around them: the voices of their parents and caregivers, animal sounds, a doorbell ringing, or a clock ticking. They respond by turning their heads toward a sound, smiling, laughing, or moving an arm or leg. Some infants are very sensitive to sounds and may be startled or cry at unexpected or loud sounds. Others respond with curiosity and interest but may be afraid of a particular noise such as a vacuum cleaner or a siren.

Infants are naturally drawn to music. They notice the music in their environment—the sound of wind chimes brushing together, the radio playing, the kettle whistling, and birds singing. Caregivers quickly discover that a lullaby can soothe a crying baby and that dancing with a baby in one's arms can brighten a cranky afternoon. Infants enjoy making sounds. Some children hum or sing from very early on.

Movement is the natural partner of music. When infants listen to a song, they may turn their heads in the direction of the music, smile or laugh, or sway from side to side. Mobile infants typically move their arms or feet.

Music and movement enhance infants' creativity by contributing to the development of their motor and listening skills.

- Young infants become conscious of what their bodies can do.

- Mobile infants begin to imitate simple action rhymes and finger plays, which develop eye-hand coordination and fine motor skills.

- Infants develop an ability to listen to sounds. Eventually they will learn to identify and distinguish among different sounds, rhythms, and volumes.

Toddlers, with their newly developed skills, can participate in a wide range of music and movement activities. You can sing songs, chant, or hum with toddlers throughout the day.

When planning music and movement experiences for toddlers, it helps to remember the following general characteristics of this age group.

- **They are discovering cause and effect.** They love to be the cause. Using their own voices to sing or making a sound with an instrument enables them to experience cause and effect firsthand: "I hit the drum and it makes a sound. I sing a song and my caregiver smiles and sings with me. I can make things happen with music."

- **They are sharpening their motor skills and coordination.** Toddlers can begin to use rhythm instruments to make their own music. In movement activities they enjoy exploring what their bodies can do.

- **They are striving to be competent.** They take pride in their ability to make sounds, sing, and move in different ways. Their self-expression takes many forms, and they are able to make choices during music and movement activities (what instrument to play, how to move across the room, and so on). Caregivers can reinforce that there are no right or wrong ways to sing, dance, or make music.

- **They are developing social skills.** The relationship between a child and his or her special caregiver grows as they enjoy music and movement activities together. Many music and movement activities for toddlers occur in small groups—for example, dancing to a record, singing a song, and experimenting with ways in which bodies can move. Although the children are engaged in the same activity, they can express themselves in unique ways.

- **They are increasing their language skills.** Listening, making sounds, singing songs, and learning new words are all part of music experiences. These activities contribute to language development, which in turn promotes children's creative expression.

Planning Music and Movement Activities

Although children change a great deal in their first three years of life, you can plan some general types of activities that will appeal to most children, including listening to music and sounds, finger plays, and singing and dancing. It is important to remember that regardless of the ages of the children in your care, music and movement should be an integral part of your schedule, not just a special activity.

Listening to Music and Sounds

You can provide many opportunities throughout the day for infants and toddlers to hear and learn about various sounds and different types of music. Try pointing out sounds in your room and during walks. "The clock goes tick, tick, tick." "Do you hear the birds singing, Kadija?"

Toys that make sounds are very appealing to young children—for example, rolling balls that chime or jingle, wind-up radios, and rattles. You can also make "sound boxes" by filling small containers with different types and amounts of dried beans and peas. (You can use film containers that have very tight lids or plastic yogurt containers that are securely sealed. Check these frequently to make sure children can't open them.)

Young children are fascinated by sounds animals make. When reading to infants and toddlers, begin to identify and imitate various animal sounds. For example, you might point to the cat and say, "What does the cat say, Sheila? The cat says *meow*." By the time they are 15 to 18 months old, most children can supply the sounds themselves. Children will enjoy hearing songs that include animal sounds, such as "Old MacDonald." Don't forget other sounds such as the telephone (ring, ring), the train (choo, choo), and the bell (ding, ding).

Infants and toddlers enjoy listening to different types of music, including children's songs, classical music, jazz, popular music, and instrumentals. Many public libraries have a selection of children's songs on records and tapes as well as other types of music that children will enjoy. Ask parents to tell you what kinds of songs or music their children like to listen to at home, and try to incorporate these into music experiences at the center. Each type of music has a different effect on children's moods: classical music or quiet children's songs might be relaxing at naptime, while a march or a jazz piece can prompt dancing.

You can introduce music at different times throughout the day. You may want to promote children's ability to concentrate by encouraging them to listen with you for a few minutes. Most infants and toddlers do not have the attention span or the ability to sit still and listen to music for very long, but they might enjoy hearing it while they do something else. Sometimes a child will stop what she or he is doing to listen to a favorite song or to a melody that is particularly appealing. Remember: play music selectively. If it is on all the time, it will become background noise rather than something to listen to and enjoy.

Making Sounds and Singing

Infants and toddlers are a great audience for caregivers who like to sing. They are responsive, clap their hands, and really don't care if you can carry a tune. They especially enjoy hearing their own names. Try making up rhymes or songs to a familiar tune and include the child's name. To the tune of "Alouette" you might sing "Jenny, penny, little Jenny penny," or "Edward, Edward, where is little Edward?"

Older infants and toddlers enjoy trying to make sounds. When reading to a child or when outside, you might ask: "What does the clock say?" "What does the fire engine sound like?" "What does the cow (horse, pig, cat, dog) say?" "How does the car sound?" "Can you gobble like a turkey?" or "Can you meow like a cat?"

Children's attempts at singing can be enjoyable for everyone. Their songs might consist of a sound repeated over and over, such as "B B B B" or "DADADADADA." Gradually they can sing the words to a song, or half-babble, half-talk through a familiar song such as "Happy Birthday." "Happy, happy, happy, BBBBBB." Make a list of all the simple songs you know and keep it handy to remind you of songs that infants and toddlers like to sing. Singing songs often improves everyone's mood.

Dancing and Moving Creatively

Even the youngest infants enjoy dancing and movement experiences. Try dancing with a child in your arms and moving to a song. When infants begin to stand and walk, you can hold their hands and move to the music. Some begin to move up and down as soon as the music begins. When they are able to walk well, you can play "Ring Around the Rosie." Some children enjoy sitting in your lap, facing you, and playing musical games such as "Row, Row, Row the Boat" while holding hands and rocking back and forth.

As they become steady on their feet and their balance improves, older infants and toddlers often become very creative in their movements. They enjoy holding a caregiver's hands and moving to the music, and they also enjoy experimenting with what their bodies can do. You might ask them:

- "What can your feet do?"
- "How can you move your arms?"
- "What noises can your hands make?"

You might make suggestions such as these:

- "Let's bend our waists."
- "Let's wiggle fingers."
- "Let's stamp our feet really loudly."
- "Let's clap our hands softly."

Older toddlers will enjoy simple musical games such as "Bluebird, Bluebird" and "Ring Around the Rosie." If you do "The Hokey Pokey," remember to adapt it—"Put one foot in," "put your other foot in" and so on—because toddlers won't know which is their left foot and which is their right.

Finger Plays

Infants and toddlers enjoy watching adults do finger plays and will gradually try to imitate the movements. Some well-known finger plays are "Itsy-Bitsy Spider," "Two Little Blackbirds," and "Open-Shut Them." Children enjoy the combination of song and movement, but most can try only one at a time—either singing or moving their hands. They don't yet have the coordination needed to do both.

When doing finger plays, try placing a child on your lap, facing you, or sit with one or two children on the floor. There are many books available that include finger plays—for example, *Fingerplays and Action Chants* by Tonja Weimer or *Fingerfrolics* by Liz Cromwell and Dick Hibner.

Playing with Rhythm Instruments

Infants and toddlers love to make their own music. You can begin by encouraging them to use their bodies as their first rhythm instruments. Start clapping and invite children to join you: "Let me hear you clap. How softly can you clap? How loudly can you clap? Can you clap slowly like this? Can you clap really fast?"

Later you can introduce simple instruments. When you first introduce them, give each child the same kind. When you bring out others, provide duplicates to help avoid conflict over sharing. The following are rhythm instruments that infants and toddlers enjoy:

- drums
- xylophones
- bells
- clackers
- rattles and shakers

- rhythm sticks
- tambourines
- sand blocks
- wood blocks
- pots and pans with wooden spoons

Allow plenty of time for children to explore the instruments. Remember that young children are not interested in actually performing with the instruments. Don't expect them to march to music and play instruments at the same time. It's too difficult for them to do several things at once. Just making different sounds is exciting by itself.

In this learning activity you will plan and implement a music or movement activity for the infants or toddlers in your room. The activity can be for an individual child or for a small group of children. Begin by reading the example that follows.

Promoting Creativity with Music and Movement
(Example)

Child(ren) _Jill and Yolanda_ **Age(s)** _18, 21 months_ **Date** _March 2_

Setting _Free play_ **Activity** _Listening to different kinds of music_

Describe the activity:

One morning I asked Jill if she wanted to listen to music. We walked over to the tape recorder. I put on a tape.

What did the child(ren) do?

As soon as the music started, Jill pointed to the tape recorder and smiled. I said, "The tape recorder is playing music for us to listen to."

As we listened for a few seconds to a piece of classical music, Jill took my hand and began dancing—moving her hands in the air and swaying back and forth. Yolanda came over and began dancing too. We all danced, each in our own way, as we listened to the music.

How did this activity encourage creativity?

The children are learning that listening to music is enjoyable. This will encourage them to listen to sounds and music around them.

Jill experienced cause and effect: when the tape recorder is turned on, there is music.

Each of us had the opportunity to respond to the music in our own way through our dancing.

Would you do this same activity again? What type of changes would you make?

I will do this again. It is so simple, and I hadn't thought of it before. I will work on expanding our tape collection so we have different kinds of music to listen to.

Promoting Creativity with Music and Movement

Child(ren) _____ Age(s)_____ Date _____

Setting _____ Activity _____

What did you do?

_____

_____

_____

_____

What did the child(ren) do?

_____

_____

_____

_____

_____

_____

How did this activity encourage creativity?

_____

_____

_____

_____

Would you do this same activity again? What type of changes would you make?

_____

_____

_____

_____

Discuss this activity with your trainer.

IV. Planning Art Experiences That Promote Creativity

In this activity you will learn:

- to recognize how art experiences foster creativity in infants and toddlers; and

- to provide a variety of appropriate art experiences for infants and toddlers.

Experiences with a variety of art materials encourage infants and toddlers to use their senses, to explore, and to be creative. Young children are most interested in the process of playing with art materials; they have little interest in the end products. The joy of causing crayon marks to appear on a piece of paper, or creating small pieces of paper by tearing up a large piece, will encourage children to continue exploring and creating.

A good way to introduce **infants** to the process of art is to provide them with many opportunities to explore different textures, shapes, sights, and colors.

- Hang a patchwork quilt or piece of fabric on the wall at infants' eye level.

- Provide textured balls or bean bags to play with on the floor.

- Float soap bubbles in the air—indoors or out.

- Provide books made of different textures: cardboard, cloth, plastic, and so on.

- Give seated infants pieces of paper to tear; try magazines and junk mail, too.

- Cut pieces of terrycloth or felt into different shapes and make them into a mobile.

- Collect a box of ribbons and large pieces (at least 5" x 7") of felt or other fabrics for infants to play with. Be sure all pieces are large enough to they won't be swallowed and short enough to avoid tangling.

- Scatter a variety of different sized or brightly colored fabric or carpet pieces around an area of the room for infants to crawl to or over.

- Older infants can kneel or stand at a low table. Give each infant a large nontoxic crayon and a large piece of paper. Let them explore and discover what the crayon can do. An infant's scribbling will be more successful if the paper is anchored to the table with tape.

For **toddlers**, art opens up a whole new world of experiences. At the center toddlers are introduced, many for the first time, to drawing, painting, and playing with dough. As their fine motor skills develop, toddlers gradually learn to make marks and scribbles with crayons, to hold paintbrushes, and to enjoy the sensation of using finger paint. For toddlers, the process of using art materials is far more important than the final product.

Art experiences for toddlers should be based on the following general characteristics of this age group:

- **They are exploring cause and effect**. Each time toddlers use art materials, they make a change and create something uniquely their own.

- **They are increasing their fine motor skills and coordination**. Almost all art experiences enhance eye-hand coordination and fine muscle development—tearing paper, using a crayon, holding a paintbrush, finger painting, or poking a hole in dough.

- **They are striving for competence.** Art experiences should provide many opportunities for toddlers to make choices. Caregivers can show respect and appreciation of the process rather than the product.

- **They are developing social skills**. Through art experiences toddlers can practice their emerging skills. They can trade crayons, talk together about what they are doing, or work side by side at an easel.

- **They are increasing their language skills**. Caregivers can model the use of descriptive language: "I see you filled your paper with bright blue squiggly lines." They can encourage toddlers to talk about their art experiences by asking them questions such as these: "How does the dough feel?" or "What color of the finger paints would you like to use?"

Art Experiences for Infants and Toddlers

Art experiences can be grouped into five major categories: painting, finger painting, drawing, using dough, and tearing and pasting paper. As you do any activity, it is important to remember that older toddlers (24 to 36 months) will have better coordination, longer attention spans, and better verbal skills than will younger children.

Painting

Painting requires smocks, easels, paintbrushes, paint, and paper. A low table is probably better than an easel for infants and toddlers. Plan for a messy activity. Protect the painting area with newsprint or an old shower curtain taped to the floor. Put a small amount of paint in sturdy containers. Remember that young children like to paint both on and off the paper, and they like to paint their hands and fingers.

For beginners, paintbrushes with flat bristles and short handles (5 to 6 inches) are recommended. They are easier to handle than brushes with longer handles. If you cannot find short-handled brushes, longer ones can be cut down and sanded. Sponges cut into shapes, small rollers, and straws can also serve as brushes.

Liquid tempera paint comes already mixed. It lasts a long time and the colors are very vibrant. Watercolor sets are not appropriate for this age. The children don't have the muscle control to use small brushes, and mixing the paint with water to make bright colors is too difficult for them.

Toddlers will enjoy painting on different kinds of paper, such as:

- newsprint (you can get the ends of rolls from a newspaper),

- computer paper (from businesses, government or university computer centers),

- wallpaper samples (from your local wallpaper store), or

- odd sizes and shapes of white and colored paper (from a printer).

Finger Painting

Finger paints offer another painting experience. Whenever possible, children should use finger paint directly on a table top rather than on glossy paper. This gives children lots of room and emphasizes experimenting with paint and fingers rather than making a picture. Children can also paint on cafeteria trays or on a large piece of plastic stretched across the table and taped in place.

Give each child two or three tablespoons of paint, then put the paint containers out of their reach. It is best to begin with one-color paintings. Demonstrate for first-time painters how to make scribbly lines and how to use their fingertips and hands to make different kinds of designs. Experienced finger painters will have developed their own finger-painting techniques.

Some toddlers don't want to use finger paints because they do not like to get messy. Encourage these children by giving them just a dot of paint to begin. If they are still reluctant, offer a different art experience and try the finger painting again in a few weeks.

Drawing

Provide large, good-quality crayons that color evenly and steadily and large sheets of paper. Children respond to a lot of color; less expensive crayons are made with more wax and have less color. Using them might be frustrating and less rewarding for children.

Chalk allows children to draw with another texture. Colored construction paper is a good surface for chalk. For a different experience, children can dip the chalk in water, then draw using the wet chalk. They like drawing on a chalkboard and using erasers to make the marks disappear. Chalking on sidewalks and pavements is a traditional activity in many communities.

Playing with Dough

Dough introduces children to a new texture. Given a clump of dough for the first time, most children will smell it, taste it, poke it with a finger, or pat it. They need plenty of time to explore this new material and see what it can do and what they can make it do. They will feel its texture, push it around the table, and pound it with their hands. Helping to make the playdough becomes another creative experience.

Give each child his or her own playdough; do not expect them to share. They can play with dough directly on a table top. Some children like to stand at the table; others will want to sit down. They might enjoy using simple props such as a wooden spoon or a wooden mallet.

Some older toddlers (24 to 36 months) might have the small muscle skills needed to make "snakes" or "balls." Toddlers are not ready for rolling pins or other props that preschoolers can manipulate.

Tearing and Pasting Paper

Children love to tear paper. You can provide magazines, scrap mail with colorful pictures, old calendars, or left-over pieces of colored construction paper.

Some older toddlers might be ready for pasting. You can give them a large piece of paper, a clump of paste, and some of the pieces they have torn. Show them how to put paste on the back of the pieces and attach them to the large piece of paper. Don't be surprised if they become more involved with how the paste feels and smells than with the process of pasting something. If they aren't interested in pasting something on the piece of paper, they probably are not yet ready for this activity.

Planning Successful Art Activities

Here are some tips for planning successful art activities for infants and toddlers.

- Have everything you need for the art activity ready ahead of time, including smocks. You will not be able to leave the children unsupervised while you go get something you forgot. Make sure you have enough materials so that each child has his or her own crayons, paper, brushes, and so on.

- Plan activities such as finger painting on days when you have lots of time and patience.

- Work in small groups to cut down on confusion and make activities more enjoyable for everyone.

- Allow plenty of time for children to get used to the materials and enough time to use them.

- Have all clean-up supplies easily accessible, including a change of clothes when needed.

- Organize space for children's creations—a low shelf where toddlers can put their pasted papers to dry flat, a low clothesline and some clothespins where they can help you hang their paintings.

- Be sure that children have the skills needed for a particular art activity. If they are having trouble, or if you end up doing the activity for them, the activity is too difficult. If necessary, redirect a child to a more appropriate activity. If you plan an activity for a small group of children and it turns out to be too difficult for them, change the activity.

In this learning activity you will observe one child participating in art activities and record your observations. You will then plan and implement an art activity based on the child's interests and skills. Begin by reading the examples that follow. Then conduct your observation, plan your activity, try it out, and record what happens.

Art Experiences Observation
(Example)

Child _Kara_   **Age** _32 months_   **Date(s)** _June 7-9_

Setting _Toddler free play, indoors and out_

ART EXPERIENCE	TIME	WHAT HAPPENED?
Marking with crayons on the easel	_5 minutes_	_Kara used a blue crayon at the easel. She made straight marks all over the paper. Then she moved her arm in circular motions to make circular marks (not closed circles). Then she left her paper on the easel._
Easel painting outside	_10 minutes_	_Kara used a brush made from a small piece of sponge clipped to a clothespin. First she used blue paint to make more circular marks. Then she covered the whole paper with red paint. When she was done she asked me to hang up the paper to dry._

Art Activity Plan
(Example)

Child _Kara_   **Age** _32 months_   **Date(s)** _June 10_

Setting _Indoors at table_   **Activity** _Sponge painting—different shapes_

Why have you planned this experience?

Kara seemed to like painting with a sponge. I think she'd like to paint with sponges cut into different shapes.

What materials are needed?

Two pie pans, two colors of tempera paint, three sponges cut into assorted shapes, large pieces of paper.

How many children can be involved at one time?

Two or three

What happened during the activity?

I set up the activity and waited to see if any toddlers would come over by themselves. Two children came and had fun smearing paint on their paper. Then Kara came over. She used a square sponge to draw circles on her paper. Then she smeared them all together. I suggested that she might try to use the round sponge to make dots on her papers. She tried it but went back to using the square sponge.

How did this activity promote creativity?

Kara had the experience of being the cause of changing the paper by making circles and smearing the paint. I showed respect for her ideas by stepping back and letting her use the materials her way even though it wasn't what I had in mind.

Art Experiences Observation

Child _____ Age _____ Date(s) _____

Setting _____

ART EXPERIENCE	TIME	WHAT HAPPENED?

Art Activity Plan

Child _____ Age _____ Date _____

Setting _____ Activity _____

Description of activity:

_____
_____
_____
_____

Why have you planned this experience?

_____
_____
_____

What materials are needed?

_____
_____

How many children can be involved at one time?

_____

What happened during the activity?

_____
_____
_____
_____

How did this activity promote creativity?

_____
_____
_____

Discuss this learning activity with your trainer.

V. Using Sand and Water to Promote Creativity

In this activity you will learn:

- to plan developmentally appropriate experiences for infants and toddlers using sand and water; and

- to promote children's creativity as they play with sand and water.

Children are naturally drawn to sand and water play. These activities let children be messy in a world that usually demands neatness and order. Think back to your own childhood. Can you remember how much fun it was to blow bubbles through a straw or bury your feet in cool, wet sand? These experiences were enjoyable, and they were times of learning as well.

When splashing in a tub full of water, infants and toddlers learn what water feels like and how it moves. By sifting, pouring, and poking sand, they also learn about sand's special qualities. As they grow and develop, children apply their knowledge of what sand and water are like in their play. Instead of just splashing water, they create a rhythm of splashes to propel a toy boat through a tub of water. Instead of just filling and emptying pails of sand, they'll form the sand into a castle and in time will refine their activities to add such things as tunnels and a moat.

Through their play, children learn many things. By burying a shovel and digging it up again, children learn about object permanence. By pouring four cups of water into an empty quart-size milk carton, children gain a foundation for math. By pouring sand through a funnel, they learn coordination skills. When digging a tunnel into a sand hill, they use their imaginations to run cars through the tunnel they've created. The skills children learn through sand and water play help them think, improve their physical powers, and get along with other children and adults.

Introducing Water Play

When infants are able to sit independently and manipulate toys—at around 6 to 9 months—they may begin to enjoy water play. While the setting for water play is often in a bathtub at home, there are other ways to introduce it in your room.

- Place the infant on a large towel on the floor. Give the infant a shallow plastic tub filled with about 2 inches of water. Put the tub directly in front of the infant. Have a separate tub for each infant.

- When infants can stand independently and maintain their balance (usually at 14 to 18 months), they can try water play in a shallow plastic tub placed on a low table or at a water play table lowered to the appropriate height. Toddlers enjoy playing at the water table with two or three others, watching each other and talking about what they are doing.

- When introducing water play, give children lots of time just to explore the water—to see how it feels and sounds. Later on you can introduce water toys to further stimulate play.

- To keep the floor reasonably dry, use a large towel or waterproof (vinyl) tablecloth; newspaper can be hard for children to walk on, and pieces of plastic may be too slippery. Keep a mop handy.

- In the summer or in mild climates, water play can be moved outdoors. Shallow swimming pools or plastic tubs can be used, with only one to two inches of water. A makeshift low water table can be made with plastic baby baths.

- For toddlers who no longer put everything in their mouths, you can introduce soapy water. Let them add the soap to the water to discover for themselves what happens.

To make water play more interesting, try adding different kinds of props such as the following:

Rubber duckies	Boats
Sponges	Squeeze bottles
Corks	Eggbeaters
Paint brushes	Whisks
Food coloring	Soap (liquid, solid, and flaked)
Funnels	Set of plastic dishes
Measuring cups	Boats
Plastic jugs	Plastic basters
Water wheels	

Introducing Sand Play

You can include sand play in your room when the infants will play with sand without eating it, usually at 15 to 18 months. While most infants will end up tasting sand at some point, infants who want only to eat sand and not to play with it are too young.

Sand play can be an indoor as well as an outdoor experience. Outdoors, be sure the sandbox is covered when not in use to prevent animals from using it as a litter box. Indoors, you can use a sand table if the height can be adjusted. Or try placing a few inches of sand in a plastic tub to create a miniature sand box. Cover the floor with a large towel or sheet to make clean-up easier.

As children play with sand, talk to them about how it feels. If they taste it, you might say, "This is sand, Rebecca. We don't eat it, we play with it. Here, give me your hand and we'll touch the sand." Or you could say, "I don't think that tastes very good, Alex. Let's see what else we can do with the sand. Try poking your fingers in it."

Vary the experience by sometimes using dry sand and then adding water. Children will discover that they can mold and shape the wet sand but that it is easier to pour the dry sand.

Here are some suggestions of props you might include with sand play:

Muffin tins	Whisk brooms
Pails	Scoops
Shovels	Measuring cups
Molds	Funnels
Sprayers (to wet sand)	Ice cube trays
Small cars and trucks	Coffee scoops
Rakes	

In this learning activity you will plan, implement, and evaluate a sand or water play activity. Begin by reviewing the examples that follow.

Sand and Water Play Activity
(Infant Example)

Child(ren) _Karen_   **Age(s)** _12 months_   **Date** _October 12_

Setting _After naptime_   **Activity** _Water play_

What materials did you provide?

I gave Karen a plastic tub of water with a rubber duck. She was sitting on the floor, and I placed the tub in front of her. The tub had about 2 inches of water in it.

What did you and the child(ren) do?

Karen put her hand in the water, took it out, and then put both hands in. She splashed the water and it hit her face. She looked surprised. She put the duck in the water, took it out, and repeated this again. She put the duck in her mouth. Then she poked the water with her finger. After she did all this, I put the duck in the water and said, "Look, Karen, the duck is floating in the water!"

How did this activity encourage creativity?

Karen explored the water with her hands and fingers and by splashing. She put the duck in and saw what happened—the duck got wet. She tasted the wet duck and saw it float. She used her senses of taste, sight, and touch to discover things about water.

Would you do this same activity again? What changes would you make?

I would add other props that float, such as boats, corks, and plastic dishes. We could try to make them sink and watch them pop back to the surface.

Sand and Water Play Activity
(Toddler Example)

Child(ren) _Ricky and Melissa_   **Age(s)** _24, 30 months_   **Date** _August 24_

Setting _Outdoors in the yard_   **Activity** _Bubbles_

What materials did you provide?

Plastic tubs with soapy water, large plastic bubble blowers, and plastic berry baskets from the supermarket.

What did you and the child(ren) do?

First we made the bubble solution by mixing dishwashing detergent with water in a big plastic tub. Dick and Melissa played with the soapy water for a while. Then I said, "Look at all the bubbles we made! Would you like to blow bubbles?" They both laughed and started jumping up and down. I gave each of them a large plastic blower, but neither of them could blow very well. So I said, "Let's move the blower and see what happens." They did and were so excited to see the bubbles. Then I gave them the berry baskets to dip in the soapy water. "Let's wave these around," I said. They seemed really surprised by all the tiny bubbles that came out. They both played with the bubbles for 10 minutes, and then I had to help them stop to give other children a turn.

How did this activity encourage creativity?

By making their own bubble solution, Dick and Melissa got to see what happens when you mix soap and water together. Waving instead of blowing the blower and berry baskets instead of blowing showed them new ways to do things.

Would you do this same activity again? What changes would you make?

Yes. And I liked doing it outside, but I guess we could do it indoors, too. Next time I'll ask Ms. Terry to take turns with me. We can make enough bubble solution and provide more baskets so the toddlers don't have to wait for a turn. I didn't realize how much fun it would be for them.

Sand and Water Play Activity

Child(ren) _____ Age _____ Date _____

Setting _____ Activity _____

What materials did you provide?

_____
_____

What did you and the child(ren) do?

_____
_____
_____
_____
_____

How did this activity encourage creativity?

_____
_____
_____
_____
_____

Would you do this same activity again? What changes would you make?

_____
_____
_____
_____
_____
_____

Discuss this learning activity with your trainer.

Summarizing Your Progress

You have now completed all of the learning activities for this module. Whether you are an experienced caregiver or a new one, this module has probably helped you develop new skills in promoting infants' and toddlers' creativity. Before you go on, take a few minutes to summarize what you've learned.

- Turn back to Learning Activity I, Using Your Knowledge of Infant and Toddler Development to Promote Creativity, and add to the chart specific examples of how you promoted creativity during the time you were working on this module.

- Next, review your responses to the pre-training assessment for this module. Write a summary of what you learned and list the skills you developed or improved.

_____

_____

_____

_____

_____

_____

_____

_____

Your final step in this module is to complete the knowledge and competency assessments. Let your trainer know when you are ready to schedule the assessments. After you have successfully completed these assessments, you will be ready to start a new module. Congratulations on your progress so far, and good luck with your next module.

Answer Sheet: Promoting Children's Creativity

Arranging the Learning Environment to Support Creativity

1. **How did Ms. Bates arrange the environment to promote creativity?**

   a. There were many ways for the infants to interact with the mobile; they could bat it with their hands, kick it with their feet, watch it move, and listen to the noise it makes.

   b. There was no wrong way to use the mobile, and it appealed to most of the senses.

2. **What do you think the infants will do with the spoons on the floor?**

   a. They may roll them, taste them, and shake them.

   b. Some of the infants might use them to make sounds by banging the spoons on something else.

Providing a Variety of Activities and Experiences to Promote Creativity

1. **Why are cooking activities such as making playdough good opportunities to promote creativity?**

   a. Children feel proud to participate and make something real.

   b. Children can use their senses to explore ingredients.

2. **How did Mr. Jones support creative thinking?**

   a. He asked Emily to think and express her ideas.

   b. He modeled a creative way of solving a problem.

   c. He commented that there are many ways to stir.

Interacting with Infants and Toddlers in Ways That Encourage Creative Expression

1. **What did Ms. Gonzalez teach Tara about creative expression?**

   a. It's fun to make up your own songs about people you know.

   b. You can make your own music to dance to.

2. **How did Ms. Gonzalez encourage Tara's creative expression?**

   a. She gave Tara the diaper so she could move creatively to the music.

   b. She admired Tara's creative movement.

Using Your Knowledge of Infant and Toddler Development to Promote Creativity

WHAT YOUNG INFANTS DO (0-8 MONTHS)	HOW CAREGIVERS CAN USE THIS INFORMATION TO PROMOTE CREATIVITY
They learn by using their senses.	Provide many opportunities for infants to see different things, hear a variety of sounds, and manipulate objects. Use daily routines to show infants toys, sing songs, or talk with them. Expose them to a variety of colors, sounds, textures, and sights indoors and outdoors.
They develop motor skills.	Give infants the freedom to move around. Provide space and time for them to practice and develop their motor skills. Praise them for their efforts and encourage them to keep trying.
They learn through their interactions with others.	Help infants develop a sense of trust and security by responding to their needs. Be consistent so they will know what to expect. When they feel secure they will be confident enough to try new things—which is the beginning of creativity.
They grow and change rapidly, each at his or her own rate.	Learn to recognize the differences in infants' abilities and respond to them as individuals. No two infants develop at the same rate. They have different eating and sleeping patterns, like to be held in different ways, require varied amounts of stimulation, and cry in different ways.
They can focus for a long time as they explore their world.	Help children learn to concentrate. If they look absorbed in an activity, assume they are taking in information. Try not to interrupt them. Learn to watch and wait to give them time to gain a sense of completion.

WHAT MOBILE INFANTS DO (9-17 MONTHS)	HOW CAREGIVERS CAN USE THIS INFORMATION TO PROMOTE CREATIVITY
They want to do things for themselves.	Recognize infants' early attempts to be independent—for example, reaching for toys, taking off clothes, or feeding themselves. Encourage them and be patient as they try to master new skills. As their independence grows, remember that there will be many times when they will need and want your help.
They are learning to communicate with language.	Encourage families to tell you about their observations of the infant's communication at home. Provide many opportunities for conversation. Talk with infants when you change them and feed them, and name things. Listen carefully to the different sounds infants make, and respond to early efforts to talk. Play simple games such as "where is the...?" and "show me your...."
They are curious about other children.	Let infants play alongside others, and help them learn to interact. Realize that they will want to touch other infants and may treat them as objects; for example, an infant may try to put another infant's foot in his or her mouth as if it were a toy. Help infants learn acceptable ways of touching others.
They respond to stimulation in different ways.	Observe infants and note how they respond to loud and soft noises, hot and cold temperatures. Learn to recognize when their body language is asking you to handle them more and when they are objecting to too much handling.
They enjoy playing games.	Introduce simple games that have no right or wrong ways of being played. Follow their cues to begin, extend, or change a game.

WHAT TODDLERS DO (18-36 MONTHS)	HOW CAREGIVERS CAN USE THIS INFORMATION TO PROMOTE CREATIVITY
They become more independent, and they have their own ideas about how to use materials and toys.	Recognize that toddlers want to do more things themselves; they are trying to become their own persons, separate from others. Offer lots of opportunities for toddlers to do things their ways. Encourage and support their creative problem solving. Accept their ideas about how to use materials or toys so they will develop positive attitudes about creativity.
They have trouble sharing toys and materials that interest them.	Provide more than one of the most popular toys and plenty of crayons, paper, paintbrushes, and so on so that toddlers can be creative without having to share or wait for turns.
They rely on familiar routines to organize their world.	Develop consistent yet flexible routines so that toddlers know what happens next. Introduce new materials and activities one at a time. Be sensitive to individual differences in the way toddlers experience activities and materials.
They begin to engage in dramatic play.	Provide the materials and encouragement to stimulate toddlers' imaginations. Recognize their early efforts at make-believe play. For example, a 21-month-old may pick up a purse, say "bye-bye," and walk away. Talk with toddlers about such dramatic play: "Have a nice trip. I'll see you later."
They thrive on exploration and are intensely curious.	Provide many opportunities for toddlers to learn by doing. Toddlers are beginning to recognize cause and effect; they can make things happen. Through trial and error they discover many things about the world around them and about their place in it. Encourage them to try new activities as well as new ways of doing things.
They enjoy making their own music with instruments or by chanting or humming as they play.	Introduce toddlers to rhythm instruments; show them how to beat a drum, bang a tambourine, or shake maracas. Make up your own hums or chants as you change diapers, serve snacks, or perform other routine tasks.

WHAT TODDLERS DO (18-36 MONTHS)	HOW CAREGIVERS CAN USE THIS INFORMATION TO PROMOTE CREATIVITY
They like to dance and move to to music.	Play different kinds of music for toddlers so they can move and dance. Share their excitement by moving your own body to the music.
They are developing and refining their fine motor skills.	Provide many opportunities for them to practice their fine motor skills, including holding crayons, using paintbrushes, working with dough, tearing paper, and playing dress-up.
They are developing language and communication skills.	If you do not speak the same languages as the children, try to find some volunteers who do. You might also learn a few community-used words and phrases. Recognize toddlers' progress in creative verbal expression. Play rhyming games and read nonsense rhymes and books such as those by Dr. Seuss. Encourage toddlers to tell about the events of the day, and help them learn to express their ideas with words. Introduce simple songs and finger plays.

Glossary

Closed question   A question for which there is only one right answer.

Creativity   An attitude or way of looking at things that involves being willing to try out new ways of doing something and realizing that there is more than one way to solve a problem.

Flexibility   A willingness to change the way one does something or to try a new approach when making something or completing a task.

Open-ended question   A question that can be answered in many ways; one for which there isn't one right answer.

Problem solving   The process of thinking through a problem and coming up with one or several possible solutions.

Self-esteem   A sense of worth; a good feeling about oneself and one's abilities. Someone with strong self-esteem feels respected, valued, and able to do things successfully and independently.

Unstructured materials   Materials that can be used in many different ways.

CARING FOR INFANTS AND TODDLERS

Module 8
Self

What Is Self-Esteem and Why Is It Important?

Self-esteem is a sense of one's own worth. People with self-esteem are proud of who they are and what they can do. People who have self-esteem feel:

- **connected** to others—to friends and to families;

- **respected** and **valued** by others; and

- **powerful**—able to do things on their own.

Our self-esteem grows when most of our daily experiences confirm who we are and what we are capable of doing. When they don't, we begin wondering if there is something wrong with us. Our self-esteem is lowered.

The development of a sense of self begins in infancy. The early experiences that infants have with their primary caregivers set the stage for viewing themselves as worthy, valuable individuals. This is the time when infants begin establishing trust because they learn that they can count on others to meet their needs.

During the first three years of life, young children start to form pictures of who they are, what they can do, and what they think and feel. This is a picture that will evolve throughout their lives.

How children feel about themselves will affect every area of their development—their ability to play, to relate to others, and to explore and learn. Their feelings are strongly and continuously influenced by their important adults at home and in child care.

You are very important to the infants and toddlers in your program. How you interact with them colors their feelings about themselves. By treating children respectfully, you will help them learn to respect themselves and eventually others. In the course of daily life at the center, you have countless opportunities to do this. As you take a minute to talk with an infant about the rattle she is shaking or invite a toddler to help you push chairs to the snack table, you support the development of self-esteem that will serve children throughout their lives.

Building self-esteem involves:

- developing trusting and supportive relationships with each child;

- helping young children accept and appreciate themselves and others; and

- providing infants and toddlers with opportunities to feel successful and competent.

Listed on the next page are examples of how caregivers demonstrate their competence in building children's self-esteem.

Developing a Trusting and Supportive Relationship with Each Child

Here are some examples of what caregivers can do.

- Acknowledge children's developing skills in ways that help children feel special. "Danny, will you be my helper today and wipe the tables?"

- Laugh and talk to an infant as you change his diaper. "Where is Evan's foot? Here it is!"

- Listen to the feelings of a crying infant and offer comfort. "Let's see what's wrong, Sara. There, there, we can take care of that problem."

- Understand that it's hard for children to say goodbye to their parents and help them feel better. "It's hard to say goodbye to Daddy. We'll take good care of you, and Daddy will come back to get you after snack."

- Identify and respond to children's feelings. "I know you want to play with the truck now. It's hard to wait. Let's see if we can find another truck for you."

- Use gentle physical contact—a hug, a touch, a lap to sit on—to show you care.

Helping Infants and Toddlers Accept and Appreciate Themselves and Others

Here are some examples of what caregivers can do.

- Express surprise and joy when an infant makes a new discovery. "Look at what you can do! When you kick the mobile, the horses move."

- Show by what you say and do that you respect each child's individuality. "Gwen, I see you like peaches. Nan, I see you like pears."

- Include pictures and toys that reflect the ethnic backgrounds of the children in your room.

- Avoid sexist remarks such as "little girls don't" or "boys always do."

Providing Infants and Toddlers with Opportunities to Feel Successful and Competent

Here are some examples of what caregivers can do.

- Sit on the floor and roll a ball to an infant. "Here it comes, Mark. Catch it! Can you roll it back?"

- Give children the opportunity to dress themselves even if this takes a long time. "You worked hard to zip your coat."

- Accept mistakes as natural. "Oh, the paint spilled. Let's get a sponge and clean it up."

- Select materials that children are ready to master. Comment on their success. "You filled up all the holes in the pegboard. That was good work."

- Repeat activities so children can master skills and experience success.

Building Self-Esteem

In the following situations caregivers are supporting the development of children's self-esteem. As you read each one, think about what the caregivers are doing and why. Then answer the questions that follow.

Developing Trusting and Supportive Relationships with Each Child

It is lunchtime. Ms. Bates is feeding Pam (8 months) some yogurt. "Your mommy told me you love yogurt," she says to Pam. Pam coos and reaches for the spoon. Ms. Bates knows that Pam's parents have begun letting Pam feed herself sometimes, so she gives Pam the spoon. Yogurt slips to the highchair tray as Pam lifts it to her mouth. Pam begins smearing the yogurt around the tray with the spoon. Ms. Bates reaches for another spoon and begins feeding Pam some yogurt. "We'll each have a spoon," she says. "I want to be sure you get some yogurt inside you because I don't want you to get too hungry." Pam looks up at Ms. Bates and smiles.

1. **What are three things Ms. Bates knew about Pam?**

   _____

   _____

   _____

2. **How did she use this information to help Pam feel good about herself at lunch?**

   _____

   _____

   _____

Helping Infants and Toddlers Accept and Appreciate Themselves and Others

Jerry (32 months) places a wooden block on the tower he is building. "Look, I did it!" he calls to Mr. Jones. "That's a very tall tower you've built," says Mr. Jones, bending down for a closer look. Jerry smiles proudly. Just then, Sandy (24 months) walks by, swinging her arms. Crash! Jerry's tower tumbles to the floor. "No!" shouts Jerry. He lifts his arm to hit Sandy. "Jerry," Mr. Jones says, reaching up to stop Jerry's swing. "I know you're angry, but I won't let you hit Sandy. *Tell* her how you feel." Jerry turns to Sandy and says, "Don't knock my building!" Mr. Jones puts his arm around Sandy and tells Jerry, "Sandy didn't mean to knock down your building. You did a good job with your words. Maybe Sandy and I can help you rebuild your tower."

1. What feelings did Jerry have in the block corner?

_____

_____

_____

2. How did Mr. Jones help Jerry learn how to express his feelings in appropriate ways?

_____

_____

_____

Providing Infants and Toddlers with Opportunities to Feel Successful and Competent

Velma (20 months) is sitting on the floor playing with a shape box. She is holding a cube in her hand. Ms. Gonzalez watches from a few feet away as Velma goes from hole to hole trying to find where the square fits. She tries to force it into the triangular space and begins looking frustrated. Ms. Gonzalez decides to step in. "Try again, Velma," she encourages. "You can do it." Velma looks up at her. Ms. Gonzalez smiles. On her next try, she finds the right space. The cube falls into the box. "Good job!" says Ms. Gonzalez clapping. "I knew you could do it." "My do!" says Velma proudly.

1. Why do you think Ms. Gonzalez decided to step in and encourage Velma to try again?

_____

_____

_____

2. How did Ms. Gonzalez help Velma feel good about herself?

_____

_____

_____

Compare your answers with those on the answer sheet at the end of this module. If your answers are different, discuss them with your trainer. There can be more than one good answer.

Your Own Self-Esteem

Self-esteem is very important to all of us. Growing up, we have many experiences that help shape our feelings about ourselves. Often, we learn to value who we are and what we can do. Yet in each situation our self-esteem is tested. In situations where we feel capable and trusted, we do well. Our self-esteem is high. In other situations we may feel less skillful. We are unsure of what support we will get. If we fail, our self-esteem may suffer.

Think of times when you have felt really good about yourself. Perhaps you had some of the following feelings.

- You felt good about an accomplishment. "Look at this closet. It took me all day, but now I know where to find everything."

- You were ready to accept responsibilities. "I'll organize the staff party."

- You were independent. "I haven't been there before, but I have a map and I'll find it."

- You didn't give up easily. "This reading assignment is really hard to understand. I think if I take notes, I'll get the important points."

- You weren't afraid to express your feelings. "I felt hurt when you questioned my word."

You also probably can remember times when you felt bad about yourself. Your self-esteem was at a low. Perhaps you had some of these feelings.

- You put yourself down. "Oh, I'm so stupid. I can never get it right."

- You felt powerless. "I don't have any idea what I'm supposed to do. I'm hopelessly lost."

- You avoided difficult situations. "I'm not going to work if she's there today."

- You blamed others. "How could I help it? He didn't tell me where the paint was."

- You felt that no one valued you. "They'll never pick me."

A caregiver with low self-esteem may tend to pass on these feelings to the children in his or her care. As we have been taught, so we tend to teach. "I'm stupid" and "I can't" easily become "you're stupid" and "you can't."

It is important to focus on building your own self-esteem and to remember people who have helped you achieve positive feelings about yourself. How were you helped to feel sure of yourself and able to try new things? And how can you pass on those positive feelings to the children you care for? Many different people in your life have encouraged your self-esteem. Think back to a teacher you had in school who made you feel especially good about yourself. Picture yourself in the classroom. Respond to the questions below.

What did the teacher do or say to build your self-esteem?

_____

_____

_____

_____

How did you feel about yourself at the time?

_____

_____

_____

_____

How has this experience affected how you feel about yourself today?

_____

_____

_____

_____

Positive self-esteem makes people happier and more productive. Your feelings about yourself influence your behavior as you care for children each day. The more capable and positive you feel about your skills as a caregiver, the more rewards you will have from your profession. The children you care for will sense that you are a positive person, and that will help them to feel good also.

When you have finished this overview section, you should complete the pre-training assessment. Refer to the glossary at the end of this module if you need definitions of the terms that are used.

Pre-Training Assessment

Listed below are the skills that caregivers use to foster infants' and toddlers' self-esteem. Think about whether you do these things regularly, sometimes, or not enough. Place a check in one of the columns on the right for each skill listed. Then discuss your answers with your trainer.

SKILL	I DO THIS REGULARLY	I DO THIS SOMETIMES	I DON'T DO THIS ENOUGH
DEVELOPING A POSITIVE AND SUPPORTIVE RELATIONSHIP WITH EACH CHILD 1. Observing children to learn their personal schedules and needs.			
2. Meeting each infant's and toddler's needs promptly and caringly.			
3. Helping young children understand and express their feelings by holding them and talking to them.			
4. Knowing what each infant and toddler is able to do and providing activities that help children practice new skills.			
5. Spending individual time with each child every day.			
HELPING INFANTS AND TODDLERS ACCEPT AND APPRECIATE THEMSELVES AND OTHERS 6. Expressing pleasure and interest in words and actions to help infants and toddlers feel good about who they are and what they can do.			

SKILL	I DO THIS REGULARLY	I DO THIS SOMETIMES	I DON'T DO THIS ENOUGH
7. Including homelike materials and pictures of families in the room so children will feel secure.			
8. Observing children to find out what they like to do, how they learn, and what they need as individuals.			
9. Helping young children deal with their feelings about saying goodbye to their parents.			
10. Helping children know that they are liked even when they are unhappy or angry.			
PROVIDING INFANTS AND TODDLERS WITH OPPORTUNITIES TO FEEL SUCCESSFUL AND COMPETENT 11. Recognizing when children are ready to learn self-help skills such as feeding themselves or using the toilet, and working with parents to provide continuity between home and child care.			
12. Giving infants and toddlers opportunities to solve problems on their own.			
13. Taking advantage of daily routines to help children master skills and feel competent.			

SKILL	I DO THIS REGULARLY	I DO THIS SOMETIMES	I DON'T DO THIS ENOUGH
14. Repeating games or activities so children can master skills and feel successful.			
15. Arranging the room so infants and toddlers can explore safely.			

Review your responses, then list three to five skills you would like to improve or topics you would like to learn more about. When you finish this module, you will list examples of your new or improved knowledge and skills.

_____

_____

_____

_____

_____

_____

_____

_____

_____

_____

_____

_____

_____

_____

Now begin the learning activities for Module 8, Self.

I. Using Your Knowledge of Infant and Toddler Development to Promote Self-Esteem

In this activity you will learn:

- to recognize some typical behaviors of infants and toddlers; and

- to use what you know about young children to help them build self-esteem.

Helping Infants Feel Good About Themselves

The most important way you can nourish the self-esteem of the infants you care for is to meet their basic needs in a caring way. When these needs are met consistently, promptly, and lovingly, infants learn to **trust** themselves and the world around them. Infants have very basic needs:

- to be fed when hungry;

- to be held and loved often, not just when they cry;

- to be changed when soiled or wet and uncomfortable;

- to be comforted when upset;

- to sleep when tired;

- to be burped after feeding;

- to be given interesting objects to look at and play with when awake;

- to be talked with in caring and soft tones; and

- to be in a safe place where they can move around and explore.

The loving attention you give in responding to these basic needs builds an infant's self-esteem. During the first months of life, infants learn if they are valued or only tolerated. They learn by how people care for them. They pick up messages from:

- how caregivers hold them—stiffly or softly and warmly;

- how they are diapered—quickly, because diapering is an unpleasant task to finish quickly, or leisurely, because diapering is a time to talk and play together; and

- how they are fed—to keep them quiet or to give pleasure as well as nourishment.

As young infants become more mobile, they develop new abilities and interests. Their needs change, and caregivers must respond to them in new ways. Knowing what infants are like at different stages allows you to respond in ways that build their self-esteem.

Helping Toddlers Feel Good About Themselves

The toddler years can be demanding ones for caregivers. Knowing what to expect can help you respond to toddlers' challenging behaviors in ways that will help children feel good about themselves.

The major task of toddlerhood is establishing a sense of **autonomy**—a sense of independence. Toddlers spend much of their time testing limits and asserting themselves. They like to be their own boss. They see things from their own point of view. If they want something, no one else could want it more. "My" and "mine" are words you often hear in a toddler room.

But their growing abilities and independence leave toddlers facing a dilemma. Although growing up has its advantages, it means leaving many good things behind. Drinking from a cup takes the place of being nursed and sucking on a bottle. Wearing underpants—even if they are decorated with dinosaurs—means taking responsibility that diapers don't require.

If toddlers could put their feelings in words, they would probably tell you, "We want to be big and we want to be little." But growing up doesn't work that way. And since toddlers don't have the words, you see their struggle in their behavior. When Jamie (27 months) screams "me do!" as he refuses to let you help put on his socks and then, five minutes later, breaks into tears of frustration and heads for the comfort of your arms, you can see the push and pull he is experiencing.

When caregivers understand that toddlers are not being naughty but rather are struggling with growing up, toddler behavior becomes easier to cope with. How you respond to their behavior is very important to a toddler's developing self-esteem.

- When a toddler says "no," do you think he or she is being stubborn, or do you recognize that this is a toddler's way of asserting independence?

- When a toddler hits or bites another child, do you treat him or her like a "bad" child, or a child having trouble controlling himself or herself—a child who needs your help?

- When a toddler wets his or her pants, do you say, "You are a baby," or do you say, "Sometimes it's hard to get to the potty on time?" Do you then ask yourself, "Is this child really ready to be out of diapers?"

- When a toddler cries and wants to be held, do you say "You are too big for this," or do you say, "You need a hug. Come, let's sit in the rocking chair."

The chart on the next page lists some typical behaviors of infants and toddlers. Included are behaviors relevant to the development of self-esteem. The right-hand column asks you to identify ways that caregivers can use this information to build self-esteem. Try to think of as many examples as you can. As you work through the module, you will learn new strategies for building children's self-esteem, and you can add them to the child development chart. You are not expected to think of all the examples at one time. If you need help getting started, turn to the completed chart at the end of the module. By the time you complete all the learning activities, you will find that you have learned many ways to help children build self-esteem.

Using Your Knowledge of Infant and Toddler Development to Promote Self-Esteem

WHAT YOUNG INFANTS DO (0-8 MONTHS)	HOW CAREGIVERS CAN USE THIS INFORMATION TO BUILD SELF-ESTEEM
They form emotional bonds with family and caregivers.	
They cry to let others know they need something.	
They need to be fed often throughout the day.	
They smile at faces nearby.	
They make sounds and respond to sounds around them.	

WHAT MOBILE INFANTS DO (9-17 MONTHS)	HOW CAREGIVERS CAN USE THIS INFORMATION TO BUILD SELF-ESTEEM
They show their attachments to certain people by becoming curious and sometimes frightened at new faces.	
They show excitement and pleasure when they perform new skills such as crawling, standing, and walking.	
They can move and get into and on top of things.	
They sometimes comfort another infant who is hurt or upset.	
They might hurt another infant.	

WHAT TODDLERS DO (18-36 MONTHS)	HOW CAREGIVERS CAN USE THIS INFORMATION TO BUILD SELF-ESTEEM
They like to do things for themselves.	
They often say "no" when adults ask them to do something.	
They are developing control of their own bodies.	
They try many new skills and sometimes have accidents.	
They might be upset when their parents leave.	
They are beginning to use language to communicate their feelings.	
They learn to use the toilet.	

When you have finished the chart, discuss your answers with your trainer. As you proceed with the rest of the learning activities, you can refer back to the chart and add examples of how caregivers can build self-esteem.

II. Responding to Each Infant and Toddler as an Individual

In this activity you will learn:

- to understand children's individual differences; and

- to foster self-esteem by getting to know individual infants and toddlers.

Children learn to respect themselves when they are respected. Each of the children you work with is a unique human being. By knowing each child and responding to his or her individual needs, you help children respect and appreciate themselves. This is the essence of self-esteem. It is also what will allow children to feel good about other people in their lives. (For more about social development, see Module 9).

Getting to know **infants** as individuals is not always easy. There is a wide range of differences in the way infants respond to the same situations. Here are some examples of how infants can differ.

- **Some infants are more adaptable than others.** They deal with changes easily. Other infants are "thrown" by the smallest change. Rico (6 months) is happy to try applesauce for the first time. Amy (6 months) spits it out and knocks the spoon away.

- **Some infants are more sensitive to light, sound, texture, and temperature.** They might become upset when something startles them. Other infants might need your help to become engaged in what is going on around them. Rob (3 months) cries when the door slams. Betty (3 months) lies quietly until a caregiver talks directly to her or plays a game of tickling her toes.

- **Some infants are more active than others.** Carla (11 months) crawls all around the room. Sally (10 months) is content to sit and play with toys or watch the activity around her.

- **Some infants are more intense than others.** Alberto (8 months) laughs with glee when he is amused and screams loudly when something upsets him. Steven (8 months) smiles when he is happy and cries for a few minutes when he is upset.

- **Some infants are more regular than others.** Frances' (5 months) parents and caregivers can predict when she will be hungry and tired or needs to be changed. Leo's (5 months) parents and caregivers are never quite sure what he will need.

- **Some infants are more fussy and hard to calm than others.** Others rarely cry. Jeremy (11 months) seldom cries. Once Sue (11 months) begins crying, it is hard to help her stop. Nothing seems to make her happy.

Because infants are small and appealing, adults may have expectations about what they need, how they should be treated, and how they will respond. For instance, imagine Ellen (5 months) crying in her crib. How would you comfort her? Most adults would probably pick her up, cuddle her, and expect that she would stop crying. Ellen might stop crying, but there are infants who do not enjoy being cuddled; in fact, cuddling can be very uncomfortable for them. Instead, they may be comforted by being placed on their stomach over your knees and gently rocked. One way of comforting is not better than another. Individual infants have individual styles.

To see individual infants clearly, we must put aside our expectations and try to understand each infant's behavior. This is important because infants' behavior can influence how caregivers feel about them. For example, think of cuddling a crying 4-month-old infant who soon stops crying, looks up at you, and smiles. This infant's response makes you feel good about yourself and about the infant.

But what if that infant tenses in your arms and screams even harder when you pick her up? This behavior can be difficult to deal with. Chances are you might find yourself feeling frustrated about not being able to comfort her and a little angry because she is still crying even though you are there to help her. Your relationship with this infant could be strained and not as close as with a cuddly infant. You must accept this as normal behavior for this child. Respecting her for who she is can help you step back and figure out alternatives. You could try changing the infant's position in your arms or holding the infant away from your body. Caregivers sometimes comfort tense infants by taking them for short walks. Your understanding of individual differences will help each of you feel better about yourselves.

Dealing with **toddlers** is not always easy. Normal toddler behavior (getting into things, testing limits, and wavering between being independent and dependent) can make it hard to manage a group, let alone focus on individuals. Toddlers often evoke strong feelings in adults. Their feelings are so intense, so on the surface, that they naturally touch off deep feelings within the adults working and living with them. Caregivers may be surprised at the anger or frustration they feel in response to a toddler's behavior. This can make it hard to observe these children objectively.

Getting to know individual toddlers means learning how each one usually behaves. How does each child react to typical situations? What is the child experiencing, and how does she or he feel? How does the child express feelings?

Your relationship with each child is influenced not only by the child's behavior but also by how you feel about that behavior. For example, imagine a 28-month-old toddler who has learned to use words to express her feelings. When another child grabs her toy, she says, "No. Mine!" You feel good about that child and proud of yourself for helping her speak up instead of hitting.

But what about the 28-month-old toddler who responds by hitting, biting, or grabbing? You might find yourself feeling frustrated about not being able to prevent this behavior and angry at the toddler for behaving this way. Your relationship with this toddler could be strained, not as close as with the child who can express her feelings in words. But the child who hasn't learned to use words, who hits or grabs, may well be the toddler who needs you most.

Here are several suggestions to help you understand individual children's behavior so you can develop positive relationships with all the children in the group.

- **Respect individual differences.** Every child is a person who needs to be respected in order to learn to respect himself or herself.

- **Be aware of your own style.** Are you a person who likes a lot of physical contact? Are you quiet, or do you enjoy excitement? Do you get angry easily? Ask yourself how your preferences influence your expectations of each child.

- **Observe children, especially those you find it hard to work with or feel you don't understand.** Record their behavior for three minutes several times a day for a week. Ask yourself what these children are experiencing. Look for patterns to give you insight into their behavior.

- **Ask a colleague or your supervisor to observe a child** whose behavior you feel you do not understand or whose behavior you are having trouble handling. Compare notes. Often a fresh perspective gives insight.

- **Take courses, attend training, or read books** to find out more about children at different ages. You may learn what a behavior might mean for a child or gain other information to help you.

- **Remember that some children will be harder for you to get to know than others.** Building relationships with infants and toddlers is part of being a professional. Although it's easy to spend lots of time with your favorite children, make a point of spending time with every child. Chances are that as you get to know each child, you will discover something interesting or appealing about that child that you didn't see at first.

In this activity you will learn to get to know a child. Think of a child in your room whose behavior you feel you do not understand or when you find it hard to work with. Next, answer some questions about that child's behavior. Plan a strategy for getting to know this child, try your strategy for a week, and see what you have learned about the child that will help you in supporting her or his developing self-esteem. First read the examples that follow.

Getting to Know a Child
(Infant Example)

Child ___Dennis___   **Age** _14 months_   **Dates** _May 11-19_

What is it about this child that is hard for you to understand or deal with?

Dennis is always moving and getting into things. He can mess up the entire room in three minutes. I never know what he is going to do next.

Think about yourself. Is there something about you that might make it hard for you to understand or deal with this child?

I know I like things to be neat and organized. Maybe I have trouble dealing with Dennis because he tends to make a mess.

List three strategies to help you get to know and deal successfully with this child. Use each strategy over the next two weeks, and record brief observations about what happens.

STRATEGY	OBSERVATIONS
I will spend time with him.	*We had a lot of fun playing "peek-a-boo" together.* *Today I took Dennis on a short walk around the center. He noticed a piece of paper on the floor.*
I will observe him.	*Dennis picked up a can of pop-beads and dumped them on the floor. Then he picked up a puzzle, turned it over, and spilled the pieces.* *Dennis sat in the rowboat and rocked for a few minutes with other children. He laughed. Then he got out and went to listen to a story. He then sat on the caregiver's lap and smiled at her.*
I will read about mobile infants.	*I learned that mobile infants love to move and explore.* *I read that mobile infants can be hard for adults to live with because they get into so many things as they explore.*

Summarize what you learned about this child:

Dennis is very curious—about things and other people.

He does mess up the room, and he moves quickly from one activity to the next.

He is busy exploring. That is why he is so active and likes to drop toys.

He can be fun to be with.

How will you use what you learned to support the development of this child's self-esteem?

I will spend more time with Dennis to develop a positive relationship. Now I know more about how to enjoy being with him. I will give him new toys to explore and try to take him on more walks. I will encourage him to join other children in activities such as rocking the boat and listening to a story. I will understand and not get upset if he stays only a short time and moves on to something else.

Getting to Know a Child
(Toddler Example)

Child ___Cathy___   Age _22 months_   Dates _May 18-28_

What is it about this child that is hard for you to understand or deal with?

Cathy never shares with other children. She holds onto her things and shouts "mine."

Think about yourself. Is there something about you that might make it hard for you to understand or deal with this child?

I guess when I think about it, sometimes I don't feel like sharing either. But because I'm an adult, I have to.

List three strategies to help you get to know and deal successfully with this child. Use each strategy over the next two weeks, and record brief observations about what happens.

STRATEGY	OBSERVATIONS
I will spend time with her.	*Cathy helped me wipe off the table before snack. She helped collect the cookie cutters we used with playdough.* *Cathy sat and rocked with me in the new rocking chair. We talked about her new baby brother.*
I will observe her.	*When Larry (25 months) slipped and fell, Cathy looked very worried.* *Cathy played in the sand box with Becky (19 months). Then both girls painted at the easel. Cathy screamed "mine!" when Becky reached for her brush.*
I will read about toddlers.	*I read that toddlers can't learn to share until they feel something is really theirs. Maybe 22-month-old toddlers don't know how to share yet.*

Summarize what you learned about this child:

Cathy has a new baby brother. She likes to help do "real work" around the center. Cathy was worried when another child tripped and fell. Cathy enjoyed playing in the sandbox and painting with Becky. Cathy screams "mine!" because she hasn't learned how to share yet.

How will you use what you learned to support the development of this child's self-esteem?

I will keep spending time with Cathy. I didn't know I could enjoy being with her. I will not force her to share. Instead, I will help her protect her things until she begins feeling secure about really having what she needs. I will keep in mind that she has a new baby brother.

Getting to Know a Child

Child _____   **Age** _____   **Dates** _____

What is it about this child that is hard for you to understand or deal with?

_____

_____

_____

_____

_____

Think about yourself. Is there something about you that might make it hard for you to understand or deal with this child?

_____

_____

_____

_____

_____

On the next page, list three strategies to help you get to know and deal successfully with this child. Use each strategy over the next two weeks, and record brief observations about what happens.

Getting to Know a Child

Child _____   Age _____   Dates _____

STRATEGY	OBSERVATIONS

Summarize what you learned about this child.

_____

_____

_____

_____

_____

How will you use what you learned to support the development of this child's self-esteem?

_____

_____

_____

_____

_____

Share what you learned with other caregivers in your room and with your trainer.

III. Supporting the Development of Trust and Autonomy

In this activity you will learn:

- how infants and toddlers develop trust and autonomy; and

- to observe yourself to see ways in which you promote the development of trust and autonomy throughout the day.

The work of Erik Erikson identifies stages in the lifelong process of developing a sense of self. According to Erikson, developing **trust** is the major task of infancy. This sets the stage for the development of **autonomy** in the toddler years.

How Infants Develop Trust

As newcomers to life, infants are totally dependent on the people around them to meet their very basic needs for food, warmth, comfort, and love. When the people who care for infants provide food when they are hungry, make them comfortable when they are cold or wet, relieve their pain, hold them, and talk to them in loving ways, they learn that the world around them is a place they can trust. When these basic needs are not met consistently by caring adults, infants develop mistrust. They become uneasy and fearful, never knowing what to expect.

By meeting infants' needs promptly and lovingly, you can promote a sense of trust that is the beginning of self-esteem. You do this by:

- **Knowing children's individual schedules.** Knowing when Deena (3 months) is usually hungry or sleepy helps her caregiver meet her needs promptly, which allows Deena to develop a sense of trust in the world.

- **Understanding and responding to children who are at different ages.** As children grow, they experience the world differently and need different things from you. At 5 months, Andy seemed to get along with everyone. Now that he is 8 months old, he shows how attached he is to his "important people" by getting upset around strangers. Because she understands and respects Andy's fears, his caregiver, rather than the substitute caregiver working in the room, takes him out of his crib after his nap.

- **Encouraging a "special relationship" between a child and caregiver.** Feeling attached to a caregiver provides infants with a base, helping them feel safe and secure in child care.

- **Talking with infants.** Infants are drawn to the human voice and face. Having face-to-face conversations with children—even though they are too young to understand what you are saying—tells them they are valued and encourages them to communicate.

- **Being responsive.** Infants feel competent when they communicate their needs and someone responds. Because they cannot yet talk, they communicate through actions and crying. When you respond to their efforts to communicate, infants learn that they are separate people and that they are respected.

- **Encouraging infants to move and explore.** Infants learn as they grasp, reach, pull, push, let go, crawl, and move on their own. By providing a safe environment and interesting things to see and do, you help children learn to trust their own bodies and invite them to move out into their world.

How Toddlers Develop Autonomy

As you watch toddlers walk around the room and listen to how much they have to say, it is easy to feel they are all "grown up." Though they have come a long way from when they were infants, toddlers still need your help to sustain the sense of trust they began developing in infancy. They need you to respect them as individuals, understand who they are at different ages, continue special relationships, talk with them, respond to their needs, and encourage them to move and explore. By nourishing their trust, you support their self-esteem, which in turn allows them to accept new challenges and become increasingly autonomous.

During the second and third years of life, a toddler's new cognitive and physical skills set the stage for developing a sense of autonomy. As toddlers make choices and learn to do new things, their self-esteem grows.

Here are some ways you can help toddlers develop a sense of autonomy:

- Allow toddlers to **take risks** by creating a safe environment that offers new challenges. Self-esteem grows when toddlers can try out new feats and succeed.

- Provide opportunities for toddlers to **make decisions** whenever possible. Give children clear alternatives when the choice is theirs, such as "Do you want to read the book about the bear or the one about the bunny?"

- **Set clear limits** to help toddlers begin to develop self-control.

- Create opportunities for toddlers to **say "no!"** For example, ask silly questions such as these: "Do you wear your shoes on your head?" or "Does our fish say bow-wow?"

- **Be patient.** Toddlers like to do things on their own: "Me do it." Though it's faster and easier for you to put on shoes or wipe a table, there's no need to rush. Give toddlers time to do things for themselves. Their accomplishments help them feel good about themselves.

- **Observe** to know how best to support a child learning a new skill. Some children may need your direct involvement, while others may need a wave or smile of encouragement.

- **Observe** to see that a toddler is ready for toilet training. Often parents and caregivers are more ready than children are. Look for signals such as a child's ability to stay dry for long periods of time and to let you know when he or she needs to urinate or have a bowel movement.

- **Offer respect and encouragement** when toddlers attempt new skills. A smile and comment such as "thanks for helping me carry the cups back from the supply closet" nurtures autonomy. A grimace and comment such as "how did you crush so many cups?—next time I'll carry them" can shame a child and cause self-doubt.

- **Have realistic expectations.** Growing up is a process of steps forward and steps back. Even the most skillful, verbal toddler at times reverts to acting like a baby. This is especially true during times of physical or emotional stress. Offering toddlers the nurturing they need shores up their sense of self.

You are your own most valuable resource in helping children develop a sense of trust and autonomy. In this activity you will identify interactions you have with individual children and describe how these interactions promote trust and autonomy. Review the examples, then complete the activity.

Supporting the Development of Trust/Autonomy Through Your Interactions with Children

(Infant Example)

Observation Dates _____March 26-29_____

CHILD	AGE	INTERACTION
Darren	7 months	Darren began crying. I went over to help him instead of asking the substitute working with me to do it so Darren wouldn't be upset by a stranger's face.
Sanjev	3 months	At our staff meeting we decided I would be Sanjev's special caregiver. I will work to develop a special relationship with him.
Lani	10 months	I encouraged Lani to crawl through the cloth tunnel. I waited for her at one end and cheered when she got to me. I think she knew I would be there if she needed me.
Shau Lee	4 months	Knowing Shau Lee usually wants a bottle when she wakes up, I had one ready for her so she wouldn't get hungry and have to wait.

Supporting the Development of Autonomy Through Your Interactions with Children
(Toddler Example)

Observation Dates _____March 26-29_____

CHILD	AGE	INTERACTION
Gregory	26 months	When I saw Gregory making a line of blocks, I commented on what a long line he was making. He smiled and added more blocks.
Helen	28 months	I talked with Helen's mother about toilet training. Because Helen lets us know when she has to urinate, we think it is time to encourage her to use the potty.
Wei Fen	30 months	I asked Wei Fen if she wanted to wear her blue socks or her yellow socks.
Oscar	22 months	Even though it took a long time, I let Oscar help me wipe off the table after snack.

Supporting the Development of Trust/Autonomy Through Your Interactions with Children

Observation Dates _____

CHILD	AGE	INTERACTION

Discuss your observations and how you might use the information to meet each child's needs with your trainer.

IV. Helping Toddlers with Toilet Training

In this activity you will learn:

- to recognize the signs that a toddler is ready for toilet training; and

- to work with parents to help toddlers experience success.

As a caregiver you spend much of your day doing things for children that they cannot do themselves. It is important, however, to recognize when children can help themselves and to provide many opportunities for them to be and feel successful. You can do this by letting 6-month-old Sheila hold her own bottle while cuddling her, by encouraging 2-year-old Arturo to use the toilet, or by putting some spreading knives next to the peanut butter and crackers so the children can try making their own snacks. Children feel good about themselves when they can practice and master their skills. They also enjoy learning new skills in a safe and accepting environment.

Each child develops according to a personal clock. Each child has his or her own style, capacity to learn, and fears. As a caregiver you need to provide an environment that both challenges and supports each child in your care. You can use your knowledge of individual capabilities and limitations to provide the right kind of support and guidance as children approach new tasks. This allows them to learn new skills in a way that builds their self-esteem.

One of the hardest things to know is when to offer help to a child learning a new skill, and when to withdraw this support gradually so that the child can manage independently. Caregivers observe children closely so they can learn who needs assistance, who needs words of encouragement, and who simply needs a caregiver's wave or smile as they practice a new skill.

The infants you care for are learning to do new things every day. During the first 18 months of life, infants go from being totally dependent on adults for their care to being quite capable and independent toddlers. Sometimes caregivers and parents don't notice right away when their young children learn to do new things. It's important to take time to observe each infant and toddler and record the new skills they have learned.

One of the most important self-help skills that a toddler will master is using the toilet. Most children show signs of being ready to use the toilet by the time they are 24 to 36 months old. This important activity is part of the toddler's learning to develop self-control and establish independence.

Caregivers need to work with parents to make sure that the home and center use the same approach to toilet training. When parents are concerned because their child has not learned to use the toilet, it is helpful to talk with them about signs that may indicate when a toddler is ready to be toilet trained. Here are some signs that parents and caregivers can look for that show that toddlers may be ready.

- They stay dry for long periods of time.

- They can remove their clothing by themselves or with a little assistance from others.

- They tug on their diapers and/or tell you when they are about to urinate or have a bowel movement.

- They can push when having a bowel movement.

- They say they want to learn to use the toilet.

As a caregiver of toddlers, you will face the issue of toilet training throughout the year, because children will show their readiness at different ages. Some children have a harder time with learning to use the toilet than others. Your focus should be on providing the right kind of support so that each toddler can have a successful experience learning to use the toilet.

In this activity you will learn to identify signs of a toddler's readiness for toilet training. You will also think of ways to assist parents in helping their child learn to use the toilet. First read the following example of how one caregiver helped a child learn a new skill. Then think of a child in your care, and answer the questions that follow.

Helping a Toddler with Toilet Training
(Example)

Child _____Susannah_____ **Age** _____24 months_____ **Date** _____January 16_____

What signs have you observed that let you know the child is ready to use the toilet?

> *She has been watching other children who know how to use the potty. She stays dry at naptime. She can pull her pants up and down.*

How will you work with the parents to help the child succeed at learning to use the toilet?

> *I will let them know the readiness signs I have seen. I'll ask them if they have seen similar signs and how they have responded. I'll suggest that we talk regularly. I'll let them know how she does each day. I'll praise Susannah in front of them so they can have an idea of how to build her self-esteem. I'll suggest some books to read themselves and some for Susannah.*

What kinds of support do you think this child will need? How can you provide this support?

> *She may get frustrated when she has accidents. I will let her know that everyone does. I'll encourage her independence.*

How will you respond when the child has an accident? What will you do and say?

> *I will say, "Susannah, it's okay. Get your clean clothes out of the cubby. You can put on the clean ones yourself. Wash your hands when you're done." I will check to see that she has changed into clean clothes and has washed her hands, and will praise her if she has. I'll seal the soiled clothes in a plastic bag and encourage Susannah to help carry them home to be laundered.*

Think of one toddler in your care who is ready to learn to use the toilet. Answer the following questions.

Helping a Toddler with Toilet Training

Child _____   Age _____   Date _____

What signs have you observed that let you know the child is ready to use the toilet?

_____

_____

_____

_____

How will you work with the parents to help the child succeed at learning to use the toilet?

_____

_____

_____

_____

What kinds of support do you think this child will need? How can you provide this support?

_____

_____

_____

_____

How will you respond when the child has an accident? What will you do and say?

_____

_____

_____

_____

Discuss this learning activity with a colleague or with the child's parents.

V. Helping Infants and Toddlers Deal with Separation

In this activity you will learn:

- to observe how individual children react to separation;

- to communicate with children in ways that help them deal with their feelings about separation; and

- to provide an environment that helps infants and toddlers deal with their feelings about separation.

Each day in a child care setting begins with parents and children saying goodbye to each other. This can evoke many deep feelings from everyone. Think about how you feel when you have to say goodbye to someone you love. Sad? Angry? Guilty? Afraid? Excited? Parents and children have these feelings, too. It can be tempting to want to get separations over with as quickly as possible.

But separation deserves the same care and planning as every other aspect of your program. When children are supported with separation, their self-esteem grows. They begin to learn that they can manage even painful feelings and that you, someone they trust, is there if they need help. They begin to feel more confident and capable as they move into the world.

How infants and toddlers experience separation is closely tied to their stage of development. Looking at the world through their eyes can help you better understand behavior that can seem baffling at times.

Infants at 4 to 5 months have begun to learn that they are separate human beings. At around 8 months of age, they show that they have become attached to their parents or a special caregiver by responding to strangers. Some children are curious. Others hide their eyes or shriek. What they are telling us is that they know the difference between their important people and others. Children this age often have a difficult time saying goodbye to their parents.

As they begin walking, the world opens up to children. Toddlers between 10 and 16 months are joyful explorers who appear to be in love with the world around them. Duane, who just weeks ago was very upset when his parents left, might be so busy climbing up and down the slide that his parents have to go over and wave in front of him. They might say, "He doesn't care if I am here or not." This isn't true. He is aware of them and he cares. Their presence fuels his activities and joy.

At around 18 months Duane may return to being clingy and very upset at being left. He has been out in the world and has discovered that it is big and he is very little. At about 24 to 26 months, children's response to separation can be very intense. The 2-year-old is old enough to know how important his or her parents are. These feelings may cause the 2-year-old to feel very scared when parents are away. Depending on the child, these frightened feelings may be expressed in different ways. One toddler's withdrawn silence may mean the same thing as another toddler's kicking and screaming.

Here are some suggestions of ways you can help children handle separation and promote their self-esteem.

- **Build a partnership with parents.** Get to know each other. Learn to work together. Encourage parents to spend time in your center. If parents feel good about you and your program, their children will sense this.

- **Help parents foster their child's trust by saying goodbye.** It can be tempting to sneak out. Though it may seem the easiest thing to do, imagine how you would feel if your most important person disappeared with no warning. Saying goodbye gives children the security of knowing they can count on their parents to let them know what is happening.

- **Encourage parents to develop goodbye rituals with their children.** The familiar actions of walking to the front door or having a giant love hug are reassuring and can give children a sense of control.

- **Listen to children's feelings.** Sharing feelings makes them more manageable. No one likes to hear crying, but by listening, you show respect. You help children learn that no matter what they feel, they can tell you.

- **Examine your own feelings about separation.** What separation experiences do you remember from your childhood? How do you feel about parents saying goodbye and leaving their infants and toddlers? How do your feelings influence your responses to parents and children?

- **Make your space as homelike as possible to help children feel secure.** Encourage parents to bring a child's special blanket or stuffed animal from home. Hang pictures of children's families to help them feel connected to their parents even when they are away.

- **Encourage children to participate in daily routines to help them feel connected with their parents.** By doing things they do with their parents, such as preparing food, picking up toys, and carrying a letter to the mailbox, you help children build a bridge from home to child care.

- **Talk with children about their parents during the day.** Look at family pictures. Encourage children to make pretend calls to their parents. Comments such as "did your mommy put that bow in your hair?" or "is that the sandwich you made with your daddy?" can help children feel connected to their absent parents.

- **Encourage play that helps children gain a sense of mastery over separation.** Encourage "peek-a-boo" games. Provide props such as hats, briefcases, and empty food boxes that will lead to games of coming and going to the office and supermarket.

- **Read books with toddlers that deal with separation.** *The Runaway Bunny* by Margaret Wise Brown is one favorite.

- **Help parents understand what can be confusing end-of-day behavior.** Reunions are the often-forgotten other side of separating. Some days children will run gleefully into their parents' arms. Other days a child might burst out in tears or have a tantrum about putting on her coat. Help parents understand that sometimes children save their deepest feelings for them—the people they trust most.

Separation isn't a problem to be solved. It isn't a goal to be achieved. Rather, it is a lifelong process we are all dealing with. By supporting children with their early separations, you have the opportunity to enhance their self-esteem and color their separation experiences throughout their lives.

In this learning activity you will identify ways in which you help infants and toddlers deal with separation. Begin by reviewing the example that follows.

Helping Infants and Toddlers Deal with Separation
(Example)

List five ways in which you help young children cope with their feelings about separation.

1. *I work with parents to develop a partnership to help them get to know me and the program.*

2. *I ask each parent to say goodbye to his or her child each morning and to not sneak away, to enhance trust.*

3. *I listen to children's feelings and let them know that I understand that they are sad and miss their parents.*

4. *I encourage children to call their parents on our toy phone.*

5. *I talk with children about their parents during the day.*

What materials and activities in your room help children deal with their feelings about separation?

1. *We hang pictures of each family at the children's eye level.*

2. *I explain to parents how a special soft toy or "comfie" from home may help their child find comfort during the day; and I provide a place for the child to keep the "comfie" while at the center.*

3. *We do the same kinds of daily activities, such as sharing a banana and taking neighborhood walks, which children do with their parents.*

4. *We have made our room as homelike as possible. We have a sofa, children can play with pots and pans kept under the sink, and we have an aquarium of fish that we feed each day.*

Helping Infants and Toddlers Deal with Separation

List five ways in which you help infants and toddlers cope with their feelings about separation.

1. _____

_____

2. _____

_____

3. _____

_____

4. _____

_____

5. _____

_____

What materials and activities in your room help children deal with their feelings about separation?

_____

_____

_____

_____

_____

Discuss your responses with your trainer.

VI. Using Caring Words That Help Build Self-Esteem

In this activity you will learn:

- to use caring words to let infants and toddlers know they are respected and understood; and

- to use caring words to help young children learn to accept themselves and others.

Some people feel that it's not important to talk to infants because they don't understand what you're saying. But infants do respond and learn from adults who talk to them. They sense how much you enjoy taking care of them. They discover that their actions can make you laugh and talk more. They feel good when they hear a soft tone of voice. They like to hear soothing words. They are especially interested if the person talking to them looks directly into their eyes. A smile, a laugh, and a look of surprise on your face also attract their attention. Your language environment is as important as your physical environment.

One way in which infants and toddlers develop positive feelings about themselves is from listening to what you say to them and how you say it. Caring words throughout the day help build young children's self-esteem.

Your early-morning greeting to each child conveys how much you care and how important each child is to you. Your words and tone of voice are as important to the child as they are to the parent. Here are some examples of what you might say when greeting children and their parents.

- "You're the first one here this morning. You and I can spend some quiet time together—rocking in the rocker and listening to music."

- "Robin, you're smiling at me this morning. Maybe you're feeling more comfortable staying with me now when your mommy goes to work."

- "Sarah, look at you waving and saying, 'Bye-bye, dada.' I bet your daddy will be thinking of your big smile all day until he picks you up after your nap."

- "Mommy tells me you stood up all by yourself over the weekend. Hooray! Your legs are getting stronger."

- "Grandpa brought you today on his way to work. He wants to know where his special boy is during the day."

Using caring words takes some practice. It may be a while before new ways of talking to infants and toddlers feel natural. You will be rewarded when the children you care for let you know how much better they feel because of your understanding and care.

During the day you have many opportunities to talk to the children in your group. In this learning activity you will read the caring words in the example. Then you will think about what you might say in different situations to build infants' and toddlers' self-esteem.

Using Caring Words to Build Self-Esteem
(Example)

What do you say when comforting a cranky child?

"Katie, you're having a hard time. I can tell by your tears that you're feeling sad. Let's sit here in the rocking chair and we'll rock a while. I'll help you feel better."

What do you say when playing with a child?

"Paul, you like crawling after this ball, don't you? You're a good crawler and you can really get to the ball fast."

What do you say when a child is trying to master a new skill?

"You crawled under the table, Keith, and now you're stuck. You backed yourself in. I'm right here if you can't get out yourself. I can help you, but you try first."

What do you say when one child accidentally hurts another?

"Your hand was too hard on Cindy's face. Now she's crying because she's hurt. I know you were just trying to touch her, John. It's okay to touch, but you need to be a little more gentle. Cindy, you're okay, just a little sad because John's touch was too hard. He didn't mean to hurt you."

What do you say when you are soothing a child, but another one is crying for your attention?

"I hear you crying, Sammy. You want me to pick you up. Right now I'm holding Beth, but I can see you. Beth, let's take this rattle to Sammy. Here, Sam, shake this—you can make the bell ring. I can hold you soon, Sammy."

What do you say to a child who is sad because Mommy or Daddy has left?

"I know you're feeling sad because Mommy left you and went to work. Mommy will come back to get you like she always does. She still loves you when she is at work. Let's find something for you to do that will help you feel not so sad."

What do you say when a child has been crying or fussing most of the day?

"You've had such a hard time today, Frank. We tried to make you feel happy but we couldn't. We like you even when you're fussy. We hope you feel happier soon."

What do you say to a child who says "no" when you ask him or her to help put away the toys?

"I heard you say that you didn't want to put away the blocks now. It's hard to stop when you're having fun. Let's do it together, Todd. You hand me the blocks and I'll put them on the shelf."

What do you say to a child who climbs up on the shelves?

"I have to take you down from the shelves, Betsy. The shelves are for holding our puzzles, toys, and blocks—not for climbing on. It's not safe. Come here to the climber. This is where you can climb. That's what it's for."

Using Caring Words to Build Self-Esteem

What do you say when feeding a child?

_____
_____
_____
_____

What do you say when a child cries?

_____
_____
_____
_____

What do you say when playing with a child?

_____
_____
_____
_____

What do you say when a child leaves at the end of the day?

_____
_____
_____
_____

What do you say when a child is angry about something?

_____
_____
_____
_____

What do you say when a child wets his or her pants?

_____
_____
_____
_____

Share your words with your trainer. You could also display your caring words in your room to help you get used to using them.

VII. Providing an Environment That Helps Build Self-Esteem

In this activity you will learn:

- to recognize how the physical environment of the room affects the development of self-esteem; and

- to choose materials, toys, and activities in your room to help build infants' and toddlers' self-esteem.

The environment of your room—its furniture and toys, along with the activities you plan—can help build a child's self-esteem. As a consistent caregiver, you are the most important factor in the environment. Your caring is what promotes self-esteem. The children who grow to trust you will be free to explore and learn from their environment—and to trust themselves as well.

How can the environment build self-esteem? First, the furniture and equipment must be the right size, sturdy, and safe to help infants and toddlers learn to trust and to encourage them to explore. If infants feel unsafe on a rickety changing table, they will find it hard to trust. If infants must lie flat on their backs in carriages, they will be less likely to explore their world during walks. If children can't reach the things they need— toys, blocks, books—they will feel frustrated and angry. If a climber is too large for toddlers to use safely on their own, you will have to be there to help constantly. If you insist that toddlers sit on the swing seat rather than swinging on their bellies, they will be unable to control their own explorations of the swing. Rather than feeling competent and capable, children will learn that they have to depend on an adult. By providing a trustworthy environment they can explore on their own, you help build their self-esteem.

Toys and materials should be appropriate for the age group and growing abilities of infants and toddlers. If the toys are broken or too simple to be of interest, the children will become frustrated or bored. Too many toys can make children confused. Too few can lead to fights or boredom. Toys or materials that are for older children will lead to frustration and failure. Children need opportunities to experience pleasure and success with materials and toys to enhance their self-esteem.

The activities you plan can also help build self-esteem. Knowing what will interest infants and toddlers at each stage of their development will help you to plan activities that are right for them. Because you know each child, you have discovered their special interests. When you plan activities that you know will interest a child, you are saying to that child, "You are important to me, and I know you will like this." You are building self-esteem.

The children you care for will change a lot while they are in your room. Every day they are learning new skills and developing new interests. To build self-esteem, the environment, materials, and activities should change to reflect these new skills and interests.

Infants are curious. They spend a lot of time looking even before they can reach out for things and move around on their own. By providing interesting and colorful things to look at, you invite infants to move out into their world.

As you hold, move, dress, and change young infants, you help them learn about the boundaries of their bodies. Mirrors placed at eye level give infants the chance to see themselves. Games you play, such as "This Little Piggy" and "Where Is Baby's Nose?," help infants learn about their physical selves while telling them they are special.

Infants feel competent and powerful when they make a noise with a rattle, set a mobile spinning, or cause a toy to drop to the ground. By providing toys that respond to infants' actions and by being willing to pick up the ball that has been dropped from the highchair for the fifteenth time, you help children feel competent and powerful.

Mobile infants want to get around and explore the environment. They need sturdy furniture to grab when they want to stand up. Objects within their reach encourage them to explore more. They are also beginning to learn self-help skills. Giving infants opportunities to feed themselves helps to build self-esteem. Having them help put toys back in a basket or on a shelf is another way to help infants feel good about themselves.

Toddlers are striving for independence. They love to do things for themselves. This strong desire gives clues to planning an environment that will build their self-esteem.

It's very important to toddlers that they can reach the things they want. Select sturdy low shelves to display their toys. Provide a sturdy stepstool for toddlers to use independently when they want to reach higher. Keep toys in good repair and neatly arranged. Toddlers can help to put toys away. This makes them feel important.

Chairs should be the right size so that toddlers' feet are firmly on the floor. Low tables enable toddlers to stand or sit while playing with toys or materials.

Toddlers who are ready for toilet training should have access to low potty chairs or toddler-sized toilets they can use on their own. Low sinks or basins with water and a low table with paper towels nearby give toddlers a chance to wash their hands on their own.

Toddlers need to experience success when they play with the toys you select. Be aware of their growing abilities. Ask yourself whether a particular toy is likely to interest toddlers. Can they use it on their own? Will they be successful?

In this learning activity you will think about how the materials in your environment help children develop self-esteem. First review the example. Then use the blank chart that follows to list five toys or materials you use in your room, what children do with them, and how this helps build their self-esteem.

Providing an Environment That Promotes Self-Esteem
(Example)

TYPICAL TOYS OR MATERIALS	WHAT CHILDREN DO	HOW THIS HELPS BUILD SELF-ESTEEM
Rattle	*Shake it* *Put it in their mouths* *Bang it on the floor or table*	*They like making noise* *I can show pleasure at the noises they make*
Ball	*Hold it* *Roll it, push it* *Hug it* *Mouth it* *Throw it*	*They feel powerful* *It's fun* *I can play with them* *They learn about their bodies as they chase the ball*
Plastic stacking rings that can stack in any order	*Take them on and off the ring* *Roll them* *Put them on their arms* *Chew on them* *Stack them up*	*They are trying out ideas on their own* *They feel grown up when wearing a "bracelet"*
Wagon	*Load it up with toys* *Pull it around* *Sit in it* *Pull other children*	*They feel powerful pulling a loaded wagon* *They are learning to play with others* *They can play independently*

Providing an Environment That Promotes Self-Esteem

TYPICAL TOYS OR MATERIALS	WHAT CHILDREN DO	HOW THIS HELPS BUILD SELF-ESTEEM

Discuss your completed chart with a colleague or your trainer.

Summarizing Your Progress

You have now completed all of the learning activities for this module. Whether you are an experienced caregiver or a new one, this module has probably helped you develop new skills for building children's self-esteem.

Before you go on, take a few minutes to summarize what you've learned.

- Turn back to Learning Activity I, Using Your Knowledge of Infant and Toddler Development to Build Self-Esteem, and add to the chart specific examples of what you have learned about building self-esteem while you were working on this module. Read the sample responses on the completed chart at the end of this module.

- Next, review your responses to the pre-training assessment for this module. Write a summary of what you learned, and list the skills you feel you developed or improved.

_____

_____

_____

_____

_____

_____

_____

_____

_____

_____

_____

_____

Your final step in this module is to complete the knowledge and competency assessments. Let your trainer know when you are ready to schedule the assessments. After you have successfully completed these assessments, you will be ready to start a new module. Congratulations on your progress so far, and good luck with your next module.

Answer Sheet: Building Self-Esteem

Developing Trusting and Supportive Relationships with Each Child

1. **What are three things Ms. Bates knew about Pam?**

    a. She loved yogurt.

    b. She was beginning to feed herself at home.

    c. She got cranky when she was hungry.

2. **How did she use this information to help Pam feel good about herself at lunch?**

    a. She fed Pam yogurt.

    b. She gave Pam a spoon so she could practice feeding herself.

    c. She fed Pam some yogurt so she wouldn't get hungry and cranky.

Helping Infants and Toddlers Accept and Appreciate Themselves and Others

1. **What feelings did Jerry have in the block corner?**

    a. Pride

    b. Frustration

    c. Anger

2. **How did Mr. Jones help Jerry learn how to express his feelings in appropriate ways?**

    a. He told Jerry he understood what Jerry was feeling.

    b. He helped Jerry not to hit by holding his arm.

    c. He gave Jerry another way to express his feelings: using words.

Providing Infants and Toddlers with Opportunities to Feel Successful and Competent

1. **Why do you think Ms. Gonzalez decided to step in and encourage Velma to try again?**

    a. She knew Velma had the skill to get the cube into the square hole.

    b. She thought it would be rewarding for Velma to master the challenge of matching the shape to the right hole.

2. **How did Ms. Gonzalez help Velma feel good about herself?**

    a. She offered encouragement when Velma was getting frustrated.

    b. She stepped back and let Velma fit the block herself.

    c. She shared her pleasure and excitement at Velma's success.

Using Your Knowledge of Infant and Toddler Development to Build Self-Esteem

WHAT YOUNG INFANTS DO (0-8 MONTHS)	HOW CAREGIVERS CAN USE THIS INFORMATION TO PROMOTE SELF-ESTEEM
They become attached to family and caregivers.	Care for a small number of infants over a long period of time so the infants can get to know and trust you.
They cry to let others know they need something.	Try to pick up crying infants promptly and comfort them to let them know you care and can be trusted.
They need to be fed often throughout the day.	Follow each infant's schedule for eating, holding each child close to your body during feedings to help him or her feel secure.
They smile at nearby faces.	Face infants when talking to them so they can see you, smile with you, and feel special.
They make sounds and respond to sounds around them.	Talk with infants even if they don't understand the words you are saying. They will feel important and good about themselves.
WHAT MOBILE INFANTS DO (9-17 MONTHS)	
They show their attachment to certain people by becoming curious and sometimes frightened at new faces.	Limit the number of people who come in and out of the room (other than parents) so infants won't be frightened by new faces. Help them accept strangers gradually.
They show excitement and pleasure when they perform new skills such as crawling, standing, and walking.	Praise and applaud infants' efforts, showing that you share their joy, so they continue to learn new skills.

WHAT MOBILE INFANTS DO (9-17 MONTHS)	HOW CAREGIVERS CAN USE THIS INFORMATION TO PROMOTE SELF-ESTEEM
They can move and get into and on top of things.	Arrange the room to allow infants to crawl and climb safely without always being told "no," so that they learn that the world is safe and interesting and so that they develop new skills.
They sometimes comfort another infant who is hurt or upset.	Show concern and kindness when an infant is hurt or upset so that they will learn to show concern and kindness, too. Support their attempts to comfort one another.
They might hurt another infant.	Comfort the hurt infant and tell the infant who hurt him or her that it is not all right to hurt people. In a caring tone, say, "Be gentle with the other children." Don't yell at or spank the infant who has done the hurting. Make sure both infants feel cared for.
WHAT TODDLERS DO (18-36 MONTHS)	
They like to do things for themselves.	Allow toddlers to participate in daily routines so they can feel good about doing things for themselves. Provide a sturdy stepstool that they can use independently.
They often say "no" when adults ask them to do something.	Realize that this is the toddler's way of asserting independence. Sometimes offer two "yes" choices for them to select an activity or toy. Play games where the answer is a laughing "no!"
They are developing control of their own bodies.	Work together with parents on toilet training so it is consistent at home and in child care. Be relaxed and give plenty of time to toddlers who are ready to learn this skill.

WHAT TODDLERS DO (18-36 MONTHS)	HOW CAREGIVERS CAN USE THIS INFORMATION TO PROMOTE SELF-ESTEEM
They try many new skills and sometimes have accidents.	Praise toddlers' efforts and help them clean up spills (without scolding) after accidents so they will feel good about trying new things.
They are often upset when their parents leave.	Comfort upset toddlers, letting them know that it's okay to feel sad. Tell them that their parents will come back to get them and that you will take care of them. Play "peek-a-boo," hide-and-seek, and other games about leaving and returning.
They begin to use language to communicate their feelings.	As a natural part of everyday activities, talk about feelings you think a child might be having. Let children see and hear you express your own feelings. Offer books, materials, and games that show facial expressions and body language associated with different feelings.
They learn to use the toilet.	Recognize the signs that a toddler is ready for toilet training. Work with the child's parents to ensure that both home and child care use a positive, developmentally appropriate approach to help the toddler learn this exciting self-help skill.

Glossary

Autonomy

Independence; the stage when children want to make choices and try to have control over their own actions.

Environment

The complete makeup of a classroom and outdoor area, including furnishings, toys, and planned activities.

Observation

The act of systematically watching what a child says and does to learn more about that child. The information gained from observation is used to plan activities that address the child's needs, strengths, and interests.

Self-esteem

A sense of worth; a good feeling about oneself and one's abilities. Someone with strong self-esteem feels connected to others, respected and valued, and able to do things successfully and independently.

Separation

The process children go through as they grow up and become independent from their parents. Children often have strong feelings about separating from their families, and caregivers can help children understand and express these feelings.

Temperament

The nature or disposition of a child; the way a child responds to and interacts with people, materials, and situations in his or her world.

Trust

The stage at which infants develop deep feelings of comfort and confidence because their basic needs are met promptly, consistently, and lovingly.

CARING FOR INFANTS AND TODDLERS

Module 9
Social

What Is Social Development and Why Is It Important?

Social development refers to the way children learn to get along with others and to make friends. As children develop socially, they learn to share, cooperate, take turns, and negotiate with other children and adults. Children's social development is strengthened when they have secure relationships with their parents and caregivers, when they have many opportunities to play with other children, and when they feel good about themselves. Although they may argue and fight, most children really enjoy playing with others. They learn to cooperate so that play can continue.

Social development begins when an infant responds to a familiar voice or the special touch of a parent or caregiver. It continues as toddlers first enjoy playing alongside each other and as preschool children learn to play in groups. Dramatic play gives children the chance to explore living with others as they try out different roles, practice their social skills, and learn to take turns being the cook, the firefighter, or the baby.

Caregivers play an important role in promoting infants' and toddlers' social development. As a caregiver you let children know that they are loved and accepted; you meet their needs as consistently and promptly as possible. This helps children feel good about themselves, which will allow them to appreciate and respect others. (Because the ways in which children feel about themselves will determine how they feel about others, you may want to review the material in Module 8, as you begin thinking about social development.) In addition, you provide an environment where children can play alone or with others. You also help them begin to understand their feelings and learn acceptable ways to express them.

Infants and toddlers first develop relationships with their parents and caregivers and then begin to make friends with their peers. The development of a social being takes a long time. As you help children feel good about themselves and others, you are planting the seeds of social skills that will serve children throughout their lives.

Promoting infants' and toddlers' social development involves:

- helping children begin to learn to get along with others;

- helping children understand and express their feelings and respect those of others; and

- providing an environment and experiences that support social development.

Listed on the next page are examples of how caregivers demonstrate their competence in promoting social development.

Helping Infants and Toddlers Learn to Get Along with Others

Here are some examples of what caregivers can do.

- Respond to infants' sounds and gestures to help them learn how people communicate. "Karla, do you want me to pick you up? I can see your new tooth when you smile at me."

- Encourage children to help each other. "Peter, can you help me find Todd's bottle?"

- Model cooperation to help children learn what cooperating feels like. "Cynthia, I see you really want to stay outside and play in the sand. I'll wait for you while you fill your bucket one more time."

- Encourage children's awareness of others by talking about what they are doing. "Tyrone, I see you and Donna are both playing with the playdough."

- Model positive ways to interact with others. "Ms. Bates, thank you for lending me your extra pair of gloves. My hands stayed nice and warm on our walk."

Helping Infants and Toddlers Understand and Express Their Feelings and Respect Those of Others

Here are some examples of what caregivers can do.

- Identify some of your own feelings when appropriate. "This beautiful, sunny day makes me feel very happy."

- Respect children by listening to their feelings and responding appropriately. "Sally, I hear you crying. I just changed your diaper, so I know you are dry. Are you hungry or sleepy?"

- Encourage children to be aware of how their peers are feeling. "Karen is happy because Sandy gave her some of the crayons."

- Accept children's feelings while helping them control their actions. "I know, you're angry when John grabs the truck. You can tell him you're angry, but I can't let you hit him."

- State what you think children are feeling when they are having trouble expressing their emotions. "I wonder if you are having a hard time today because you miss your mom a lot when she goes away on a trip."

- Give children words they can use to express how they feel. "Tell Michael 'no!' when he takes your noodles."

and Experiences That Support Social

givers can do.

cooperation. "The plants in our garden are very
you please help me carry this bucket of water to the

more children to enjoy together, such as playing in a
n a rocking boat. "Heather, let's ask Corinna to sit
g boat. Then you can have fun together."

even if they have already eaten. "Here, Cordell.
seat and be with us."

ay by joining in for a while. "Thank you for the
tle more, please?"

plicate toys so that children who cannot yet share
"Here is a green truck for Bernice and one for Shau

the same and different. "Lottie eats applesauce
teeth yet. You can crunch on an apple with your

that children have the opportunity to be in small
to take a walk with Sandy and me?"

Promoting Social Development

In the following situations caregivers are promoting the social development of infants and toddlers. As you read each one, think about what the caregivers are doing and why. Then answer the questions that follow.

Helping Children Learn to Get Along with Other Members of the Group

Ms. Gonzalez is sitting in the rocking chair with Rochelle (11 months), looking at some pictures in a book and talking about them. "That's a cup, Rochelle. Do you drink milk in a cup? And there's a wagon, like our wagon. But ours is red and this one is blue." Rochelle looks up at Ms. Gonzalez and touches her face, and Ms. Gonzalez smiles at Rochelle. Ms. Gonzalez looks up from the book, then down at the floor. She had felt someone pulling on her pants. There is Carrie (10 months), sitting on the floor with her arms raised. "Hi, Carrie. Do you want to sit up here too?" Ms. Gonzalez turns to Rochelle and says, "Carrie wants to sit here too. I think my lap is big enough for both of you." Rochelle looks at Carrie and reaches out with her hands. Ms. Gonzalez says to Carrie, "Stand up and I will lift you." Ms. Gonzalez first moves Rochelle to the other side of her lap and makes sure she's comfortable. Then she reaches down, lifts up Carrie, and places Carrie in her lap. "Now we can all read the book together. Now what's that on the next page? Can you show me the apple, Carrie? We had apples at snack time." Carrie pats the book and laughs. "Now Rochelle, you show me the banana." Rochelle laughs too.

1. **How did Ms. Gonzalez encourage Rochelle's social development?**

   _____

   _____

   _____

   _____

2. **How did Ms. Gonzalez encourage the two infants to get along with each other?**

   _____

   _____

   _____

   _____

Helping Infants and Toddlers Understand and Express Their Feelings and Respect Those of Others

"What's the matter, Leroy?" Ms. Bates asks as she picks up Leroy. Tears are streaming down 5-month-old Leroy's cheeks. "I wonder why you are crying." Ms. Bates lets Leroy know she is there to help him while she tries to learn what his crying means. She can feel that he is not wet. She looks at the daily chart hanging on the bulletin board to see how much sleep Leroy has had: plenty. He shouldn't be sleepy. She sees on the chart that he ate most of his breakfast and lunch. His crying has stopped. "I wonder if you were bored and wanted a little companionship and a change of scene," Ms. Bates says. She sits on the floor, holding Leroy in her lap, and tickles his tummy. He giggles and reaches up to grab her necklace. "You wanted some company, didn't you?" she asks. "Well, you've got some now."

1. How did Ms. Bates figure out what Leroy was feeling?

_____

_____

_____

_____

2. How did Ms. Bates help Leroy begin learning about respecting others' feelings?

_____

_____

_____

_____

Providing an Environment and Experiences That Support Social Development

The children are getting ready to go outside. "Where's your other shoe?" Mr. Jones asks Becky (25 months). "Shoe?" she says, lifting her sneaker in an "I don't know" expression. Jerry (30 months) and Sally (32 months), jackets on, ready to go out, are standing by the door. "We have to find Becky's shoe before we go outside," Mr. Jones explains. "Jerry and Sally, will you two help Becky find her sneaker? Then we can all get outside faster." They begin searching. "Here," Sally calls. "It was under the pillows." She holds up the sneaker proudly and hands it to Mr. Jones, who helps Becky put it on. "Thank you both for helping," he says. "Who would like to help carry this big bag of balls? Now, if we all work together we can carry it outside." The three children help Mr. Jones lift the bag. "We are all ready now," he announces. "I like it when we work together to help each other."

1. How did Mr. Jones use the daily routine of getting ready to go outside to help the children develop social skills?

_____

_____

_____

_____

2. What social skills did the children practice as they prepared to go outside?

_____

_____

_____

_____

Compare your answers with those on the answer sheet at the end of this module. If your answers are different, discuss them with your trainer. There can be more than one good answer.

Your Own Social Development

Adults use social skills every day. When you yield to another car in traffic, share your lunch with a colleague who forgot hers, or wait for a turn to offer your opinion at a staff meeting, you are using the social skills you learned as a child and will continue to use throughout your life.

Sometimes you find yourself in situations where you need to use your social skills to adapt to a new group of people. Perhaps you just joined a choir or started a new exercise class. In both of these situations you use social skills to get to know the other group members and to adjust to the group's accepted ways of doing things.

Some adults find it very difficult to adjust to new situations. Although this difficulty may stem from their personalities, perhaps these adults never really learned, when they were children, how to get to know new people.

Infants and toddlers learn about how society expects them to behave by watching adults interact with each other as well as with children. Therefore, it is very important that young children see their caregivers working cooperatively, sharing feelings and ideas, having friendly conversations, and enjoying each other's company. Sometimes caregivers are so busy that it's hard for them to find time to be "friends"—but when caregivers model social behaviors for children, everyone benefits. The caregivers can feel positive about their jobs and the people they work with, and the children can gain a more complete picture of their caregivers. They see adults working out problems, sharing happy experiences, and cooperating throughout the day.

Think about how you and your colleagues model social skills. Give some examples below.

Sharing:

_____

_____

_____

Cooperating:

_____

_____

_____

Taking turns:

_____

_____

_____

Solving problems:

_____

_____

_____

Helping:

_____

_____

_____

Appreciating each other:

_____

_____

_____

Showing concern:

_____

_____

_____

Social development is an ongoing process. As adults, we continue to learn about ourselves and ways of relating to others. Your social skills help you enjoy working as part of a team that provides a valuable service to children and families. These are skills that you refine each day, on the job and elsewhere.

When you finish this overview section, you should complete the pre-training assessment. Refer to the glossary at the end of this module if you need definitions for the terms that are used.

Pre-Training Assessment

Listed below are the skills that caregivers use to promote the social development of infants and toddlers. Think about whether you do these things regularly, sometimes, or not enough. Place a check in one of the columns on the right for each skill listed. Then discuss your answers with your trainer.

SKILL	I DO THIS REGULARLY	I DO THIS SOMETIMES	I DON'T DO THIS ENOUGH
HELPING INFANTS AND TODDLERS LEARN TO GET ALONG WITH OTHERS			
1. Talking, making eye contact, and playing with infants and toddlers to show them how it feels to interact with another person.			
2. Giving a warning when an activity must be ended to show your respect for what children are doing.			
3. Being there in times of stress to offer children comfort.			
4. Providing toys and other materials that can be used by more than one child at a time.			
5. Encouraging infants and toddlers to help each other.			
6. Including children in the "real work" of group life, such as making snacks and putting away toys.			
7. Modeling positive ways to cooperate, share, and interact with others.			

SKILL	I DO THIS REGULARLY	I DO THIS SOMETIMES	I DON'T DO THIS ENOUGH
HELPING INFANTS AND TODDLERS UNDERSTAND AND EXPRESS THEIR FEELINGS AND RESPECT THOSE OF OTHERS 8. Meeting young children's needs according to their personal schedules.			
9. Talking with children about their feelings throughout the day.			
10. Identifying your own feelings when appropriate so children can learn about expressing their feelings.			
11. Verbally expressing infant's feelings for them when they are crying, laughing, gurgling, and so on.			
12. Helping infants and toddlers learn words they can use to express their feelings, instead of hitting, biting, or pinching.			
13. Praising children to show your respect and appreciation for their accomplishments.			

SKILL	I DO THIS REGULARLY	I DO THIS SOMETIMES	I DON'T DO THIS ENOUGH
PROVIDING AN ENVIRONMENT AND EXPERIENCES THAT SUPPORT SOCIAL DEVELOPMENT 14. Creating a homelike environment where infants and toddlers can explore safely.			
15. Arranging the environment so young children spend some time alone or in a small group.			
16. Developing and continuing special relationships with children so they will feel secure.			
17. Having more than one of favorite toys so children can play together without having to share.			
18. Providing simple, homelike props that encourage dramatic play.			

Review your responses, then list three to five skills you would like to improve or topics you would like to learn more about. When you finish this module, you will list examples of your new or improved knowledge and skills.

_____

_____

_____

_____

_____

Now begin the learning activities for Module 9, Social.

I. Using Your Knowledge of Infant and Toddler Development to Promote Social Development

In this activity you will learn:

- to recognize some typical behaviors of infants and toddlers; and

- to use what you know about children to promote their social development.

A child's social development begins at birth. Infants and toddlers learn about themselves and how to relate to other people through daily interactions with their parents and caregivers. They learn how to treat others by noticing how they are treated; therefore, developing a nurturing, loving relationship with each infant and toddler is the most important way in which caregivers can promote social development.

How Infants Relate to Others

From birth, infants show a preference for the human face and voice. During the first 3 months of life, infants relate to others by crying, smiling, grasping a finger, and cuddling. They turn their head when someone speaks, focus more and more steadily on faces and objects, and make noises in response to sounds and words they hear around them. From 3 to 6 months, infants who receive loving and consistent care respond to their caregivers by smiling, hugging, and showing that they feel good. They want to be around others and may cry when left alone.

Infants 6 to 9 months are becoming increasingly mobile. They show their increasing awareness of being separate people as they put their hands in your mouth, touch your hair, and pull your earrings or glasses. They imitate sounds and gestures. They have become attached to their special caregiver and show this by being curious about, and sometimes frightened of, strangers. Some children may scream or try to hide from an unfamiliar person. Children this age are becoming more interested in the world around them, including other children.

Mobile infants 9 to 18 months old have clear likes and dislikes and show you how they feel. They are becoming more independent, are able to crawl and walk where they want to go, and are eager to explore. They enjoy watching other children and may imitate what they see others do. They can crawl after you and climb up on your lap. They point to things they want and begin saying a few words.

By noticing infants' cues, playing "peek-a-boo," and rolling a ball back and forth, you help infants learn how it feels to respond and be responded to. They learn that they can have a good time with another person. They discover that relating to another person is interesting, fun, and rewarding.

How Toddlers Relate to Others

Toddlers work very hard to figure out who they are. When they run, climb, jump, test limits, and shout, "No! Me do!" they are saying, "This is me!" The experiences of being loved, cooperated with, and cared for help toddlers feel good about themselves and let them know what it means to love and care for another person.

Toddlers are very curious about each other and very observant. Toddlers cared for in a group setting quickly learn whose mommy and daddy, bottle, and shoes belong to whom. Their curiosity often leads them to establishing friendships.

Because toddlers are trying to make sense of a world that can seem very big and confusing to them, they need caregivers to set clear limits for them. If toddlers can depend on the fact that an adult is in charge, they can feel free to explore and learn about themselves and other people.

Toddlers are rapidly learning to use language to communicate with others—an important social skill. Just as some toddlers are very interested in practicing their physical skills by constantly moving, others want to practice their language skills by talking nonstop. Caregivers can foster language development by listening to toddlers, talking with them, asking them questions, and answering their questions. In short, caregivers can engage toddlers in conversations to model for them the give and take involved in communicating with others.

To foster toddlers' social interactions, caregivers need to give them many opportunities to interact with each other. Toddlers tend to have strong feelings and often don't know how to express them. They might hit, bite, pinch, or push instead. But they can also show tremendous sensitivity and ability to work things out with each other, without adult assistance.

The chart on the next page lists some typical behaviors of infants and toddlers. Included are behaviors relevant to social development. The right-hand column asks you to identify ways that caregivers can use this information about child development to promote social development. Try to think of as many examples as you can. As you work through the module, you will learn new strategies for promoting social development, and you can add them to the child development chart. You are not expected to think of all the examples at one time. By the time you complete all the learning activities, you will find that you have learned many ways to promote social development.

Using Your Knowledge of Infant and Toddler Development to Promote Social Development

WHAT YOUNG INFANTS DO (0-8 MONTHS)	HOW CAREGIVERS CAN USE THIS INFORMATION TO PROMOTE SOCIAL DEVELOPMENT
They cry to express their needs.	
They make eye contact and like to look at faces.	
They gradually learn to recognize primary caregivers.	
They show a wide variety of feelings.	
They begin to initiate interactions and games with adults.	
They are interested in other children.	

WHAT MOBILE INFANTS DO (9-17 MONTHS)	HOW CAREGIVERS CAN USE THIS INFORMATION TO PROMOTE SOCIAL DEVELOPMENT
They are sensitive to and interested in the moods and activities of others.	
They understand more language than they are able to use.	
They look to adults for encouragement, support, and approval.	
They may begin to demonstrate fear of strangers.	
They are increasingly aware of their own possessions.	
They enjoy helping caregivers because they like to imitate adults.	

WHAT TODDLERS DO (18-36 MONTHS)	HOW CAREGIVERS CAN USE THIS INFORMATION TO PROMOTE SOCIAL DEVELOPMENT
They have strong feelings but might not have the words to express them. They may hit, bite, push, or pinch instead.	
They are beginning to understand what personal property is.	
They enjoy helping to do chores.	
They can become overwhelmed in a busy environment.	
They are beginning to enjoy playing with others.	
They are aware of adults who are important to them, and they want to be like them.	

When you have completed as much as you can do on the chart, discuss your answers with your trainer. As you proceed with the rest of the learning activities, you can refer back to the chart and add examples of how caregivers can promote social development.

II. Helping Infants and Toddlers Learn Caring Behaviors

In this activity you will learn:

- to recognize caring behaviors in infants and toddlers; and

- to help young children develop caring behaviors.

Children learn caring behaviors by being cared for in a loving and consistent manner. As a caregiver you let children know how much you value them throughout the day by talking to them while changing their diapers, helping them put on their jackets, singing silly songs, and giving hugs. In doing so, you are helping children learn to show positive feelings toward others.

Caring behaviors begin very early in life. Between the ages of 1 and 2, children show concern for others. When this concern is recognized and reinforced by caregivers, children continue to develop caring behaviors. "Sammy, you look worried about Donna. Let's pat her back to help her feel better." Between the ages of 2 and 6, children begin to develop skills for responding to the needs of others.

Caring behaviors are sometimes called "prosocial" behaviors. They include certain social skills such as sharing and taking turns as well as behaviors such as the following:[1]

- **Showing Empathy**

  - Feeling and acting concerned when another person is upset or hurt
  - Sharing another person's happiness or excitement

- **Showing Generosity**

  - Giving a toy or other possession to another person
  - Sharing with another person

- **Helping**

  - Helping another person do a job
  - Helping when another person needs assistance

One can think of caring behaviors as "Golden Rule" behaviors. People who act caringly behave toward others as they would like others to behave toward them. Some techniques to encourage prosocial behavior in infants and toddlers follow.

---

[1]Based on Janice J. Beaty, *Observing Development of the Young Child* (Columbus, OH: Charles E. Merrill, 1986), pp. 111-127.

- **Remember that children learn how to treat others by imitating how they are treated.** Respond to a young infant's crying promptly to help him or her learn about caring for others. Help a mobile infant practice walking up and down the steps to help the infant learn about helping another person. If a toddler is hesitant about joining a new activity, allow him or her to watch for a while instead of forcing the child to participate.

- **Encourage and acknowledge cooperation and thoughtfulness.** Dress older infants as if they are partners in the task. When 16-month-old Ricky holds out his right arm, put that arm through a sleeve first. Suggest that Ben (32 months) help Tim (29 months) peel his orange at lunch. Later in the day Tim might be able to help Chris (19 months) turn on the water in the bathroom sink.

- **Give children opportunities to help you and other children.** Ask Fred (18 months) if he would bring you 4-month-old Lisa's blanket from across the room. Thank him for helping you and Lisa. Let mobile infants and toddlers help you do "real work." They will enjoy helping you carry some blocks outside or carrying a small bag of fruit back from the store.

- **Use each child's name often.** Call children by their given names when you talk with them. Practice pronouncing each name the way it is pronounced by the family. Hang pictures of children, caregivers, and families on the wall at child's eye level, and talk about who is who. Sing songs with everyone's name. Label cubbies with children's names and pictures, and display their names along with their artwork.

- **Model prosocial behavior as you interact with the children, parents, and other caregivers.** Say things such as these: "We missed you yesterday" or "Let's see if we can figure out something to make you feel better" or "Ms. Perez, can you please help me put the art supplies back in the cupboard?"

- **Read and write books for mobile infants and toddlers with themes of helpfulness and friendship.** Be sure your books are about real events and the children in your room—for example, "Jeremy Shares His Cheese" and "Kim Helps Larry Find His Shoe."

- **Share with children your excitement and pleasure in the things they do.** Stop to watch Sarah, a mobile infant who is learning to pull herself to standing, or Travis (29 months), who is learning how to put together a new puzzle.

- **Help children learn that there are words for their feelings.** Although a young infant won't understand the words "I think you are angry," she or he will feel your caring and understanding. Mobile infants may use your words to help make sense of their feelings. One day you may find Henry (17 months) looking into the mirror and frowning at himself, saying "sad." Help toddlers learn to use their words to let each other know their feelings: "Use your words to tell Jeff you are angry that he took your book."

- **Provide mobile infants and toddlers with plenty of opportunities to interact.** Be aware of what they are doing and be available to step in if they need help. Children need practice to learn how to get along with each other.

- **Divide the group occasionally to give children opportunities to interact in small groups.** Sometimes children who spend a lot of time watching feel more comfortable playing with other children and toys in a small group of two or three.

In this learning activity you will observe the infants and toddlers in your group and record three examples of caring behaviors. Then you will identify five examples of how you demonstrated caring behaviors or helped children learn caring behaviors. Begin by reading the example on the next page.

Caring Behaviors of Infants and Toddlers
(Example)

Observation Dates _____ *March 26-29* _____

Describe examples of caring behaviors of these children.

Child ___*Bonita*___ **Age** ___*23 months*___

> *As I comforted Susan, who fell down outside, Bonita came over and patted her back.*

Child ___*Ben*___ **Age** ___*8 months*___

> *Ben looked up when he heard laughing. He smiled and clapped his hands.*

Child ___*Maddie*___ **Age** ___*16 months*___

> *Maddie picked up a sponge and helped me wipe off the table.*

How I Demonstrate and Promote Caring Behaviors

1. *I noticed that Aaron (19 months) handed Michael (same age) a shovel in the sandbox. I told Aaron I liked the way he shared his things with Michael.*

2. *I bumped my knee hard and said, "Ouch!" David (12 months) came over as I was rubbing it. I said, "Can you help me rub it?" and he did.*

3. *Karen (3 months) was crying hard when she woke up. Leroy (12 months) came over to us and looked puzzled. I knelt down, holding Karen. Leroy stroked her hair. I said, "Thank you for helping Karen feel better."*

4. *I was putting the toys in a box and asked three toddlers to help me. They did and I said, "Thank you for being such good helpers. I couldn't have done it all myself."*

5. *I took photographs of the children and made a book about how everyone helps each other in our room. The toddlers love it!*

Caring Behaviors of Infants and Toddlers
(Example)

Observation Dates _____

Describe examples of caring behaviors of these children.

Child _____   **Age** _____

_____

_____

_____

_____

Child _____   **Age**_____

_____

_____

_____

_____

Child _____   **Age**_____

_____

_____

_____

_____

Child _____   **Age**_____

_____

_____

_____

_____

How I Demonstrate and Promote Caring Behaviors

1. _____
   _____
   _____
   _____
   _____

2. _____
   _____
   _____
   _____
   _____

3. _____
   _____
   _____
   _____
   _____

4. _____
   _____
   _____
   _____
   _____

5. _____
   _____
   _____
   _____

Discuss this activity with your trainer.

III. Promoting Infants' and Toddlers' Play

In this activity you will learn:

- to observe how infants and toddlers learn and develop through play; and

- to guide children's play in ways that promote their social development.

Play is a child's work, and it helps children develop in all areas. As they play, children develop physically, learn how to think and solve problems, and develop self-esteem. Play is also one of the most important ways in which children develop social skills. It helps them learn to take turns, share favorite things, understand how a friend feels, express their own feelings, and try out grown-up roles.

For an **infant**, play can be almost anything—smiling back at a caregiver, kicking a mobile, crawling over a big floppy pillow, beating a pan with a spoon, or reaching out and touching another infant's cheek. Throughout the day there are countless natural opportunities for play. Dressing an infant can be the perfect time to point out different body parts: "Where's Bobby's nose? Here it is!" An infant crawling across the room may find a bell to ring, another infant to stop and touch, and a ball to bump and send rolling. There might also be times of the day when caregivers do special play activities with one or more infants. You might sit on the floor with an infant and roll a ball back and forth, or you might introduce a game such as "Can You Do What I Do?" to help a child become more aware of what other people are doing. Both planned and unplanned play times can be valuable opportunities for fostering an infant's social development.

As infants grow, they develop new social skills that influence how they play. For example, from a very young age, infants respond to "peek-a-boo" games that adults initiate. It doesn't take long for them to learn to keep a "peek-a-boo" game going by peeking out from behind the doorway one more time. And in their second year of life, they may learn how to begin the game by ducking behind the door or covering their faces with their blankets. Being able to take turns and knowing how to begin a game are skills that infants need for the more complex play of their toddler and preschool years.

What infants learn about objects also influences their play. At first, infants treat all objects in the same way, but between 9 and 12 months, infants learn about differences in objects. They may roll their balls and pat their dolls' heads. Knowing about objects is a necessary first step for more complex play such as pretending to drink from a cup.

Without a doubt, the caregiver is the most important influence on an infant's play in the center. Here are some guidelines to help you support infants' social development through play.

- **Interact with infants as you care for them.** Don't feel you have to entertain them. Instead, respond to them, and give them opportunities to respond to you. For instance, pause a moment when you play an imitating game to give an infant time to pat his or her head before you move on to another activity.

- **Observe young infants so you can read their cues** and adapt your play accordingly. Your observations might tell you that a tickle game is too much for a tired 5-month-old at the end of the day and that the child might enjoy quiet singing instead.

- **Change your plans to meet an infant's needs or build on an infant's skills.** If you are singing to a 4-month-old infant who begins cooing, you might stop before your song is finished and acknowledge the infant by saying, "I hear you singing, too."

- **Communicate with infants** as you play. Looking, talking, moving, holding, laughing, and singing are all ways to communicate. Respond to infants when they communicate. "I see you looking over at me. Do you want me to pick you up?"

- **Use language in interacting with an infant.** Infants are interested in language. Repeating "bah, bah, bah" can be an enjoyable game in itself. An "aah baby" can be soothing. "I think you are angry" communicates feelings, and "this is a cup" gives an infant information.

- **Recognize that each infant has a unique style of playing.** Some infants approach an activity hesitantly, while others jump right in and get involved. Respect each infant's style and adapt your play accordingly. Hiding your face and calling "peek-a-boo" may be the way to start play with one baby, while with another you may say, "Jerry, shall we play 'peek-a-boo'? Watch— I'm going to put my hands over my face now."

Toddlers spend their days playing alone, next to other children, occasionally with another child, and with caregivers. A toddler might play alone with toys that are different from those used by others in the group. Although other children might be nearby, he or she might not talk to them or move toward them. This kind of play is called solitary play. As toddlers get older, they begin playing alongside each other using the same kinds of toys. This is called parallel play. It involves some talking between toddlers. Two children sitting at opposite ends of a sand box, both using shovels and chatting with one another, are involved in parallel play. They are enjoying each other's company but are not yet ready to build a home in the sand together, which would be an example of cooperative play.

As they move around the room or outdoors, toddlers make the environment interesting for one another. The presence of other children encourages toddlers to explore. A bell ringing in the hand of another toddler is much more interesting than a bell lying on the shelf. It is the motion, sound, and, most important, the fact that another toddler is making something happen that sparks interest and leads to exploring and learning.

Here are some guidelines to help you support toddlers' social development through play.[2]

- **Allow toddlers time to simply watch other children play.** You may feel that all children should be actively engaged at all times. As long as Marcus (22 months) has other choices of activities, it is fine if he chooses to watch someone else paint or climb or put pegs in a pegboard. Here he is learning about the activity before taking action.

- **Encourage and acknowledge sharing but do not insist on it.** Children can learn to share only after they have experienced a sense of ownership. Provide multiples of favorite toys. Model sharing in your interactions with children and other adults.

- **Give toddlers opportunities to play on their own.** Be aware of what toddlers are doing and ready to step in if need be, but try to stay out of the action. It is easier for toddlers to play with adults than with each other and, given the chance, most would choose to play with an adult.

- **Give toddlers a chance to work things out among themselves.** Be ready if they need help, but keep in mind that when Katie (22 months) pulls Isolina's (19 months) hair, she might be curious, not aggressive. Isolina might be able to handle the situation by saying "no" and moving away if she doesn't like what Katie is doing.

- **Help toddlers develop an awareness of themselves and their peers.** For example, you might make comments such as the following: "Sally, you have almost finished putting that puzzle together," or "James likes tunafish but Susie prefers cheese sandwiches."

- **Encourage toddlers to help each other** in different situations even if they end up needing your assistance. For example, you might suggest that Karen (33 months) help George (22 months) zip up his coat, or you might ask Jake (32 months) to show Manuel (30 months) how to put the napkins on the table.

- **Respect children's relationships** by not insisting that everyone be friends. Friendships will develop on their own.

- **Attract toddlers' attention by getting down on the floor to play.** Calling a small group together is not as effective as sitting down yourself and starting to play. Toddlers who are curious will come over to see what's happening and will become involved quite naturally.

---

[2]Adapted with permission from Dennie Palmer Wolf, ed., *Connecting: Friendship in the Lives of Young Children and Their Teachers* (Redmond, WA: Exchange Press, PO Box 2890, Redmond Washington 98073, (206) 883-9394, 1986), pp. 18-26.

Encouraging Dramatic Play

Toddlers develop social skills by engaging in simple forms of dramatic play. Their dramatic play is usually centered around family activities they know well, such as eating, cleaning, cooking, and caring for babies. You've probably seen toddlers patting a doll as they say, "Sleep baby." Usually this will last for just a minute, but it is the beginning of dramatic play. You can encourage imaginative play by providing realistic props for toddlers to use as they are pretending. Toy food and a few dishes can prompt a party. A toy telephone might lead to a simple dialogue of "hello" and "goodbye." Longer, more detailed conversations will happen later. You might comment to a toddler holding a doll, "I see your baby needs a nap. Where should we put her?"

To encourage dramatic play, remember the following:

- **Simple props are best.** Plastic dishes and spoons, a pot or two, dolls and blankets, a few pocketbooks, briefcases, and hats will lead to hours of play.

- **Pretend play can take place any time, anywhere.** Keep your eyes open. You may discover that it isn't Duane crawling on the floor but a kitten looking for a bowl of milk. Sometimes you may decide to take a more active role in shaping children's play. At the water table you may, for example, pick up a margarine container and say, "Toot, toot! Here comes my boat." Once play has started, step back. Too much involvement can inhibit children's play. If they are going to have fun and learn, their play must belong to them.

- **Take dramatic play props outside.** A blanket draped over a picnic table makes a wonderful tent, house, or hiding place. Bowls and spoons can prompt a pretend lunch of pinecones. A box may become a car.

- **Help children use dramatic play to express their feelings.** When a toddler is missing her parents, you can pretend to call her mother or father on the telephone: "Hello, is this Rita's mommy? She'd like to talk to you." Then hand the phone to the toddler and encourage her to talk to her mother.

In this activity you will spend 5 to 10 minutes observing one or more children playing with each other or a caregiver. Record what happened and what social skills you observed in use or being developed. Read the two examples before you begin your observation.

Promoting Children's Play
(Infant Example)

Child(ren) _Toby_   **Age** _15 months_   **Date** _June 12_

Setting _In the play yard_   **Caregiver** _Ms. Lewis_

Describe the play:

Toby and Ms. Lewis are throwing a ball into a laundry basket, then taking it out to throw again. They laugh together and take turns throwing the ball. When Toby tries to get the ball out of the basket, he can't reach inside. Ms. Lewis watches to see what he will do. He tries to climb in the basket, but he doesn't fit. Then he tips it over and the ball rolls out. He picks it up and runs back to Ms. Lewis. She hugs him and tells him he is very clever.

What social skills were used or being developed?

Toby learned that it was fun to play with someone else. He learned about taking turns. He learned that he could solve problems on his own and that Ms. Lewis was there if he needed her. He learned that Ms. Lewis enjoyed playing with him.

What did the caregiver do to promote the child(ren)'s play?

Ms. Lewis took turns with Toby. She laughed with him and let him know she liked playing with him. She let him solve his own problem.

Promoting Children's Play
(Toddler Example)

Child(ren) _Carlos and Joanie_   **Age(s)** _24 and 30 months_   **Date(s)** _June 12_

Setting _Morning free play indoors_   **Caregiver** _Ms. Moore_

Describe the play:

Joanie is jumping on the pillows. Carlos watches her. She smiles at Carlos and says, "Jump." Then Carlos begins jumping on the pillows next to Joanie. He jumps on the green pillow, and she jumps on the red one. They look at each other and laugh. Joanie jumps off her red pillow and onto the green one. Carlos looks at Joanie and says, "No." Ms. Moore is playing with some children in the block area. When she hears the loud "no," she looks up. Joanie returns to her red pillow, and Carlos stays on the green one. Ms. Moore watches them bounce for a while; then she continues playing with the block builders.

What social skills were used or being developed?

The children were learning to play alongside each other. They were learning that playing together is fun. Carlos uses his words to tell Joanie that he doesn't want her to jump on his pillow. Joanie responds to him and returns to her pillow.

What did the caregiver do to promote the child(ren)'s play?

She watched them from a distance. When she saw that they could manage without her help, she returned to what she was doing. By staying out of their conflict, she let them learn how to play together.

Promoting Children's Play

Child(ren) _____ Age(s)_____ Date(s) _____

Setting _____ Caregiver _____

Describe the play:

_____

_____

_____

_____

_____

What social skills were used or being developed?

_____

_____

_____

_____

_____

What did the caregiver do to promote the child(ren)'s play?

_____

_____

_____

_____

_____

Discuss this learning activity with your trainer.

IV. Creating an Environment That Supports Social Development

In this activity you will learn:

- to set up the environment to help infants and toddlers be comfortable in a group setting; and

- to plan the environment so that young children are encouraged to interact with adults and each other.

You are the most important part of the environment for the infants and toddlers in your room. You provide the base from which they can explore and learn about themselves and other people. The ways in which you arrange the furniture and equipment and display the toys and other materials can help children feel comfortable interacting. The following are some of the ways that you can create an environment that encourages the social development of infants and toddlers.

- **Be sure that each child has a special relationship with a caregiver.** A special relationship, which is hard to see and can't be neatly arranged like a toy shelf, is the most important way in which the environment enhances a child's social development. Through special relationships with their caregivers, children learn to trust other people and to feel good about themselves.

- **Create a homelike environment.** Infants and toddlers in the center spend most of their waking hours away from their home and families. By creating a homelike environment, you help children feel safe and comfortable in the center. (See Module 3 for suggestions.)

- **Arrange space and activities so children have opportunities to spend time alone or in a small group during the day.** Living all day in a group can be stressful for infants and toddlers as well as for caregivers. Being alone with a caregiver or in a small group of two or three children offers opportunities for social interaction that a large group doesn't. An infant seat, a corner piled with pillows, a large cardboard box, and a large, comfortable chair are examples of physical spaces that can provide children with a break from group life. Short walks inside the building or outside, playing at the sand table, or preparing snacks are examples of activities that children can do with a caregiver alone or with one or two other children.

- **Provide young infants with safe places from which to watch mobile infants and caregivers interact.** An infant seat (used only for a short period of time) and a caregiver's lap are examples of such places.

You can use the environment in many ways to encourage mobile infants and toddlers to interact with each other. Here are some suggestions.

- **Provide clear limits so mobile infants and toddlers can be free to explore and play.** Set up your environment so you don't have to constantly say "no" and chase after children. A closed door lets children know they should not go in, and a pile of large, soft pillows invites them to jump safely.

- **Offer a variety of activities so infants and toddlers can choose what they want to do.** Keep in mind that no matter how much you like the activity you have planned, some children may choose not to participate.

- **Create places where children can watch what is going on.** Children in group care often need private spaces where they can get away for a while. Some children like to watch before they join in an activity. A platform or a window seat are ideal places from which to observe the action in the room.

- **Arrange spaces where two or three children can play together** or close to each other, such as a sandbox or a rocking boat. Toddlers can easily become confused and overwhelmed in large groups.

- **Put out duplicates of toys** and offer enough choices so that toddlers who are not ready to share can still play happily together.

- **Make sure that toys and equipment are developmentally appropriate.** If young children are constantly frustrated by puzzles that are too difficult, interlocking toys that they can't fit together, or blocks that fall down because the rug is too bumpy, they may express their frustrations by lashing out at others. You can promote positive relationships by making sure that toys and materials are ones that children can use successfully.

- **Include materials that two or three children can use together.** Large boxes, tunnels, a water play tub, and bins filled with shape blocks are examples of materials that two toddlers can use at the same time. Activities such as sand and water play hold children's attention and can encourage social interactions.

- **Plan small group activities.** Ask several children to help you prepare a special snack, or hang a large sheet of paper for several children to color together. These types of activities encourage interaction among several children working side by side. Children enjoy them because they don't require sharing of toys or materials.

- **Encourage dramatic play.** Provide simple props such as hats, bags, plates, pans, and wooden spoons. Caregivers can enhance children's play by asking them questions such as these: "Where are you going?" or "What are you making for dinner?"

In this learning activity you will identify ways that your environment supports social development. Then you will plan two changes to your indoor or outdoor environment and note how these changes affect children's social interactions. Read the example before completing the activity for your environment.

Creating an Environment That Promotes Social Development
(Example)

Setting _Infant play room_   **Age Group** _8-18 months_   **Date(s)** _April 2-6_

What materials and furniture in your room encourage social development?

There are large open spaces where infants and toddlers can crawl safely and climb.
We have mirrors at floor level and lots of things to play with and explore. Also,
we have a large mattress to climb on. We offer plenty of toys so there's enough
for everyone.

What will you change or add to the environment to encourage social skills?

I will bring in a large cardboard box from a water heater we just received. I'll
open it at both ends so the children can crawl through it and also put in some new
bright-colored pillows and stuffed animals.

What did the children do after you made this change or addition to the environment?

Charles (12 months) went to the box immediately, looked through one end, and
then crawled through the box and out the other end. Ella (15 months) followed
right behind. They laughed together and then repeated this over and over. This
attracted the attention of two other children who joined them. Some children
preferred to stay inside, sitting on the pillows, and that created a problem because
the other children wanted to move through the tunnel. So I brought in a smaller
box and put the pillows in there for the children who just wanted to sit.

How did these changes encourage children's social development?

Going through the "tunnel" became a very popular game, one that several children
could do together. Sometimes they even played "Follow the Leader" through the
tunnel so they really learned to cooperate and play together. Having two boxes,
one for a hideaway and one used as a tunnel, meant that there was something for
everyone, and the children didn't need to fight over turns.

Creating an Environment That Promotes Social Development

Setting _____ Age Group _____ Date(s) _____

What materials and furniture in your room encourage social development?

_____
_____
_____
_____
_____
_____

What will you change or add to the environment to encourage social skills?

_____
_____
_____
_____
_____

What did the children do after you made this change or addition to the environment?

_____
_____
_____
_____
_____

How did these changes encourage children's social development?

_____
_____
_____
_____
_____

Discuss this activity with your trainer.

Summarizing Your Progress

You have now completed all of the learning activities for this module. Whether you are an experienced caregiver or a new one, this module has probably helped you develop new skills for promoting social development. Before you go on, take a few minutes to summarize what you've learned.

- Turn back to Learning Activity I, Using Your Knowledge of Infant and Toddler Development to Promote Social Development, and add to the chart specific examples of how you promoted social development during the time you were working on this module.

- Next, review your responses to the pre-training assessment for this module. Write a summary of what you learned, and list the skills you developed or improved.

_____

_____

_____

_____

_____

Your final step in this module is to complete the knowledge and competency assessments. Let your trainer know when you are ready to schedule the assessments. After you have successfully completed these assessments, you will be ready to start a new module. Congratulations on your progress so far, and good luck with your next module.

Answer Sheet: Promoting Social Development

Helping Infants and Toddlers Learn to Get Along with Other Members of the Group

1. How did Ms. Gonzalez encourage Rochelle's social development?

    a. She gave her some individual attention in the rocking chair.

    b. She smiled back at Rochelle when she touched her face.

2. How did Ms. Gonzalez encourage the two infants to get along with each other?

    a. She let Rochelle know that Carrie would be joining them.

    b. She made room in her lap so that both children would be comfortable.

Helping Infants and Toddlers Understand and Express Their Feelings and Respect Those of Others

1. How did Ms. Bates figure out what Leroy was feeling?

    a. She picked him up.

    b. She checked his diaper.

    c. She checked the daily record for sleep and eating.

    d. She was playful with him, and he responded by giggling.

2. How did Ms. Bates help Leroy begin learning about respecting others?

    a. She responded to his crying by holding him.

    b. She tried to figure out why he was crying.

    c. She talked to him about the steps she was taking to find out why he was crying.

    d. She offered the explanation that maybe he wanted some companionship and a change of scenery.

    e. She changed his scene and played with him.

Providing an Environment and Experiences That Support Social Development

1. **How did Mr. Jones use the daily routine of getting ready to go outside to help the children develop social skills?**

    a. He asked two children to help another child find her missing shoe.

    b. He said the bag of balls was so big that he needed help to carry it.

    c. He said he likes it when children work together.

2. **What social skills did the children practice as they prepared to go outside?**

    a. They learned to work together and help each other.

    b. They learned to feel good about themselves because Mr. Jones thinks all the children are important, and he will wait until everyone is ready before going outside.

Using Your Knowledge of Infant and Toddler Development to Promote Social Development

WHAT YOUNG INFANTS DO (0-8 MONTHS)	HOW CAREGIVERS CAN USE THIS INFORMATION TO PROMOTE SOCIAL DEVELOPMENT
They cry to express their needs.	Try to learn what children are saying when they cry and respond appropriately. This helps them learn how it feels to be in nurturing, caring relationships.
They make eye contact and like to look at faces.	Look at children when you talk with them to let them experience what attentive communication feels like.
They gradually learn to recognize primary caregivers.	Be aware that children need a consistent special adult so they can feel secure and experience a positive relationship with an adult who really knows and cares about them.
They show a wide variety of feelings.	Recognize and respect children's feelings. Take advantage of daily routines to talk with children about feelings they may be expressing.
They begin to initiate interactions and games with adults.	Be aware of children's cues and signals that they want to interact. Talk with them and play games such as "peek-a-boo" and looking in the mirror. Show them that it is fun to interact with another person.
They are interested in other children.	Provide opportunities for children to see each other. Be close by to ensure their safety, but let them touch each other and be together so they will learn about being with other people.

WHAT MOBILE INFANTS DO (9-17 MONTHS)	HOW CAREGIVERS CAN USE THIS INFORMATION TO PROMOTE SOCIAL DEVELOPMENT
They are sensitive to and interested in the moods and activities of others.	Provide opportunities for children to watch each other and interact. Explain in words what children might be feeling. Talk about what others are doing to encourage children's interest in others. Talk about your feelings. Share your pleasure in and excitement about things children do.
They understand more language than they are able to use.	Show children respect by including them in conversations.
They look to adults for encouragement, support, and approval.	Be available as a "home base" for children to check back to if necessary when they are interacting with other people. Share your pleasure and interest in children's new relationships. Say, for example, "It looked like you and Chris were having lots of fun rowing that boat together."
They may begin to demonstrate fear of strangers.	Encourage strangers to approach slowly. Support children by being sure a special caregiver is there when a visitor arrives or when a child is getting to know a new person.
They are increasingly aware of their own possessions.	Acknowledge an infant's possessions and help children define who they are by helping them protect their things. Sharing can be encouraged, but it is learned at a later age.
They enjoy helping caregivers because they like to imitate adults.	Provide opportunities for children to help you so that they can feel good about themselves and their ability to help.

WHAT TODDLERS DO (18-36 MONTHS)	HOW CAREGIVERS CAN USE THIS INFORMATION TO PROMOTE SOCIAL DEVELOPMENT
They have strong feelings but might not have the words to express them. They may hit, bite, push, or pinch instead.	Be aware of what toddlers are doing so you can step in and help if necessary. Provide materials and toys (such as a sandbox or rocking boat) that can be shared easily to encourage positive social interactions. Give toddlers words for their feelings ("I am angry," "I am sad") to help them use words instead of hitting, biting, or pushing.
They are beginning to understand what personal property is.	Provide spaces where toddlers can store their things, and help toddlers protect their projects (block buildings, paintings). Help them know how it feels to have their property respected.
They enjoy helping to do chores.	Help toddlers feel that they are valuable members of the group by including them in the "real work" of taking care of the room (such as cleaning the table, putting away supplies, and setting a table).
They can become overwhelmed in a busy environment.	Provide spaces where toddlers can spend time alone. Divide the group during the day to give toddlers the opportunity to interact with each other and caregivers in small groups of two or three children.
They are beginning to enjoy playing with others.	Have more than one of their favorite toys so toddlers can play together without having to share. Encourage toddlers to interact by providing activities that more than one child can do at once. Encourage toddlers to help each other—for example, carrying something heavy, finding a lost shoe, or getting a tissue.
They are aware of the adults who are important to them, and they want to be like them.	Model caring behaviors. Share, take turns, help, and talk about what you're doing. Encourage toddlers' caring behaviors by saying, "I saw the way you shared with Michael. That was very generous of you. Thanks!"

Glossary

Cooperative play	Two or more children playing together, using the same toys or materials, or making believe.
Parallel play	Two or more children playing side by side, using the same or similar kinds of toys or materials but not interacting.
Peer	A friend or companion who is the same age or at the same developmental level.
Prosocial behavior	Accepted behaviors, such as sharing or taking turns, which children learn and use to get along in society.
Social development	The gradual process through which children learn to live as members of a group.
Solitary play	The first stage of play, when infants and young toddlers play alone, independent of other children.

Module 10
Guidance

What Is Guidance and Why Is It Important?

Children need adults to guide them—to help them learn what is acceptable behavior and what is not. How you offer this guidance depends on your goals for the children you care for. What kind of people do you want them to become? Do you want them to behave out of fear or because they have learned what is acceptable and want to live cooperatively with others?

Because adults are powerful, they can make children behave in certain ways. But children who are punished or forced to "be good" learn the following lessons:

- I am a bad person.

- I need to watch out for adults.

- I had better not get caught.

These children become like puppets whose behavior is controlled from the outside. They are likely to behave well only when someone is watching, because they don't want to be punished. They do not learn to value acceptable behavior for itself. They do not learn self-discipline.

Self-discipline is the ability to control one's own behavior. People who are self-disciplined make independent choices based on what they believe is right. They are able to balance their own needs with those of others. They can accept the results of their actions.

Adults who want children to learn to make their own decisions, to know the difference between right and wrong, and to correct their own mistakes need to provide positive guidance. That is what this module is about.

Positive guidance takes many forms. Sometimes caregivers take actions such as covering outlets or providing duplicates of favorite toys to prevent dangerous or unacceptable behavior before it occurs. At other times caregivers intervene to redirect behavior as they guide an infant to chew on a rubber toy rather than a piece of paper or a toddler to climb on the climber instead of the table. And sometimes caregivers must step in and stop a behavior such as hitting or biting.

By developing a trusting, caring relationship with the infants and toddlers in your room, you are already doing a lot to help them achieve the goal of self-discipline. Because the children you care for feel close to you, they imitate some of your actions and attitudes. How you behave helps them learn what is acceptable and what is not. They depend on you and want your approval. Your smile of encouragement when a toddler uses the potty inspires that child to sit on the potty next time. By learning some techniques of positive guidance, you can continue to help children take their first steps toward self-discipline.

Guiding infants' and toddlers' behavior in ways that promote self-discipline involves:

- providing an environment that encourages children's self-discipline;

- using positive methods to guide individual children; and

- helping children understand and express their feelings in acceptable ways.

Listed below are examples of how caregivers demonstrate their competence in guiding the behavior of infants and toddlers.

Providing an Environment That Encourages Self-Discipline

Here are some examples of what caregivers can do.

- Encourage safe exploration by making sure there are no safety hazards. "Mr. Jones, that was a good idea to replace the indoor climber. It was just too large for the children in this group."

- Store toys and equipment on low shelves. "Sammy, please put the big blocks back on their shelf now. You can take them down again tomorrow."

- Prepare children for changes in advance. "Felicia, I'm going to change your diaper next. As soon as you go up and down the slide, it will be your turn."

- Organize daily routines to keep waiting time to a minimum. "Sandra is going to wake up soon. I will get her bottle ready now because she's usually very hungry after her nap."

- Arrange the room to provide children with private spaces. "When Marty wants to be alone, she likes to sit in the refrigerator-box house."

- Follow children's cues when planning activities. "Jamie is still talking about the digger we saw on our walk yesterday. Let's go by it again today."

Using Positive Methods to Guide Each Child's Behavior

Here are some examples of what caregivers can do.

- Try to understand why an infant is crying. "I wonder if your diaper is wet, Tamika. Let's change you and see if that helps you feel better."

- Help children see the consequences for their actions. "Carla, there's a sponge by the sink. You can use it to clean up the juice you spilled."

- Redirect children to acceptable activities. "Susan's holding that doll, Bobby. Here's another doll for you to hold."

- Be there for a child having a tantrum. "Laura, I'm going to sit here with you to help you calm down."

- Use simple, positive reminders to restate rules. "Use the crayons on the paper, Jerry, not on the table."

- Gently move children while accepting their need to say no. "I'm going to carry you inside today because you're having such a hard time coming in by yourself. I know you really want to stay outside, but it's lunchtime."

Helping Infants and Toddlers Understand and Express Their Feelings in Acceptable Ways

Here are some examples of what caregivers can do.

- Make it easier to wait for a turn. "I know it's hard to wait. Do you want to help me hold the bowl until it is your turn to stir the pancake batter?"

- Offer an angry child a soothing activity. "Jane, you look so angry. I think playing at the water table might help you feel happier. We have some new funnels you can use."

- Give children words for their feelings. "Tricia, I know you feel angry when Debby pushes you. Tell Debby *no!*"

- Model acceptable ways to express anger. "Barbara, I've asked you three times to please use your inside voice. Your loud voice really hurts my ears."

- Listen to children's crying or words that tell how they are feeling. "Corey, are you sad because Daddy had to say goodbye?"

Guiding Children's Behavior

In the following situations, caregivers are providing guidance to help infants and toddlers develop self-discipline. As you read each one, think about what the caregivers are doing and why. Then answer each one of the questions that follow.

Providing an Environment that Encourages Self-Discipline

It is a stressful day in the infant room. Carrie (3 months) is finding life very frustrating, and she is letting her caregivers know by crying. Ms. Bates and Ms. Jackson are working together to try to find out why Carrie is distressed. Ms. Bates changes her diaper, feeds her a bottle, and puts her down in her crib. Fifteen peaceful minutes pass before she starts crying again. This time Ms. Jackson takes a turn while Ms. Bates plays with the other children. She calmly picks her up and rocks her for a while. "Carrie, dear. I know you want me to help you feel better. Let's see if rocking works. I'll hold you in my arms." Carrie settles down and almost falls asleep. All of a sudden she starts crying again. Ms. Bates says, "I'll take her for a while. I've noticed that she likes it when she lies across my lap on her belly." Ms. Bates sits down in the rocking chair and carefully places Carrie across her lap. Then she rubs her back. Ms. Jackson puts on some soft music before she goes to take care of the other children. In a few minutes Carrie is asleep. Ms. Jackson and Ms. Bates look at each other and sigh with relief.

1. How did Ms. Jackson and Ms. Bates support each other?

_____

_____

_____

2. What did Ms. Bates and Ms. Jackson do to help Carrie?

_____

_____

_____

3. Why did Ms. Bates place Carrie across her lap?

_____

_____

_____

Using Positive Methods to Guide Each Child's Behavior

Mr. Jones and the group of 2-year-olds are outside in the play yard. Travis, a very active child, has collected some pine cones and is throwing them at other children. Mr. Jones walks over to him. He bends down, looks at him, and says, "Travis, you are learning to be a good thrower. But if you hit someone with a pine cone, they might be hurt or angry. You can practice your throwing safely on the grass, or you can do something else. Shall I help you carry your pine cones over where there aren't other children?" Travis nods yes. He and Mr. Jones carry the pine cones over to the grass. Mr. Jones watches for a few minutes and then goes over to the sandbox to play with other children.

1. What did Mr. Jones know about Travis?

_____

_____

_____

2. How did Mr. Jones let Travis know that he respected him?

_____

_____

_____

Helping Infants and Toddlers Understand and Express Their Feelings in Acceptable Ways

"No!" screams Billy (18 months). With arm extended, he leans over ready to hit Sam (15 months), who has just grabbed a piece of orange from Billy's plate. "Billy," says Ms. Lewis, extending her hand between Billy's hand and Sam's arm. Billy looks up at Ms. Lewis. "That was good stopping," Ms. Lewis says. "I know you don't like it when someone takes your things. Tell Sam not to take your orange. You can talk to people when you are angry, but I can't let you hit them." Billy looks at Sam and says, "Mine." Sam puts the piece of orange down and goes back to eating his lunch.

1. How do you think Billy felt when Sam grabbed his piece of orange?

_____

_____

_____

2. How did Ms. Lewis help Billy learn to express his feelings in acceptable ways?

_____

_____

_____

Compare your answers with those on the answer sheet at the end of this module. If your answers are different, discuss them with your trainer. There can be more than one good answer.

Your Own Self-Discipline

Often your behavior is automatic. You don't stop to think about what you should do; you just do it. When you put money in a parking meter, come to work on time, or thank a store clerk, you are probably acting without thinking about what you are doing. You have learned and accepted certain rules of behavior, and because you have self-discipline, you don't need to be reminded of them.

Your self-discipline guides your behavior at work in many ways.

- You let the center director know when you're sick so a substitute can be called.

- You let a colleague know you are angry with her by telling her what you feel and why.

- You volunteer to help a colleague who's having difficulty understanding the needs of a child.

- You don't make long-distance calls on the center phone.

List below a few other examples of how self-discipline guides your behavior at work.

_____

_____

_____

_____

_____

Self-discipline also guides your behavior at home.

- You remember to water the plants because you know they'll die if you don't.

- You check the car's oil and fill the tank with gas so you won't be stranded by the side of the road.

- You clean the frying pan so it will be ready to use in the morning.

- You say no to a second piece of cake because you shouldn't have so much sugar.

List below several other examples of how self-discipline guides your behavior at home.

_____

_____

_____

_____

_____

Think of a time when you did not show self-discipline. What affected your loss of control?

_____

_____

_____

_____

_____

What does this tell you about what children need to gain self-discipline?

_____

_____

_____

_____

Some adults have problems making their own decisions about how to behave. They are most comfortable when they have rules and guidelines to follow. They may respond only to promises of rewards or threats of punishment. Perhaps they come to work on time only because they're afraid of being fired or having their pay docked.

When these adults were children, they probably didn't have many opportunities to make their own decisions. They weren't able to develop inner controls.

Being in control of your own behavior usually results in higher self-esteem. Having good feelings about yourself will make you a more effective and skilled caregiver. Your self-discipline is a good model for the children. They will learn a lot from being cared for by a responsible and competent person.

When you have finished this overview section, you should complete the pre-training assessment. Refer to the glossary at the end of this module if you need definitions for the terms that are used.

Pre-Training Assessment

Listed below are the skills that caregivers use to guide infants' and toddlers' behavior. Think about whether you do these things regularly, sometimes, or not enough. Place a check in one of the columns on the right for each skill listed. Then discuss your answers with your trainer.

SKILL	I DO THIS REGULARLY	I DO THIS SOMETIMES	I DON'T DO THIS ENOUGH
PROVIDING AN ENVIRONMENT THAT ENCOURAGES SELF-DISCIPLINE			
1. Planning the schedule so children don't have to wait too long for their needs to be met.			
2. Removing temptations or dangerous objects from young children's reach.			
3. Helping young children learn to get along with each other.			
4. Anticipating dangerous situations and providing a safe environment so infants and toddlers can explore freely.			
5. Keeping the room well-organized so there is more time to spend with children.			
6. Keeping toys and other safe materials on low shelves so children can reach them and help put them away.			

SKILL	I DO THIS REGULARLY	I DO THIS SOMETIMES	I DON'T DO THIS ENOUGH
USING POSITIVE METHODS TO GUIDE EACH CHILD'S BEHAVIOR			
7. Separating children who are hurting each other.			
8. Using the word "no" sparingly.			
9. Giving infants and toddlers chances to make real decisions and choices.			
10. Using positive words to explain rules or limits and telling children what they can do (for example, "You can read the books but I can't let you tear our books.")			
11. Using facial expressions and tone of voice to express feelings.			
12. Trying to understand why a child is crying.			
13. Trying to understand the reasons for an infant's or toddler's behavior.			
14. Letting children say "no" because it helps them feel independent.			
15. Anticipating when problem behaviors might occur and taking steps to prevent them.			

SKILL	I DO THIS REGULARLY	I DO THIS SOMETIMES	I DON'T DO THIS ENOUGH
HELPING INFANTS AND TODDLERS UNDERSTAND AND EXPRESS THEIR FEELINGS IN ACCEPTABLE WAYS 16. Listening to children as they express their sad, hungry, or frustrated feelings.			
17. Providing soothing activities.			
18. Working with parents and other staff to plan a supportive strategy for dealing with a challenging behavior such as biting.			
19. Modeling appropriate ways to express feelings.			
20. Encouraging children with language skills to use words to express their feelings.			

Review your responses, then list three to five skills you would like to improve or topics you would like to learn more about. When you finish this module, you will list examples of your new or improved knowledge and skills.

_____

_____

_____

_____

_____

_____

_____

_____

Now begin the learning activities for Module 10, Guidance.

I. Using Your Knowledge of Infant and Toddler Development to Guide Behavior

In this activity you will learn:

- to recognize some typical behaviors of infants and toddlers; and

- to use what you know about child development to help infants and toddlers develop self-discipline.

Understanding children's behavior is the first step in providing guidance and promoting self-discipline. By learning what children can and can't do at each stage of development, caregivers can develop realistic expectations for children's behavior. They also can learn how to adopt daily routines or the environment to meet children's needs rather than expecting the children to change their behavior.

Infants need what they need when they need it. They do not cry because they are trying to annoy you or because they are "bad." They cry to let you know that they need you—to feed them, change their diapers, or turn off the lights that are shining in their eyes. Studies have shown that when an infant's cries are met quickly, the infant cries less often than an infant who has to wait for a caregiver to respond.

At about 6 to 8 months, infants begin to have more control over their actions. They are fascinated with what their hands, fingers, legs, and feet can do. They grasp, pull, squeeze, poke, and kick objects (and people) within their reach. Caregivers might need to step in so that infants do not get hurt. For example, you should remove a mobile from a crib when an infant is strong enough to pull it down, and you should step in when an infant is about to poke another child in the eye.

Between 10 and 12 months of age, infants begin to realize that their caregivers don't approve of some of the things they do. A caregiver's tone of voice or firm "no" can help these older infants learn what the limits are. The infant room should be arranged so that the children can explore safely.

Toddlers can try your patience. One minute they want to be independent and do everything themselves; the next, they want to be babies. Sometimes the intense feelings of push and pull that are part of being a toddler explode in a tantrum. Because a tantrum often signals loss of control, it can be frightening for children—and adults. Children need you to be there for them. Sometimes you can help children pull themselves together by holding them. At other times the best thing to do is to sit near and wait out the storm.

As toddlers move out into the world, they need their caregivers to set limits. Ironically, limits give children the freedom to be active, curious explorers. Knowing someone is there to help them stop makes the world a safer place. Although toddlers often forget what you tell them from one minute to the next, they are beginning to learn what is acceptable behavior and what is not.

The chart on the next page lists some typical behaviors of infants and toddlers. Included are behaviors relevant to self-discipline. The right-hand column asks you to identify ways that caregivers can use this information about child development to help children develop self-discipline. Try to think of as many examples as you can. As you work through the module, you will learn new strategies for guiding children's behavior, and you can add them to the child development chart. You are not expected to think of all the examples at one time. By the time you complete all the learning activities, you will find that you have learned many ways to guide children's behavior.

Using Your Knowledge of Infant and Toddler Development to Guide Behavior

WHAT YOUNG INFANTS DO (0-8 MONTHS)	HOW CAREGIVERS CAN USE THIS INFORMATION TO GUIDE BEHAVIOR
They like to be held.	
They respond to faces and listen to voices.	
They cry (sometimes a lot).	
They reach out and grab things (for example, mobiles, toys, and eyeglasses).	
They can become bored.	

WHAT MOBILE INFANTS DO (9-17 MONTHS)	HOW CAREGIVERS CAN USE THIS INFORMATION TO GUIDE BEHAVIOR
They experience and express a wide range of feelings (such as happiness, sadness, anger, and frustration).	
They are interested in other children. They can accidentally hurt another child while saying hello or exploring.	
They may show fear of strangers.	
They like to feed themselves.	
They watch and know their important adults—you are one of them! They learn from being around you.	
They know how you feel about them.	

WHAT TODDLERS DO (18-36 MONTHS)	HOW CAREGIVERS CAN USE THIS INFORMATION TO GUIDE BEHAVIOR
They are eager to please adults.	
They want to make decisions for themselves.	
They sometimes lose control and start kicking and screaming.	
They can be very possessive.	
They test limits and say "no" often.	
They sometimes hit out in anger at other children or at adults.	

WHAT TODDLERS DO (18-36 MONTHS)	HOW CAREGIVERS CAN USE THIS INFORMATION TO GUIDE BEHAVIOR
They may suck their thumbs.	
They may touch their genitals or masturbate.	

When you have completed as much as you can do on the chart, discuss your answers with your trainer. As you proceed with the rest of the learning activities, you can refer back to the chart and add more examples of how caregivers guide children's behavior.

II. Guiding Infants' and Toddlers' Behavior

In this activity you will learn:

- to use positive approaches to guide the behavior of infants and toddlers; and

- to use strategies tailored to meet the needs of individual children.

Often the words *discipline* and *punishment* are used to mean the same thing. They are actually very different. Discipline means guiding and directing children toward acceptable behavior. The most important goal of discipline is to help children gain inner controls. Caregivers use discipline to guide children and help them learn the consequences of their actions.

Punishment means controlling children's behavior through fear. Punishment makes children behave well because they are afraid of what might happen to them if they don't. Punishment may stop children's negative behavior temporarily. But it doesn't help the children develop self-discipline. Instead, it might reinforce their bad feelings about themselves.

Caregivers can use a variety of approaches to guide children's behavior. No single approach works for every child or every situation. The approach used should relate to the child and to the problem. Positive disciplinary approaches are based on the following beliefs:

- **The goal of guiding children's behavior is to help them develop self-discipline.** Caregivers should guide behavior in ways that show respect and help children feel good about themselves. "I'm going to pick you up to help you stop pulling Jessie's hair. We'll find something else for you to do."

- **Very young children do not misbehave.** They are not trying to annoy or control anyone when they cry or want to be held. "You are having a fussy day, Pam. Let me get you a bottle, and let's sit in the rocking chair."

- **There is usually a reason for children's behavior.** Caregivers should try to find out why a child is crying or frustrated. "Maria's mother told me she is drooling a lot and chewing on her toys. Maybe she is crying because she is teething and is in pain."

- **Children begin learning how it feels to have inner control by having some help from the outside.** "I am going to hold you to help you stop throwing books."

- **Many problems can be avoided by anticipating dangerous situations and setting up a safe environment.** "You are getting to be a strong crawler. You can crawl in this area of the room, inside these pillows."

- **Many problem behaviors can be avoided by effective planning.** "Put on one of the smocks hanging by the easels, Francia. That way you won't get paint all over your clothes."

175

- **It's best to focus on a child's behavior instead of on the child.** "Thank you for putting your milk carton in the trash can, Annette" (rather than "you're a good girl for cleaning up your place.")

- **Consequences should logically follow a child's actions.** "Paul, I told you, you might hurt someone if you keep swinging that toy around. I'm going to put it away and help you find something else to do."

- **Children can learn from hearing positive language about what behaviors are acceptable.** Use simple, clear language to help children understand you. Be sure that your facial expression and body language reflect what you are saying. "You may use the crayons on the paper."

- **Children's behavior is affected by the atmosphere in the room.** Because children pick up on the feelings of their important adults, caregivers need to figure out ways to support each other when they feel overwhelmed and tense. "Ms. Gonzalez, will you please help Frank? I need a breather."

How you guide a child's behavior depends in large part on the child's age and stage of development. In the first three years, children grow and develop very quickly. How you guide their behavior changes as they become more mobile, develop new skills, and learn new ways to communicate.

Guiding Infants' Behavior

Guiding the behavior of young infants means keeping them safe.

- Keep infants away from potential problems. If an infant is climbing up on the table, move him or her to pillows on the floor or a low padded platform.

- Remove temptations or dangerous objects. Close the bathroom door and put pencils and other sharp objects up high.

- Distract an infant by offering a different toy if another child is playing with the one the infant wants.

- Separate children who are hurting each other. If they are pulling each other's hair, sit down between them and show them how to be gentle.

Around the age of 10 months, children begin understanding how their actions affect others. You can begin to discourage certain behaviors. Here are some specific techniques you can use.

- Express your feelings with your facial expressions and tone of voice, rather than with lots of words.

- If no one will be hurt, give infants a chance to work things out themselves. One child may not even notice or care when another picks up the toy he or she had been playing with.

- Use "no" sparingly. Save this word for dangerous situations so that it will be effective.

- Always respond in ways that help infants feel good about themselves.

Guiding Toddlers' Behavior

The following techniques can help you guide toddlers' behaviors in positive ways.

- When you want toddlers to do something, make a positive suggestion. For example, toddlers are more likely to go along with your request if you say "let's all hang up our coats" rather than "hang up your coats."

- Pay close attention to a toddler who has a tendency to hit, bite, or hurt when angry or frustrated. This will allow you to redirect the child to an acceptable outlet for his or her feelings before another child gets hurt. Make sure to praise children when you see them using self-discipline. "That was good stopping, Jake."

- Ask toddlers silly questions so they can have opportunities to say "no." You might ask questions such as these: "Do we eat dinner in the morning?" or "Can we go swimming in the snow?"

- Show toddlers that you don't like it when they express their anger by hurting people or things. "I know that you feel angry, Josh. It looks like you want to hit Sarah. I like you but I don't like it when people hurt each other. You can hit the pillows instead."

- Be sure that your facial expression and body language reflect the seriousness of your request. Toddlers are making great progress in their understanding and use of verbal language, but they understand and respond to body language with even more precision.

- To get a toddler to give you an object that you do not want the child to have, say, "Give me the_____." Using simple, clear language lets toddlers know what you want them to do.

- Encourage toddlers to participate in daily routines to support their growing need for independence. "Thank you for pushing that chair over to the table. Now we all have a place to sit."

- Understand that toddlers are not ready to share. They must feel a sense of ownership before they will feel secure enough to share their belongings. Provide duplicates of favorite items so that sharing is less of an issue: "Will is using this telephone. You can get one of the other telephones off the shelf."

It is important for parents and caregivers to talk to each other about how to use positive guidance techniques to help infants and toddlers learn self-discipline. Many of the approaches to positive guidance described above are appropriate for use at home as well as at the center. You can help parents develop appropriate expectations for their children's behavior, based on an understanding of child development. Consistency between what is done at home and what is done at the center is crucial in helping children learn self-discipline.

In this learning activity you will review some typical behaviors of children and suggest positive guidance approaches that can be used to guide their behavior.

Using Positive Guidance Techniques

WHAT INFANTS AND TODDLERS DO	HOW YOU WOULD RESPOND
Betty (4 months) has been crying off and on all day.	
Reggie (8 months) has just fallen asleep. A maintenance worker walks in to change a light bulb and slams the door. The noise wakes Reggie, and he begins to cry.	
Lou (9 months) pulls himself to standing and reaches for the pencil you left on the table.	
Fran (11 months) and Laura (10 months) are sitting face to face. Fran reaches out and softly touches Laura's face. Then she grabs a handful of Laura's hair.	
Ed (16 months) throws a block across the room for the third time. He looks at you and smiles.	
Sandy (20 months) is climbing on her cot and laughing as she jumps up and down.	
It is naptime. Eric (22 months) runs across the room, dragging his blanket behind him. He doesn't want to lie down on his cot.	
Lisa (28 months) hits Barry (26 months) when he bumps into her.	

When you have completed the chart, compare your answers to those on the answer sheet at the end of this module. A situation can have more than one good response. Discuss your ideas with your trainer.

III. Creating an Environment to Promote Self-Discipline

In this activity you will learn:

- to observe infants' and toddlers' behavior for clues to problems in the environment; and

- to use the room arrangement and display of materials to help children develop self-discipline.

There are times when everything seems to go wrong, no matter how hard you try. The children seem restless or frustrated. Three children are crying, the floor is covered with toys, and the kitchen counter is so cluttered that you can't find a clean spoon. Children are running across the room, playdough is being smeared in the rug, and a new crawler is heading for the toilet.

There are many reasons why these things happen. But if they seem to happen day after day, it's a good idea to check your room arrangement. How you arrange the room and organize and display materials and equipment can be working against you. The environment can encourage the very problems you want to avoid.

To the children you care for, you are the most important part of the environment. Children tend to be in tune with your feelings. If you feel happy and comfortable in your room, they are likely to feel happy and comfortable there, too. Comfortable seating for adults, a place where you can keep your things, and a vase of flowers are all things that can make your room work for you.

To make the room serve you better, you also need plenty of storage space. Shelves must be clearly marked so you and the other caregivers can find things you need. It is easier to work together if everyone knows where things are. And you can focus on being with the children, instead of searching for an extra pair of socks. You will feel less hassled and more efficient. You will be more likely to include children in daily routines when you can find what you need. Children will benefit because you will be able to spend more time with them.

Making your room safe will save you worry and energy. In addition, a safe space encourages children to explore and literally move out into the world. As they begin crawling, reaching higher, and climbing, they will—with your help—begin learning self-discipline.

Here are some suggestions for arranging your environment to promote self-discipline:

- Keep a variety of safe toys on low, open shelves so mobile infants and toddlers can select what they want to play with and help you return the toys during clean-up time. About once a month, add to or take away from the selection, based on the needs and interests of the children in the group.

180

- Schedule outdoor play times twice a day, weather permitting. Outdoor time gives children fresh air, a time to use "outdoor voices," and opportunities to use their large motor skills and burn up some energy.

- Include in your environment places where infants and toddlers can safely climb, such as a pile of pillows, a mattress, or a low climber or platform.

- Feed infants according to their own personal schedules and try to plan your daily schedule for the older children so that lunch and naptime occur before they get too hungry or too tired. If your center has a set time for serving meals, provide healthy snacks such as crackers or slices of fruit that hungry children can serve themselves.

- Try to plan the day so that children don't have to wait for the next activity to begin. If the group must wait for a few minutes, do a finger play, tell a story, or lead a movement activity to help pass the time in an interesting, relaxed way.

- Give older infants and toddlers time to move from one activity to the next and establish rituals for different routines. For example, put on special, quiet music when it's time to get ready for naps, or announce that it will be time to clean up in five minutes, then two, then one.

In this activity you will consider how room arrangement affects three common behavior problems. Then you will plan ways to change the environment so that the room arrangement helps you address these problems. Begin by reading the example on the next page.

Arranging the Room to Promote Self-Discipline
(Example)

Infant/Toddler Behavior	Possible Problems in the Environment	How You Might Change the Environment
Young infants get trampled	*Young infants do not have a safe place to play.*	*Create a safe place for young infants using pillows and furniture to shelter it from crawlers and walkers.*
Fighting over toys	*There is only one of each toy. Children are asked to take turns before they are ready to.*	*Identify which are the most popular toys and provide several of each.*

Arranging the Room to Promote Self-Discipline

INFANT/TODDLER BEHAVIOR	POSSIBLE PROBLEMS IN THE ENVIRONMENT	HOW YOU MIGHT CHANGE THE ENVIRONMENT
Crying when they have their diapers changed		
Running and tripping over furniture		
Scattering toys all around the room		

Check your answers with the answer sheet at the end of the module. There can be more than one good answer.

Think about the young children in your group. Do you see any of the same problem behaviors? If so, describe them below.

_____

_____

_____

Look at your room arrangement. Are there any changes you could make to improve the arrangement? Use the space below to note the changes you wish to make.

_____

_____

_____

Discuss your ideas with your trainer and colleagues before trying them out.

IV. Using Words to Provide Positive Guidance for Infants and Toddlers

In this activity you will learn:

- to use words to guide infants and toddlers behavior; and

- to use words to remind infants and toddlers of rules and limits.

Although children may not talk or understand everything you say, they listen and understand a great deal. The words you use, the expressions on your face, and your tone of voice are very powerful disciplinary tools. Angry, insensitive words can make children feel scared, sad, ashamed, or angry. Caregivers can use language in positive ways, however, to help promote children's self-discipline. Your words help children understand their own feelings and those of others.

Some adults use a loud, sharp "discipline voice" to talk to children. It is better to talk to children in a natural though firm tone of voice all the time. When children hear a quiet, firm tone, they feel safe and cared for. Try to get close enough to a child to speak at a normal level. When you shout, children may be so startled that they don't really hear the words. Getting close to a child by crouching or kneeling allows you to have a private discussion. Look into the child's eyes, touch an arm or shoulder, and give him or her your full attention.

If you're not sure how your voice sounds when you're talking to children, try tape recording a part of the day. Play it back for yourself and ask, "Would I like to listen to this person all day?"

The words you use also are very important. Sometimes, an adult who is angry with a child lets out a flood of words. This may make the adult feel better, but chances are the child probably does not hear the message. Try to use simple statements, spoken once, so the child can focus on the real issue. These statements should be very clear and should include brief descriptions of the following:

What happened:	"Sally, you have torn the pages in this book two times this morning."
Acceptable behavior:	"You can read a book."
Unacceptable behavior:	"I can't let you tear our books."
Suggested solution:	"Let's get some tape and fix up the book. Would you like to help me get the tape or wait here?"

In this situation the child was offered two choices. Both of these are acceptable to the caregiver. Be careful to offer choices only when you mean them. When you say to a child,

"Would you like to clean up now?" it sounds as if the child has a choice. The child could easily say, "No." Probably you really mean, "It's time to pick up now."

You can use words to give directions in a positive way. Instead of saying "no running" or "don't leave your coat on the floor," you can say "walk" or "hang your coat on the hook." Children respond well to positive directions. You can use words to show respect for children's feelings and help children feel good about themselves. Avoid comparing one child to another. Instead of saying, "Susan is nice and quiet while I'm reading this book—can you be quiet like Susan?" you could say, "Please be quiet now so I can finish the story. If you don't want to listen now, you can go do something else so that Susan and I can finish the story." Phrases such as "big girls don't suck their thumbs" should also be avoided. They make children feel bad, and they do not change behaviors.

The chart below provides more examples of words you can use to provide positive guidance.

SITUATION	YOU MIGHT SAY
Jack reaches for Sarah's rattle as she sits in the highchair next to him.	"Here, Jack, I have another rattle for you to play with. You don't need to take Sarah's. You may have your own."
Beth cries as she sees that Lisa is being pushed in the carriage.	"Beth and Lisa can ride in this carriage together. There is room for two. Let's move you up front, Lisa, and Beth, you can ride in the back."
Jim sits on the floor alone while Mr. Jones rolls the ball to Jenny.	"Crawl over here, Jim, and sit with me. We can roll the ball to Jenny together."
Bob and Franklin both want to sit in the caregiver's lap.	"There's room for both of you to sit on my lap and look at the book. You can both share my lap, and we can all share this big chair."
Linda and Casey both want all the blocks.	"There are lots of blocks on this shelf, Linda, enough for you and Casey to share. Each of you can build."
Luke and Jeffrey both want to play in the same space.	"Luke, you you can share this space with Jeffrey. One of you can drive a truck here and the other can drive his truck there.

Using words to guide children's behavior takes some practice. It may be a while before new ways of talking to infants and toddlers feel natural to you. You will be rewarded when the children you care for let you know how much better they feel because of your understanding and caring.

In this learning activity you will practice using words to guide children's behavior and help them learn self-discipline. First read the example. Then write down words that you can use in typical situations.

Words You Use to Provide Positive Guidance
(Example)

When a child grabs another child's bottle:

"This is Jim's bottle. Here is your own bottle of juice."

When a child bites another child:

"I don't like biting. Dan needs some cool water on his bite. Come help us at the sink."

When a child paints on the table.

"Eileen, your paper is for painting on, not the table. See if you can keep your design on the paper."

When a child keeps throwing a toy out of the crib:

"You might not want to sleep right now and that's okay. I can't let you keep throwing the toys out of your crib. They make too much noise when they fall on the floor. Here, you may sit on the rug and play with the toys."

When a child hurts another child out of frustration:

"Simon, I know you want the ball, but I can't let you hit Carol. We can play the rolling game together."

Words You Use to Provide Positive Guidance

When a child pushes another child:

_____
_____
_____
_____
_____
_____
_____

When a child pulls another child's hair:

_____
_____
_____
_____
_____
_____
_____

When a child takes another child's toy, making him or her cry:

_____
_____
_____
_____
_____
_____
_____

When a child keeps throwing a cup on the floor:

_____
_____
_____
_____
_____
_____

When a sleepy child whines and cries:

_____

_____

_____

_____

_____

_____

_____

When a frustrated child throws a toy:

_____

_____

_____

_____

_____

_____

_____

When (add your own example here) _____

_____

_____

_____

_____

_____

_____

Now share your words with your trainer. You could also write these words on a chart and hang it in your room to help you get used to saying them.

V. Setting Rules and Limits

In this activity you will learn:

- to use daily routines and the environment to set clear, simple limits for infants and toddlers; and

- to communicate limits to young children and enforce them consistently.

Rules and limits help both children and caregivers understand what behaviors are acceptable. Young children need simple rules that are stated clearly and positively. For example, "walk in the room so you don't hurt yourself" rather than "don't run in the room" tells children what they can do and why. Children feel safer when they know that adults have set limits. These feelings of security help children feel freer to explore and experiment.

Rules should reflect what children are like at each stage of development. For example, infants can't follow rules—not because they are bad, but because they cannot yet understand rules. It would be pointless to set rules and expect that infants would follow them. Toddlers are always on the move, say "no" a lot, and test limits to define themselves. It would be unfair to ask them to sit at the table for 10 minutes while you bring out the materials for an activity. As the children get older, they will be able to understand some simple rules. It is up to you to meet children's needs rather than to ask them to change their behavior to follow your rules.

The fact that you must meet children's needs doesn't mean you shouldn't have any rules. However, you should have realistic expectations about children's ability to follow them. Rules are important because they give order to the world. Clear, realistic limits help children make sense of the world. They learn, for example, that the table is not for climbing. This helps them create order within themselves. They learn that when they want to climb, they should climb on the pillows or platforms, and they begin to develop self-discipline.

Often the limits you set will be based on your knowledge of an individual child's development, skills, temperament, and so on. You might permit one child to engage in an activity that would not be appropriate for another child in the room. For example, you might allow Terry (30 months) to put a cassette in the tape player because he has the necessary fine motor skills to accomplish this task. For Corey (also 30 months), whose fine motor skills are not as developed, this task would be too difficult and would probably result in a mass of tangled tape and a broken machine. Instead of allowing Corey to put in the tape himself, you would hold Corey's hand, gently guide the tape into the machine, and show him how to push the buttons to make the tape play. The limits you set have to be appropriate for the children in the room.

There are many ways to set limits that help children define their world. Using caring words is one way. But words alone are not sufficient. Children don't understand everything you say, and they may not always remember rules. In addition to words, you can use your daily schedule and your environment to establish limits and minimize conflicts.

In this learning activity you will read about a caregiver setting limits for a child and answer a few questions based on the reading. Next, you will read some examples of limits and how they are communicated to the children using daily routines and the environment. Then you will list examples of the limits that you set for the children in your care.

Adam and the Waterfall[1]

While the rest of the children were busy with Mr. Jones, I found Adam (26 months) in the bathroom holding his thumb under the faucet. His thumb was making the water spray over the edge of the sink and onto the floor. "Look," he said proudly, "I'm making a waterfall."

Adam is a quiet child who rarely initiates activities. He was really enjoying himself with the waterfall. Unfortunately, the water was spraying all over the floor and it was getting wet. My first reaction was to say "no" very firmly and sincerely. However, because the other children were on a walk, I considered some other options: I could put a towel on the floor, I could turn off the faucets and remove Adam from the sink, I could divert him with the promise of another activity, or I could let Adam continue making his waterfall.

I decided to let Adam continue under one condition: "The waterfall must stay in the sink." We turned the water down a bit and put a towel on the floor to mop up the spills. Adam happily continued playing while I kept an eye on him.

What would you have done if you had found Adam making a waterfall in the sink? Why?

_____

_____

_____

How do you decide what limits to set for the children in your room?

_____

_____

_____

What are things children do that make you say "no" automatically?

_____

_____

_____

---

[1]Based on Amy Dombro, "That Waterfall Has to Stay in the Sink: A Lesson in Setting Limits," _Newsletter of Parenting_ (Columbus, OH: Highlights for Children, October 1984), p. 14.

Setting Limits for Infants and Toddlers
(Example)

LIMITS YOU SET	HOW YOU COMMUNICATE THE LIMITS THROUGH DAILY ROUTINES AND THE ENVIRONMENT
Chew on food or safe rubber toys, not small objects that might choke you.	*I make sure there are no small chokeable objects in the room.*
Climb on the climber or pillows but not on the table or other furniture.	*I provide an area with pillows for climbing, a climber, and a platform. I keep chairs pushed in at the table to make it harder to climb on them.*
Be gentle with other people, don't hurt them.	*I am gentle with children as I change their diapers and dress them. I make sure infants are in a protected space away from crawlers and walkers who might hurt them.*
Keep the floor dry so no one will slip.	*I put towels under the water table to soak up spills. I ask older children to help me wipe up spills.*
Books are important. They are for reading, not for tearing.	*I give children cloth books and cardboard books that are hard to tear. I show them I am careful with books when I read to them. I ask children to help me tape books that are torn. When we clean up, I thank the children for helping take care of our things.*
Scissors are not toys, so use them carefully.	*I keep scissors up high. I show older toddlers (34 to 36 months) how to use child safety scissors correctly during art projects.*

Setting Limits for Infants and Toddlers

LIMITS YOU SET	HOW YOU COMMUNICATE THE LIMITS THROUGH DAILY ROUTINES AND THE ENVIRONMENT

Discuss your answers with your trainer.

VI. Responding to Challenging Behaviors

In this activity you will learn:

- to look for the reasons behind a child's challenging behavior; and

- to develop a plan for responding to a child's challenging behavior.

We all have a wide range of feelings. As adults we have learned to cover up some of our feelings, and we have learned acceptable ways of expressing others. This isn't true for infants and toddlers. Their feelings—those of joy and excitement as well as those of frustration and anger—are immediate and intense.

Even after they have begun talking, children may still find it hard to express their feelings with words. As children kick, cry, bite or have temper tantrums, they may be telling you many different things.

- "I feel lonely. That's why I'm crying."

- "I am angry. That's why I bit Tory."

- "I am afraid. That's why I won't let go of your hand."

- "I need some limits. That's why I'm running around the room."

When faced with challenging behaviors such as these, caregivers need to step back and think about what a child is saying. Only then can a caregiver figure out how to respond in ways that will promote self-discipline.

To do this, caregivers first need to be aware of their own feelings. These behaviors we are talking about often stir up deep feelings such as anger, sadness, and loneliness in adults who work with infants and toddlers. It is as if the raw, intense feelings of young children reach back and touch off deep feelings from adults' childhoods. Knowing who is feeling what helps ensure that caregivers are responding to children's needs and not their own.

It can be helpful if all the adults who share the care of a child discuss what is going on in that child's life. Perhaps a change at home such as an illness or the birth of a new sibling is upsetting a child. Perhaps the environment at the center may be causing frustration. Maybe the fact that a child's special caregiver has been out sick has left a child feeling alone and angry.

By pooling information, parents and caregivers can come up with a consistent plan for dealing with a difficult behavior. Maybe Fernando (13 months), who has been feeling frustrated, needs more one-on-one time with his special caregiver. The opportunity to throw bean bags or be a growling lion may help Gabrielle (28 months) express her anger without hurting herself or someone else.

Amazingly, it sometimes happens that right after a conference, a behavior disappears. This is not magic. What happens is that talking together often helps the adults relax a bit and be available to a child in a way they couldn't when tension was building. At other times a challenging behavior takes time to resolve. Regardless of how long it takes, be sure to let a child know that she or he is still loved and cared for.

Common Behaviors That May Need Special Attention[2]

Some common behaviors of young children may be more difficult for adults to understand and to deal with than others. Two of these are throwing temper tantrums and biting. These behaviors are ways in which children release tension.

People of all ages need to cope with anger, frustration, and disappointment. Everyone—children as well as adults—needs to feel that their emotions are okay. It is okay for children to be angry, and their feelings need to be respected. They need your help finding acceptable ways to express their anger.

Temper Tantrums

Two-year-olds are learning about limits. They have to learn about the limits that you set for them, and they have to learn about the limits of their own abilities. They want to be big, but they aren't really big enough or strong enough to do everything they want. They can talk, but they don't know enough words to express everything they want. Their world can be very frustrating.

A temper tantrum is an expression of extreme rage in a child. The child is beside himself—he is so angry that his whole body screams with his frustration. Tantrums should not be encouraged, or else the child will believe that this is an acceptable way of getting what he wants. At the same time, a tantrum in a very young child needs to be understood. Decide ahead of time how you will respond to a child's tantrum.

To help prevent tantrums, take as much of the frustration out of a child's world as possible. Make your room one where the children can be fairly free. If you are always saying "no"—"no, don't touch that," or "no, don't get in there," or "no, don't open that cupboard"—then children are bound to be frustrated and will lose self-confidence.

Make sure that the toys, puzzles, games and activities are appropriate for the children in the room. If all your puzzles are made for 3-year-olds, the younger children are likely to get very frustrated. But if you provide toys that are designed for the children's developmental levels, they will learn and will feel a sense of accomplishment and pride.

Watch for signs that a tantrum is coming. Children usually have tantrums because they are tired or frustrated. Watch the children in your care: Have they been indoors too long? Are they hungry? Is it naptime? Have there been lots of visitors? Most of the time a tantrum is a

---

[2]Adapted with permission from Margaret Nash and Costella Tate, *Better Baby Care: A Book for Family Day Care Providers* (Washington, DC: The Children's Foundation, 1986), pp. 70-75.

response to the environment. If you know the children in your care fairly well, you can probably tell when they are getting tense. Have relaxing activities in mind for those times.

A child may be frightened by the power of his own tantrum. "How much power do I really have? Will someone protect me from myself?" When the tantrum subsides, he may need you for comfort and for reassurance that he is not a bad person just because he lost control. Sometimes you may need to gently stop the child if he is hurting himself or another person, or breaking something. Hold his hands or feet gently but firmly. He will feel much better about himself later if he has not caused any damage.

Although you accept tantrums as part of developing self-control, the child needs to know that there are better ways to let out his anger. After he has calmed down, acknowledge his feelings, but also get him thinking about another way to let off steam. Say, "Boy, you were really mad, Carlos. It's hard to be so mad," or "You got frustrated with that toy, didn't you? Next time, when you start getting upset, put the toy down, or else ask someone for help." A little child may not always understand what you are saying, nor will he always be able to identify the anger when it's there, but slowly your message will sink in: you accept him and accept his feelings, but you do not accept the tantrum.

Sometimes the young child will be exhausted by the tantrum and will need to sleep. Help the child to a comfortable nap place. Awakening, she or he will need your presence and a gentle touch: "You fell asleep after your tantrum. I bet you feel more relaxed and ready to play now." Help the child's transition back into the classroom and activities: "We had crackers and juice for snack while you were asleep. I saved some for you."

Biting

Biting is a very common problem among groups of young children. Any time someone bites, though, your first responsibility is the child who was bitten. Comfort that child and wash the wound. Usually the child who did the biting is willing to help you care for the bitten child; this an excellent opportunity for you to teach nurturing behavior.

Toddlers bite fairly frequently, often when they are very frustrated and are trying to get some attention. They probably don't realize the results of biting—they don't mean to hurt anyone.

Try to figure out what is happening to the toddler that is so frustrating. Is someone teasing her? Is something going on at home? Might she be jealous of a new baby at her home? Try to make her playtime more simple so that there is less to upset her.

Tell a toddler who bites that you will not allow her to bite another child. Say, "Wei Yng doesn't like to be bitten. It hurts! Wei Yng likes it when you touch her softly, like this." Show her what gentle touching is like. Then keep your eye on her as closely as possible. If you see her getting angry or frustrated, suggest another activity. If you see her move to bite someone, stop her immediately. Keep your voice and your actions as calm, quiet, and firm as possible.

Since biting can hurt so much, we tend to jump and get upset. This kind of excited attention can cause a child to repeat the behavior. Your intervention will be most effective when you are within reach of the biter and can block the bite with your own arm while saying firmly, "Stop!" and looking at her with a very serious and determined expression. As with tantrums, stop the unacceptable behavior and give the child more attention when she is playing acceptably. Encourage children to "pretend" play. Sometimes when toddlers do this, caregivers can learn a lot about what is on the child's mind. If pretend play reveals to you what is bothering the child, try to deal with the source of the unhappiness.

In this learning activity, you will think of a child in your care who has a challenging behavior. You will describe the behavior and your response. Next you will talk with the child's parents about the child's behavior. Together you will develop a plan for responding to the behavior. First review the example that follows; then fill in the chart, focusing on a child in your room.

Responding to Challenging Behaviors
(Example)

Child _____Frances_____ **Age** _____30 months_____ **Date** _____June 25_____

What behavior is challenging?

Frances bites other children. Usually on their arms.

How often does this occur?

Every other day.

How long has it been going on?

Two weeks.

When does it happen?

When Frances gets into small spaces. Sometimes when she climbs into a tunnel or into our large cardboard box and another child crowds her.

How do you respond now?

One caregiver comforts the child who was bitten and gets the child ice or, if necessary, takes the child to get first aid. The other caregiver takes Frances aside and tells her she may not bite people. Then we try to get her engaged in an activity that will allow her to release some of her feelings—for example, throwing bean bags in a box.

How does the child respond?

She cries. Then she sometimes sucks her thumb.

Did something happen at home that might have upset the child?

Frances has a new baby brother who shares her room. She does not seem very interested in him. Frances doesn't bite at home.

Did something happen at the center that might have upset the child?

We can't think of anything that has changed.

Conclusion:

Frances might feel jealous of her new brother. We need to look at the ways we are responding now to see how we could improve. We think Frances really doesn't understand that she is hurting the other children. We think she gets upset when she bites someone. We need to help her use her words to express her feelings.

Plans for responding to this behavior at home and at the center:

Frances' parents will help her express her feelings about her baby brother. They will try to set up a special place at home that is just for Frances, and they will each spend some time with her—away from the baby.

At the center we will also provide ways for Frances to express her feelings about her brother. We will be sure there are dolls for her to play with. We will offer her opportunities to help us take care of younger children. We will spend extra time cuddling and playing with her.

When Frances bites, one caregiver will still comfort the child who was bitten. The other caregiver will respond to Frances. Along with telling Frances she cannot bite, this caregiver will try to comfort Frances, since biting someone is very scary. The caregiver will then encourage Frances to join in giving comfort and first aid to the bitten child.

Responding to Challenging Behaviors

Child _____ Age _____ Date _____

What behavior is challenging?

_____

_____

_____

How often does this occur?   **How long has it been going on?**

_____   _____

When does it happen?

_____

_____

_____

How do you respond now?

_____

_____

_____

How does the child respond?

_____

_____

_____

Did something happen at home that might have upset the child?

_____

_____

_____

Did something happen at the center that might have upset the child?

_____

_____

_____

_____

Conclusion:

_____

_____

_____

_____

Plans for responding to this behavior at home and at the center:

_____

_____

_____

_____

_____

_____

_____

_____

After one or two weeks have passed, answer the following questions:

What happened at home and at the center when you tried your plans? Has the challenging behavior changed or gone away?

_____

_____

_____

_____

_____

_____

Discuss this activity with your trainer.

Summarizing Your Progress

You have now completed all of the learning activities for this module. Whether you are an experienced caregiver or a new one, this module has probably helped you develop new skills for guiding infants' and toddlers' behavior. Before you go on, take a few minutes to summarize what you've learned.

- Turn back to Learning Activity I, Using Your Knowledge of Infant and Toddler Development to Guide Behavior, and add to the chart specific examples of what you learned about helping children develop self-discipline while you were working on this module.

- Next, review your responses to the pre-training assessment for this module. Write a summary of what you learned, and list the skills you developed or improved.

_____

_____

_____

_____

_____

_____

_____

_____

_____

_____

_____

_____

Your final step in this module is to complete the knowledge and competency assessments. Let your trainer know then you are ready to schedule the assessments. After you have successfully completed these assessments, you will be ready to start a new module. Congratulations on your progress so far, and good luck with your next module.

Answer Sheet: Guiding Children's Behavior

Providing an Environment That Encourages Infants' and Toddlers' Self-Discipline

1. **How did Ms. Jackson and Ms. Bates support each other?**

    a. They took took turns taking care of Carrie.

    b. They worked together until Carrie was calmed down.

2. **What did Ms. Bates and Ms. Jackson do to help Carrie?**

    a. Ms. Bates changed her diaper, fed her a bottle, and put her down in her crib.

    b. Ms. Jackson picked her up and rocked her.

    c. Ms. Bates laid Carrie across her lap on her belly and rubbed her back.

    d. Ms. Jackson put on some soft music.

3. **Why did Ms. Bates place Carrie across her lap?**

    a. She had noticed that in the past Carrie liked to lie on her belly.

    b. She thought it would help Carrie stop crying.

Using Positive Methods to Guide Individual Infants and Toddlers

1. **What did Mr. Jones know about Travis?**

    a. Travis likes to throw things.

    b. Travis responds well when given choices.

    c. Travis is very active.

2. **How did Mr. Jones let Travis know that he respected him?**

    a. He walked over to him and bent down to talk to him.

    b. He told him he was learning to be a good thrower.

    c. He gave him a choice of throwing the pine cones on the grass or doing something else.

Helping Infants and Toddlers Understand and Express Their Feelings in Acceptable Ways

1. **How do you think Billy felt when Sam grabbed his piece of orange?**

    a. Angry.

    b. Frustrated.

2. How did Ms. Lewis help Billy learn to express his feelings in acceptable ways?

   a. She helped Billy refrain from hitting Sam.

   b. She told Billy it was okay to be angry.

   c. She told Billy not to hit Sam but instead to tell him not to take his orange.

Using Your Knowledge of Infants' and Toddlers' Development to Guide Behavior

WHAT YOUNG INFANTS DO (0-8 MONTHS)	HOW CAREGIVERS CAN USE THIS INFORMATION TO GUIDE BEHAVIOR
They like to be held.	Hold infants a lot during the day. By helping them feel happy and cared for, you are saying that they can trust the world, and you are helping them feel secure.
They respond to faces and listen to voices.	Look at infants. Talk to them as you feed them, change their diapers, or play with them. By building a relationship, you are laying the foundation for helping them learn self-discipline.
They cry (sometimes a lot).	Respond to infants immediately. Do not keep them waiting. You will not spoil the infants. Rather, you will teach them that they can trust the world and you.
They reach out and grab things (for example, mobiles, toys, and eyeglasses).	Provide safe toys within easy reach. Be sure small swallowable objects are out of reach. Let your environment set limits by making sure it is safe for infants.
They can become bored.	Offer the infants toys, move infants to new locations in the room, or talk and play with them. Young infants need your company.
WHAT MOBILE INFANTS DO (9-17 MONTHS)	HOW CAREGIVERS CAN USE THIS INFORMATION TO GUIDE BEHAVIOR
They experience and express a wide range of feelings (such as happiness, sadness, anger, and frustration).	Talk to infants in ways that show you respect their feelings. Comment on feelings expressed by other children: "Hear Joey laugh? He's happy to have a clean diaper."
They are interested in other children. They can accidentally hurt another child while saying hello or exploring.	Guide infants to touch each other gently. Say, "Be gentle." Touch infants' faces gently to let them feel what you are talking about.

WHAT MOBILE INFANTS DO (9-17 MONTHS)	HOW CAREGIVERS CAN USE THIS INFORMATION TO GUIDE BEHAVIOR
They may show fear of strangers.	Stay with infants when someone new is around. Introduce the the infant. Let the infants explore someone new in the safety of your presence.
They like to feed themselves.	Give infants finger foods. By helping infants develop new skills, you are saying, "You can do it! I have faith in you."
They watch and know their important adults—you are one of them! They learn from being around you.	Let infants see you express feelings appropriately and solve problems so they will learn from you.
They know how you feel about them.	Let infants know you care about them. Show your pride and pleasure in things they do.
WHAT TODDLERS DO (18-36 MONTHS)	**HOW CAREGIVERS CAN USE THIS INFORMATION TO GUIDE BEHAVIOR**
They are eager to please adults.	Reinforce positive behavior. Let children know you are pleased for them when they do a good job cleaning up, helping friends, or zipping up their coats, so they feel good about themselves.
They want to make decisions for themselves.	Give toddlers clear, simple choices to make. This helps toddlers feel that they have some control and that they are competent people.
They sometimes lose control and start kicking and screaming.	Be there to hold the child and stop the behavior. Stay with the child until she or he is calmed down and can listen to your words. Sometimes you might stay nearby but leave the child alone until she or he is calm. This is the start of self-discipline.
They can be very possessive.	Do not expect toddlers to share or take turns. They are not selfish but are working hard to define themselves. Let them see you share things. Have more than one of favorite toys to avoid unnecessary conflict. Comment on positive social aspects of play: "Oh, Natalia, it looks like Juan is having so much fun beside you at the water table."

WHAT TODDLERS DO (18-36 MONTHS)	HOW CAREGIVERS CAN USE THIS INFORMATION TO GUIDE BEHAVIOR
They test limits and say "no" often.	Avoid power struggles. Set limits clearly and consistently. Invite them to help you so they can feel important for the positive things they do.
They sometimes hit out in anger at other children or at adults.	Stop the hitting or kicking immediately—do not ignore it. Calmly but firmly say, "Hitting hurts. It's not okay to hit. Use your words to tell _____." Using words instead of hands and feet is part of self-discipline. Be sure that your face reflects the seriousness of your words.
They may suck their thumbs.	Try to find out if there is a reason why the toddler is sucking his or her thumb. Is anything causing him or her to feel more needy? Thumb sucking may be a way of asking for help.
They may touch their genitals or masturbate.	Avoiding paying too much attention to these activities. When toddlers are learning to use the toilet, it is very natural for them to touch their genitals. Toddlers will soon stop touching their genitals or masturbating in public because they can see that the people around them don't do these things.

Answer Sheet: Using Positive Guidance Techniques

WHAT INFANTS AND TODDLERS DO	HOW YOU WOULD RESPOND
Betty (4 months) has been crying off and on all day.	Hold her, rock her, see if she is hungry or in pain. Try to comfort her so she learns she can trust you to help her.
Reggie (8 months) has just fallen asleep. A maintenance worker walks in to change a light bulb and slams the door. The noise wakes up Reggie, and he begins to cry.	Help Reggie understand what he is feeling. Hold him or rub his back and explain, "That noise woke you up. It surprised you. You weren't ready to wake up yet." Help him relax and fall back asleep.
Lou (9 months) pulls himself to standing and reaches for the pencil you left on the table.	Remove the pencil. Put it out of reach so Lou won't be tempted again. Offer Lou something safe to hold instead.
Fran (11 months) and Laura (10 months) are sitting face to face. Fran reaches out and softly touches Laura's face. Then she grabs a handful of Laura's hair.	Move in quickly. Comfort Laura. Explain to Fran that she should touch other children gently. Touch both girls softly on their cheeks and hair so they feel what gently means.
Ed (16 months) throws a block across the room for the third time. He looks at you and smiles.	Tell him "no." Be sure your face and voice look and sound serious. Give him a rubber ball and say, "You can roll this ball on the carpet."
Sandy (20 months) is climbing on her cot and laughing as she jumps up and down.	Ask her to get down. If necessary, help her get down. Guide her to a place where she can safely climb and jump, or sit on the cot with her for a minute until she quiets down.
It is naptime. Eric (22 months) runs across the room, dragging his blanket behind him. He doesn't want to lie on his cot.	Try giving him a warning to give him a chance to get ready for his nap: "It will be naptime in five minutes." Develop a routine to help him prepare for sleep. For example, lie down on his cot, sing a song, rub his back, or let him put his clothes in a special place where he can find them when he wakes up.
Lisa (28 months) hits Barry (26 months) when he bumps into her.	Use your voice and expression to make it clear to Lisa that she may not hit someone. Acknowledge her anger and explain she can yell "no" or "move." Even though she won't understand completely, explain that hitting hurts Barry.

Answer Sheet: Arranging the Room to Promote Self-Discipline

INFANT/TODDLER BEHAVIOR	POSSIBLE PROBLEMS IN THE ENVIRONMENT	HOW YOU MIGHT CHANGE THE ENVIRONMENT
Crying when they have their diapers changed.	It is taking too long because supplies in the diaper area are not well organized. There is nothing in the area to capture the child's interest.	Rearrange the diaper area so all supplies are within reach. Put up a mobile, a wind chime, or some pictures and mirrors where infants can see them.
Running and tripping over furniture.	The room doesn't have enough open spaces for children to move about safely. There aren't enough opportunities for children to use their large motor skills.	Rearrange the furniture so there are more open spaces for children to move about. Provide some indoor large motor activities such as jumping on pillows, crawling through boxes, or dancing to music.
Scattering toys all around the room.	There are too many toys and materials on the shelves. Too many materials with small pieces are out.	Sort through the toys. Put some away. Limit the materials with many pieces. Some can be kept on higher shelves where children can see and request them.

Glossary

Challenging behaviors	Behaviors such as biting or temper tantrums that are often difficult to handle.
Consequence	The natural or logical result of a behavior.
Discipline	The actions that adults take to guide and direct children toward acceptable behavior.
Limits and rules	Guidelines set by caregivers as to what is acceptable behavior.
Positive guidance	Methods that caregivers use to help children learn to behave in acceptable ways. These methods help children develop self-discipline.
Punishment	Control of children's behavior by use of fear.
Redirecting	Offering activities that allow children to test skills in ways that are acceptable and safe.
Self-discipline	The ability to control one's own behavior. People who are self-disciplined make independent choices based on what they believe is right. They are able to balance their own needs with those of others. They can accept the results of their actions.

Module 11
Families

Why Is Working with Families Important?

Recent studies have shown that the most effective infant and toddler child care programs are those which actively promote and encourage the involvement of families. When parents and caregivers work as a team, they can share information and discuss ways to provide consistent care at home and at the center. Good working relationships with families enable caregivers to get a more complete picture of who children are and thus to be more responsive to each child's needs. (As we will discuss, there are many different models of families today. When we refer to "parents" in this module, we are thinking not only of parents but also of step-parents, foster parents, grandparents, aunts, uncles, or whoever has the primary responsibility for raising a child.)

No matter how much time children spend at the center each day, their parents are the most important people in their lives. Theirs is a lifelong relationship that will continue years after a child leaves your care. Your role is to enhance this relationship. By strengthening the connection between child and parent, you are supporting a child's development in the years to come.

You can do this in a variety of ways. Daily conversations with parents are opportunities to get to know each other and to exchange information about a child's activities at home and at the center. As you help parents feel welcome in your room and offer them a variety of ways to participate in the program, you can help parents feel connected to their children's life at the center. Often parents have questions about their child's development. They may ask you how to handle a situation. It can be easy to fall into the role of expert. Although sometimes you will respond by drawing on your own knowledge and experience, remember that your role is to help parents discover what works for them and their child. By asking parents what they try at home and encouraging them to talk with other parents, you can help them develop a sense of confidence and competence.

While building a good working relationship with families is clearly part of taking good care of children, it can be easier to talk about than to do. As caregivers become attached to children, they sometimes find themselves feeling competitive with parents, which gets in the way of the partnership. Sometimes, in fact, caregivers resent having to work with parents; they chose to be caregivers because they want to work with children. Such feelings are important and need to be acknowledged and resolved. You may find it helpful to discuss these feelings with your supervisor or trainer, or there might be an issue or incident that you need to address with a child's family. When it comes to working with families, knowing oneself is as important as knowing about how children grow and develop.

Working with families can be a very rewarding part of your job. Together you can meet the challenges that come with living and working with young children. You can also share the pleasure and excitement when a child learns to sit or say a new word.

Working with families involves:

- communicating with family members often to exchange information about their young child at home and at the center;

- offering a variety of ways for family members to participate in their infant's or toddler's life at the center; and

- providing support to families.

Listed below are examples of how caregivers demonstrate their competence in working with families.

Communicating with Family Members Often to Exchange Information About Their Child at Home and at the Center

Here are some examples of what caregivers can do.

- Encourage parents to drop in at the center at any time. "Mr. Jackson, we're looking forward to your visit at lunch today."

- Share some good news with parents every day. "Connie tried a new vegetable today. She really feels good about tasting the beets."

- Use information about infants' and toddlers' interests that was provided by parents. "Look, Teresa, this puppy has spots just like the ones on your puppy, Trixie."

- Give parents information about their child's routines and activities. "Mary wasn't very hungry this afternoon. She drank only half her formula."

- Suggest ways that parents can extend learning at home. "Mark really enjoys water play at the center. When he takes a bath, you could give him some plastic cups and bottles so he can practice pouring."

- Learn each parent's name and something about them as a way to build trust. "I thought of you last night, Mr. Parker, when I watched the television special on Houston. That's where your family lives, isn't it?"

Offering a Variety of Ways for Family Members to Participate in Their Child's Life at the Center

Here are some examples of what caregivers can do.

- Give parents opportunities to make decisions about their child's activities. "Deena seems ready to drink from a cup. What do you think?"

- Ask parents to help you include their culture in your activities. "Would you share the song you sing with Andres about making tortillas?"

- Set up workshops on topics in which parents have expressed interest. "Many of the parents wanted to know more about how to help their children with saying goodbye in the morning."

- Sponsor a weekend fix-up day when parents and caregivers work together to spruce up the center. "Ms. Hanes, the children are having a great time crawling through the old tires you set up."

- Find innovative ways for working parents to help when they can't come to the center during the day. "Thanks so much for typing this month's newsletter for us, Ms. Peterson."

Providing Support to Families

Here are some examples of what caregivers can do.

- Support families under stress. "It's often hard to adjust when one parent is away. We'll help Sherrie as much as we can at the center."

- Work with parents to figure out strategies for dealing with a behavior. "What do you do at home when Ricky says 'no' and refuses to do whatever you ask? One of the things we try is to offer choices that can't be answered 'yes' or 'no.' For example, 'What shirt do you want to wear—the red or blue one?'"

- Use what you know about development to help parents understand how much their children are learning through everyday activities. "When Jessica builds in the block corner, she is learning a lot about math concepts. Young children learn best when they can play with real objects. When she's older she'll learn to count."

- Use familiar terms instead of jargon when you talk to parents. "When Sammy plays with the pegboard and beads, that helps the small muscles in his hands and fingers develop. This is important for writing later on."

- Interpret children's behavior to their parents. "Loren is happy that her Grandma is coming to visit. I heard her talking on the play phone, 'OK Grandma, you come see me soon,' she said, nodding her head."

Working with Families

In the following situations, caregivers are working with families. As you read each one think about what the caregivers are doing and why. Then answer the questions that follow.

Communicating with Family Members Often to Exchange Information About Their Child at Home and at the Center

Yesterday was an exciting day for Janet (12 months). For the first time she stood up and took a step. Ms. Lewis watched her and gave her a big hug. Over the last few weeks, Ms. Lewis and Janet's parents, the Carters, have been sharing information about Janet's progress. First she crawled and then began cruising, holding onto furniture. Recently she let go and stood for a second before plopping down on her bottom. Ms. Lewis knew that Janet's family was very pleased that she was learning to stand alone. She decided not to say anything about Janet's accomplishment so they could see it for themselves.

1. **Why did Ms. Lewis decide not to share the news about Janet's accomplishment?**

   _____

   _____

   _____

   _____

   _____

2. **What kinds of information will Ms. Lewis and the Carters need to share, now that Janet is beginning to walk?**

   _____

   _____

   _____

   _____

   _____

Providing a Variety of Ways for Family Members to Participate in Their Child's Life at the Center

At the beginning-of-the-year orientation for parents, Mr. Bradley comes up to Ms. Bates to discuss how he can be involved in the center's program. "It's still hard for me to put my baby in child care," he says. "I want to be a part of Jerry's life at the center, but I'm not sure what I can do." Ms. Bates asks Mr. Bradley several questions about his work and other interests. Then she says, "We have wanted to build a carpet-covered platform that the babies can climb on and get another view of the room, but we don't know how to go about it. It sounds like you are pretty handy with woodworking and tools. Would you like to help us build a platform and see how the children use it?" Mr. Bradley is delighted. He draws a sketch of what he has in mind and checks it with the staff. The next week he brings a new platform, fully covered with soft carpet, to the center. He stays for an hour playing with Jerry and the other children as they explore the new piece of furniture. "Thank you for showing me a way to be involved. I'll be glad to come back again. This was a lot of fun, and it was great to see Jerry with all his friends." Ms. Bates smiles. "Come any time. You're always welcome here, and I see that it means a lot to Jerry to have his dad around."

1. **How did Ms. Bates help Mr. Bradley deal with his feelings about leaving Jerry?**

_____

_____

_____

_____

_____

2. **How did Ms. Bates help Mr. Bradley find a way to participate in Jerry's life at the center?**

_____

_____

_____

_____

_____

Providing Support to Families

"I just don't know what to do," says Ms. Thomas when she drops off 21-one-month-old Marita one morning. "Marita's been coming to the center for almost a month now, and she still cries and clings to me when I leave. I have to go to work, I can't stay with her all the time. Do you have any suggestions?" Mr. Jones says, "Marita usually stops crying a few minutes after you leave. It takes some children a while to get used to being separated from their parents. We'll keep working with her to help her feel secure. What can we do to help you? Would you like to make an appointment to talk about separation? I could tell you more about what Marita does here. You could tell me what Marita does at home." Ms. Thomas says, "That would be great. Let's talk tomorrow afternoon." Mr. Jones says he will make the necessary arrangements for a parent conference. "Remember, this is a partnership. We'll work together to help Marita deal with separation." Mr. Jones holds the crying Marita and tells Ms. Thomas, "Feel free to call me and check on her after you get to work." As Ms. Thomas leaves for work looking a lot less worried, he waves and calls "Goodbye! See you after naptime!" In a few minutes Marita calms down, and she and Mr. Jones pick out a story to read together.

1. **What did Mr. Jones do to help Ms. Thomas understand Marita's behavior?**

_____

_____

_____

_____

_____

2. **How did Mr. Jones help Marita and her mother cope with separation?**

_____

_____

_____

_____

Compare your answers with those on the answer sheet at the end of this module. If your answers are different, discuss them with your trainer. There can be more than one good answer.

Your Own Family Experiences

Infant and toddler caregivers bring many firsthand experiences to their role in working with families. Most of us grew up in a family. Some of us are now raising families of our own or have grown children. Our own experiences influence how we view families, what we think a family should look like, and how parents should raise their children.

Think for a moment about what the word "family" means to you. Do you think of a mother and father and one or more children living together? Do you think of different kinds of family relationships?

The families of the infants and toddlers you work with may resemble your own experiences, or they may look very different. Children may be growing up with a single mother or father or with step-parents. Some children are being raised by grandparents or by a teenage mother living at home with her own parents. The traditional view of a family is not always true today. Additionally, the stresses families experience today can make parenting a very difficult job.

It is not uncommon for caregivers to blame parents when their infants and toddlers are having problems. This is especially true when caregivers see parents whose behavior toward their infants and toddlers is very different from the caregivers' past experiences. It may help to remember that almost all parents want the best for their children and they are probably trying as hard as they can to be good parents. They, too, are guided by their own experiences growing up in a family.

Before you begin the learning activities in this module, spend a few minutes thinking of how your own views and experiences may affect the way you work with families. Consider the following questions:

1. Whom did you consider to be part of the family you grew up in?

_____

_____

_____

_____

_____

2. How are families of the children in your group different from your own family?

_____

_____

_____

_____

_____

3. What pressures do parents have today that your parents didn't experience?

_____
_____
_____
_____
_____

4. What pressures are the same?

_____
_____
_____
_____
_____

5. How do you think your views and experiences affect your work with families?

_____
_____
_____
_____
_____
_____
_____
_____
_____

Discuss your responses with your trainer and a group of other staff members. When you have finished this overview section, you should complete the pre-training assessment and then go on to the learning activities in this module.

Pre-Training Assessment

Listed below are the skills that caregivers use to work with families. Think about whether you do these things regularly, sometimes, or not enough. Place a check in one of the columns on the right for each skill listed. Then discuss your answers with your trainer.

SKILL	I DO THIS REGULARLY	I DO THIS SOMETIMES	I DON'T DO THIS ENOUGH
COMMUNICATING WITH FAMILY MEMBERS OFTEN TO EXCHANGE INFORMATION ABOUT THEIR CHILD AT HOME AND AT THE CENTER 1. Building trust through learning each parent's name and something about them.			
2. Providing parents with daily information about their child's routines and activities.			
3. Encouraging parents to come to the center at any time.			
4. Suggesting ways to extend the young child's learning at home.			
5. Holding parent-teacher conferences to share information about each child's progress and to make plans for the future.			
PROVIDING A VARIETY OF WAYS FOR FAMILY MEMBERS TO PARTICIPATE IN THEIR CHILD'S LIFE AT THE CENTER 6. Involving parents often in making decisions about their child's care.			
7. Surveying parents' needs and interests and providing appropriate workshops or resources.			

SKILL	I DO THIS REGULARLY	I DO THIS SOMETIMES	I DON'T DO THIS ENOUGH
8. Providing alternative ways for parents to participate when they can't come to the center during the day.			
9. Holding regularly scheduled parent meetings at times that are convenient for most parents.			
PROVIDING SUPPORT TO FAMILIES			
10. Helping parents understand the stages of development every child goes through.			
11. Working with parents to come up with strategies on how to deal with a behavior.			
12. Using knowledge of child development to help parents understand why their child may be behaving in a certain way.			
13. Providing support to families under stress, such as when a parent must travel for extended periods of time.			
14. Helping parents to recognize signs of a child's readiness to learn something new.			

Review your responses, then list three to five skills you would like to improve or topics you would like to learn more about. When you finish this module, you will list examples of your new or improved knowledge and skills.

_____

_____

_____

_____

Now begin the learning activities for Module 11, Families.

I. Developing a Partnership with Parents

In this activity you will learn:

- to develop and maintain a relationship with parents; and

- to recognize your feelings about sharing care and how they can affect your work with parents.

Every parent-caregiver relationship is as unique as the caregivers, parents, and child involved. But no matter who the parents are, your goal remains the same—to support children and families in ways that help parents develop a sense of competence and strengthen the ties between parent and child.

Your relationship with a child's parents begins when their child first enters your room. Your smile and greeting, a comfortable adult-sized chair, a pot of coffee, and labels telling what is in the drawers so parents can find what they need are all ways of letting parents know they are welcome.

Hopefully, parents will be able to spend a few days in the room getting to know you and the program as they help their child get settled. If not, find some time to meet together, perhaps in an evening or early one morning. Expect that parents will want to learn about you. After all, they will be leaving their most precious possession—their baby—in your care. Tell parents something about yourself. Explain why you enjoy working with infants and toddlers. Show parents you are interested in who they are too. Find out their interests and what kind of work they do. Reassure parents that you see them as their children's most important people. Let them know that your goal is to work together with them to support their child.

In addition to wanting to know about you, parents will want to know about the program. Knowing specific things that are happening, such as the fact that applesauce is on today's lunch menu and one of the caregivers will be on vacation next week, will help parents feel more involved and connected to their child's daily life at the center. Some of this information can be shared when you see parents in the morning and afternoon. Because these times are often brief and not conducive to long conversations, many programs use newsletters to keep parents informed.

Here are some other suggestions of ways to keep parents informed about what is going on in your program.

- Establish a **message center** where each family has a box or message pocket. These can be used to provide parents with general news and information about their child.

- Provide each family with a **journal** that can be used by both parents and caregivers to share information about the child. Notices or flyers can be tucked in the journal so parents will see them.

- Set up a **parent bulletin board** in the lobby or some other area that all parents pass by. Post articles, a calendar of events, reminders of upcoming meetings, the week's menus, and other items of general interest.

- Develop and maintain a **parent handbook**. Issue copies to each parent and provide revisions whenever necessary. The handbook can address the center's policies and procedures and list opportunities for parents to become involved.

Like any relationship, the one you build with parents needs ongoing attention. Throughout the year you need to continue to involve parents in the care of their children. Your partnership will be strengthened by continued communication and appreciation for each partner's role in caring for a child. The partnership will grow when you each see how a child benefits from your teamwork.

Here are some suggestions for maintaining a strong partnership:

- **Respond to parents' concerns or questions even though they may seem trivial.** Such concerns are important to the parents and therefore should be acknowledged. "Yes, some of the children can zip their jackets, but others, like Gregory, aren't ready yet. We will provide more chances for him to use his finger skills."

- **Try parents' suggestions,** unless you think they will hurt the child, even when they differ from what you would do. "We'll be sure to slice Jason's sandwich in four pieces if you think he likes it better that way."

- **Help parents focus on their child's accomplishments** rather than comparing their child to others the same age. "Denise always has a smile ready. All the caregivers feel good when she smiles at them."

- **Help children and parents feel good about belonging to the same family.** "Mr. Bradley, Jerry is so excited when he knows you're coming for lunch. He really likes it when the other kids talk about your visits."

- **Wait until you are asked before offering advice.** When you are asked, avoid assuming the role of the know-it-all expert. Make sure you are clear about what is fact and what is opinion. "Child development experts say that children Billy's age are too young for formal reading lessons."

- **Tell parents about the good things that happen each day.** It's not necessary to report every time their child has a fight or loses his or her temper. Share problems when you need to work together to help the child. "Erica hits children when she gets angry. When can we get together to discuss ways to help her?"

- **Acknowledge events and transitions in the child's and parents' lives.** "Congratulations on your promotion. Your husband told me the whole family had a party to celebrate."

- **Be sensitive to normal guilt feelings parents may have when they leave their children at the center.** Be careful not to make assumptions about parents or judge them because their lifestyle is different from yours.

- **Help children and parents cope when one parent is away.** Suggest sending artwork or messages to the parent who is away. Remind children that their parents love them even when they are gone.

- **Keep in touch when the child is absent or ill.** "Hello, Ms. Carson, how is Paula feeling today?"

- **Maintain confidentiality when parents share private information with you.** "I'm glad you told me about this. It will help me work with Brendan. You don't need to worry about me telling someone else. I understand that this was said in confidence."

If parents don't respond to your efforts to establish a partnership, consider the deep feelings stirred up by sharing the care of a very young child—theirs as well as yours. Put yourself in the place of parents. Try to understand their feelings about leaving their children at the center. Often parents feel guilty and concerned about not spending as much time with their child as they would like. Parents may worry that their child will end up loving you more.

You probably also have feelings about sharing care that you may be conveying through the tone of your voice, facial expressions, or the information you choose to share. Do you ever find yourself feeling competitive, jealous or even resentful that parents are leaving their small children in your care?

All of these feelings of parents and caregivers are normal and very common. They are rooted in the deep attachment you each feel to the children you care for. Recognizing such emotions can help you keep them from getting in the way of your relationships with parents. As a caregiver, you are your own most valuable resource. Because how you feel influences how you respond to parents and children, being in touch with your feelings is a vital part of your work.

In this learning activity you will examine some feelings about sharing care that may affect your relationship with parents. Begin by reading "How Parents and Teachers See Each Other." Then take some time to reflect on your own feelings about working with parents, and answer the questions that follow.

How Parents and Teachers See Each Other[1]

When I was a teacher, I used to sit in on those proverbial teacher room discussions, but I don't think it was until I became a parent that I became aware of the way that teachers talk about parents: "Can you believe the way she dresses that child?" "Why can't that father ever be on time?" I became curious as to why there is so much griping about parents. The way that teachers talk about parents seemed almost comparable to racism, a stereotypism of some sort.

I've been working on this issue off and on for ten years. Most recently, I have been surveying day care teachers to learn about their attitudes about parents. When asked to describe the parents they work with, teachers choose words that are frequently negative—*overwhelmed, anxious, demanding, struggling, busy, tired, ambitious, confused, depressed, angry*. They use some positive terms, too, but the preponderance is negative. Of course, this is not to say that their judgments may not be realistic responses to life in our time.

One of my purposes in my last book, **Between Generations**, was to help teachers understand what was normal about parental growth so that they could view issues through the eyes of parents as well as their own.

In interviewing parents across the country, I found that being a parent, especially of an infant or toddler, was often anxiety provoking. Before they had children they were sure of themselves, now with young children they are less certain. The relationship with the child changes the parent. Parental growth is affected by child growth, but the changes occur on a different level. As the child is figuring out who he or she is (that is as separate from the adult), the parent is figuring out who he or she is as a parent. The child feels dependent; the parent feels dependent.

---

[1]Reprinted with permission from Ellen Galinsky, "How Parents and Teachers See Each Other," *Beginnings: Parents and Teachers* (Redmond, WA: Exchange Press, PO Box 2890, Redmond, Washington 98073 (206) 883-9394, Fall 1984), pp. 3-5.

Feelings and Expectations

There are four factors that figure into this caregiver-parent relationship. The first factor is the possessive feelings. Parents may feel that they are the only ones capable of caring for the child. Unexpected feelings of envy or jealousy arise when other people get involved with the child. There are also possessive feelings that parents can feel toward their spouses or even the other children in the family. All of this goes into the formula when you think about the parents' relationship with the caregiver.

Teachers likewise start to get attached to the child. I think that somehow the young child who needs to be cared for, who needs to be protected, engenders these feelings. Yesterday, for example, I talked with teachers at a center who were distressed at the sudden departure of a child who had been in their care for two years. The family left without discussing it with them and they felt distressed. They had a big investment in this child, and they were expressing feelings of a very strong and normal attachment.

The second factor in the caregiver-parent relationship is the parents' expectations of what they should be doing with their child—what kind of child care the child should have, whether or not the mother should be working. These expectations, according to the research, make a critical difference in the impact of child care on children.

The third factor is the normal anxieties people have around the time of separation. When someone leaves or goes to do a new thing, the person leaving always has irrational flashes of danger or disaster—the loss becomes translated into a fear of a more permanent loss. Parents worry that the child is not going to be safe or that the child will come to love the caregiver more than the parent.

Defensive feelings are also involved. Parents and teachers are in a judgmental relationship, and both are not very high on the social hierarchical scale of important jobs in the world. Certainly there are no more important jobs than being a parent or teaching, but in terms of the outside world and

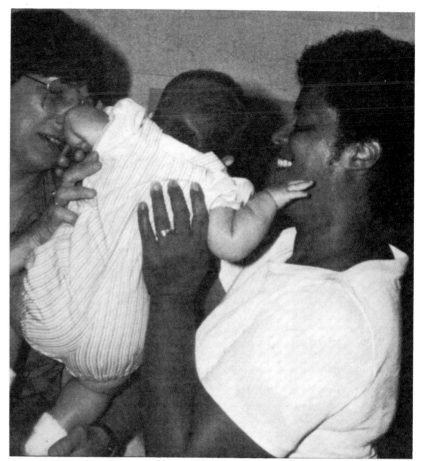

Photograph by Subjects and Predicates

the rewards and deference society gives to people, these jobs are unfortunately low.

In the beginning parents do not differentiate themselves from the children. If something wrong happens to a child, it's like something wrong happens to the parent. Even though every parenting book tells parents that they shouldn't feel this way, they do. When parents leave their child with a teacher, they know that they're going to be judged as parents; and they want to get high marks. It's a tense feeling.

Parents don't realize that the teachers (who look so secure to them) can also feel tense. They can feel that the parent is judging the way they're teaching the child.

Stronger Teacher-Parent Relations

There are several ways for parents and

teachers to establish a healthy partnership. First, both parents and teachers should learn about the normal range of feelings. If a child doesn't want to go to the center, parents have to decide if there is really something wrong or if this is just a phase. When teachers are feeling annoyed or negative toward the parents, they have to determine whether there is a problem or if these are normal feelings of possessiveness.

Also, it's important to understand that these normal feelings are positive. If teachers didn't get attached to children, they wouldn't be very good teachers. When I look at the words the teachers I surveyed used to describe parents, I don't, therefore, think of them as totally negative. They mean that teachers have made the first step—they care about the kids.

If it is clear that no problem exists, a method must be found for overcoming these normal feelings. For staff, it usually is very helpful if they can talk to each other about their feelings. Yesterday I asked teachers what they did when they were feeling mad at a parent. They all laughed and looked at each other—"We talk a lot!"

What happens in really good child care programs (and perhaps should be consciously done) is that one or more people on the staff take on the role of helping people see the world through both the parents' and the teachers' eyes. This person can help broaden people's perspective. For example, in an incident involving parent and staff, this person would ask questions that help the teacher understand how the parent is feeling.

Parents also need people to talk with about their feelings. It can be a network of people who are in the child care program or other parents. If a child is having a hard time, parents need someone they can turn to in order to figure out what's going on—

Photograph by Judy Burr

to help them determine if this is typical or if there is a problem in the program. It's a lot less anxiety producing to raise a child when one feels one has support. So it's important for parents to find people who will give them support, to help them solve problems, and to help them look at the other person's perspective. This makes them feel good. There's great potential for this type of parenting support through the child care center.

It also helps if people can see problems as outside of themselves, as situations to be resolved. If they can view things from a teamwork perspective rather than an adversarial approach, they are more likely to clear up difficulties without undue strain. This approach can be facilitated by establishing open channels of communication between parents and staff. Summit Child Care Center in New Jersey, for example, has a *parent rep* system. Representatives from each group call all the parents each month to ask for positive and negative feedback. When parents

bring up suggestions, there is the instinct to be defensive; but there is also a sense that the problem is there to be worked on together.

There is one final issue for teachers to consider in working with parents. Teachers need to be the kind of expert who facilitates the expertise of others rather than holding onto the expertise and dispensing it from a lofty position. For example, if a parent is having a very difficult time leaving her child, there are temptations to tell the parent what to do or to criticize the parent. But by helping the parent, encouraging the parent to talk, then making non-threatening suggestions, the teacher gives the parent options and lets the parent try to solve the problem. Making the parent feel competent is a particular way of being an expert. It is very constructive and builds in a partnership of people who are different but equal. Teachers are, in general, not trained for this role, yet it's part of being a child care professional (and one of the reasons teachers deserve respect).

When I was a parent in a child care class, one of the teachers began complaining early in the year about the parents. She said that the parents didn't care about the kids; they just wanted to dump their kids and run away. I knew I didn't feel this way and decided to find out how the other parents felt. I happened to be doing a study so I had the opportunity to interview the parents. I discovered that the parents were having a terrible time with the separation. There were as many different reactions as people, and most of them were uncertain about how to respond to their powerful and conflicting feelings. It wasn't that they didn't care. What the teacher interpreted as running away from children was really running away from the pain of leaving children.

It's easy to be critical of parents, to say they don't care, but that's rarely been my experience. There are very few parents who don't care. They may not express their care in a way that is useful, but they do care. It can be hard for teachers to step beyond their own feelings about parents, but when they do so, the rewards are rich—for the teachers, the parents, and, of course, the children.

Feelings About Sharing Care

How do you really feel about parents leaving their infants and toddlers with you all day long?

_____

_____

_____

_____

_____

How do you think parents feel about being away from their children?

_____

_____

_____

_____

_____

How do you feel about parents being in your room?

_____

_____

_____

_____

_____

How do you think parents feel when they are in your room?

_____

_____

_____

_____

_____

What can you do to help parents feel welcome?

_____

_____

_____

_____

_____

Whom can you talk openly with when you are feeling upset with a parent? How does talking with this person help you?

_____

_____

_____

_____

_____

How can your feelings influence your relationships with parents?

_____

_____

_____

_____

_____

Discuss your answers to these questions with your trainer or another caregiver.

II. Sharing the Care of Young Children

In this activity you will learn:

- to recognize the different information parents and caregivers have about children; and

- to better support children by exchanging information with parents.

Parents and caregivers come to their partnership with different kinds of knowledge about children. The parents' focus is their individual child. They see their child at home. Caregivers have a broader view, based on their study of child development and experience working with lots of children. They see a child in a group setting.

When parents and caregivers are able to share their information, each ends up with a more complete picture of who a particular child is. Information that parents and caregivers exchange each morning and afternoon about a child's eating, sleeping, and toileting helps each partner plan to best meet the needs of that child. Knowing, for example, that Karen (6 months) woke up three times during the night means that her caregivers can arrange the morning to offer her an earlier-than-usual nap. Knowing that Leroy (29 months) ate a big bowl of macaroni at afternoon snack means that his parents won't expect him to eat much dinner.

Here are some examples of the kinds of information that each partner can provide.

What Parents Know

A child's parents have information about the following areas in the child's life:

- **Health and growth history.** "After Ben's checkup at the pediatrician, I'll let you know how the treatment is progressing for his 'toeing in.' I know you will want to know about his condition so we can work together to continue his treatment."

- **Relationships with other family members.** "Carla really enjoys being with her brother. Every morning I feed her at the table with him, and he talks with her as much as with me. She coos and smiles with him as they eat."

- **Ways the child likes to be held or comforted.** "When Yancey is tired, he likes to have his back rubbed. It helps him settle down."

- **Which foods the child enjoys.** "Tom started eating carrots today. He really enjoyed them."

- **Which foods the child can or cannot eat.** "Donna is allergic to all kinds of berries."

- **How the child reacts to changes in routines.** "Sonia gets very upset if I ask her to dress before breakfast. She likes to eat first, then put her clothes on."

- **What the child likes to do at home.** "Timmy always wants to stay in the bathtub and play. He hates to have me lift him out."

- **What the child is afraid of.** "Travis is afraid of clowns. We're not sure why, but he always cries when he sees one."

- **What the child did last night, over the weekend, or on vacation.** "We all went to the beach for our vacation. Stacy collected buckets full of shells."

- **Who the child plays with at home.** "Our 3-year-old neighbor likes to play with Roxanne. Roxanne toddles around after her."

- **The family's lifestyle.** "We like to get outdoors as much as possible. Peter likes to ride in the backpack while we hike in the mountains."

- **How the child "used to be" as well as how the child is now.** "When he was 18 months, Nick never sat still except to eat. Now that he's 2, he'll sit down to look at a picture book alone several times a day."

What Caregivers Know

The child's caregiver has information about the following areas in the child's life:

- **Favorite play materials.** "When Tanya first comes in the morning, she goes right to the water table. She really has fun trying to catch the floating toys and looking at her fingers under water."

- **Which toys are too frustrating.** "Tory isn't ready to do the farm puzzle yet. He's learned to pick out the ones that don't have as many pieces."

- **What challenges the child enjoys.** "Shauna spent a lot of time today filling and dumping the baskets of pine cones."

- **How the child plays with others.** "Janna likes to be next to another toddler in the block center or at the easel. She watches their play while she 'does her own thing'."

- **How the child reacts to changes in the environment.** "Whenever we put on a record, Mark waves his arms in the air as if he were dancing while he lies in the crib."

- **How the child tells others what she or he is feeling.** When Gina is angry with another child, she holds her body stiffly and says in a loud voice, "Me no like."

- **What the child talks about during the day.** "Today Carlos talked about going to see his cousin, Luis. He's very excited about it."

• **What the child does when his or her parents leave.** "Today I heard Malik telling Sandy, 'Mommy come back.' I think that's his way of assuring himself that you will always come back."

Establishing a Partnership

Your relationship with a child's parents begins when their child first enters your program. Although the parents probably don't know you, you are the person who will care for their child for most of the day, five days a week. It is natural for them to want to learn as much as they can about you, the program, the other children in the group, and how their child will spend each day. Share this information and tell them something about yourself. Let the parents know what you are like and why you enjoy working with infants and toddlers. Describe the day's activities and what their child will be doing. It is also helpful to give parents a copy of the daily schedule.

Get to know the parents, too. Find out what their interests are, what kind of work they do, and how they feel about leaving their child at the center. Reassure parents that you see them as their child's most important people. Let them know how you will work with them to share information about their child and to make decisions about their child's care.

You and the parents will continue getting to know each other through brief conversations at drop-off and pick-up times. Show that you are interested in the parents by always greeting each by name. Share interesting, positive information about their child's day. Let them know by your attitude and tone of voice that their child is well cared for. "Susanna had fun today. She played with Carrie in the sand box, she painted, and she sat in my lap for a story." These kinds of daily communications will build trust and acceptance, which will lead to a stronger partnership.

In this learning activity you will focus on sharing information with the parents of one of the children in your care to better meet the needs of that child. Select a child and family with whom you feel comfortable but whom you would like to know better. Let them know that you have selected them. Then, for two weeks, record your daily communications—any information you each shared. Look for ways in which your communication helps you meet this child's needs. Begin by reading the example that follows.

Parent-Caregiver Daily Communication Record
(Example)

Child _Donna_ **Age** _Two years_ **Dates** _June 6-20_

Parents _Karen and Frank Anderson_

How long the child has been coming to the center: _4 months_

Day One

A.M. *Greeted Ms. Anderson and told her about this activity. She was pleased to hear that I am working on this module. She told me Donna went to bed later than usual. She said that lately Donna has liked carrying her grandmother's old purse around the house.*

P.M. *Mr. Anderson came to pick up Donna. I told him Donna had taken a long nap. I told him that Donna played with her friend Sheila. They filled purses with small toys and carried them around. His wife already told him I was doing this learning activity. He wished me luck.*

Day Two

A.M. *Mr. Anderson brought Donna. I told him we were going to bring the water play table outside today and that Donna really liked to use the little pitcher to fill up cups and the ice cube tray. He asked if she could do that at home. I told him she could do it at the sink, in a dishpan, or in the bathtub. He seemed pleased with my ideas.*

P.M. *Ms. Anderson picked up Donna. I told her Donna helped us carry out the water play toys today and that Donna ate a big lunch and made fruit smoothies this afternoon. She was surprised because Donna doesn't eat much fruit at home. I said that often the children eat more food when they help make it. She told me Mr. Anderson would be bringing Donna and picking her up for the next two days because she would be away at a conference. She said she was worried about Donna. We talked about the importance of her telling Donna she would be away and then would come back. I suggested she leave a picture and write Donna a love note. I assured her we would keep a special eye on Donna. Ms. Anderson said maybe she would make Donna a tape. I said that sounded like a good idea.*

First Weekly Summary
(Complete after five days)

Information you shared:

That I'm doing this learning activity.

How Donna ate and slept in child care.

Donna played with Sheila.

Donna likes to pour into different containers.

Ways Donna could play with a pitcher at home.

Donna helped carry the water play toys.

Donna likes fruit smoothies.

Information parents shared:

They were interested in my work on this module.

How Donna slept and ate at home.

Donna likes to carry her Grandma's old purse.

Donna doesn't eat much fruit at home.

Donna's mother will be away for two days.

How has sharing information helped you meet this child's needs?

Knowing more about Donna's life at home helps me plan her day at the center.

Knowing about her mother's trip means I can offer Donna extra support by talking about where her mother is and saying that she will come back like she always does.

I was able to help her mother feel competent about her idea of making a tape. Feeling good about herself will help her be more available to Donna.

Parent-Caregiver Daily Communication Record

Child _____ Age _____ Dates _____

Parents _____

How long the child has been coming to the center: _____

Day One

A.M. _____
_____
_____

P.M. _____
_____
_____

Day Two

A.M. _____
_____
_____

P.M. _____
_____
_____

Day Three

A.M. _____
_____
_____

P.M. _____
_____
_____

Day Four

    A.M. _____

          _____

          _____

    P.M. _____

          _____

          _____

Day Five

    A.M. _____

          _____

          _____

    P.M. _____

          _____

          _____

First Weekly Summary
(Complete after five days)

Information you shared:

_____
_____
_____
_____
_____
_____
_____
_____
_____
_____
_____
_____
_____

Information parents shared:

_____
_____
_____
_____
_____
_____
_____
_____
_____
_____
_____
_____
_____
_____

Day Six

    A.M. _____

_____

_____

_____

    P.M. _____

_____

_____

_____

Day Seven

    A.M. _____

_____

_____

_____

    P.M. _____

_____

_____

_____

Day Eight

    A.M. _____

_____

_____

_____

    P.M. _____

_____

_____

_____

Day Nine

A.M. _____

_____

_____

_____

P.M. _____

_____

_____

_____

Day Ten

A.M. _____

_____

_____

_____

P.M. _____

_____

_____

_____

Second Weekly Summary
(Complete at the end of another five days)

Information you shared:

_____
_____
_____
_____
_____
_____
_____
_____
_____

Information parents shared:

_____
_____
_____
_____
_____
_____
_____
_____
_____
_____

Review all your notes and complete the following.

How has sharing information helped you meet this child's needs?

(Give at least five examples)

_____
_____
_____
_____
_____
_____

Discuss this activity with the child's parents and your trainer.

III. Offering Ways for Parents to Be Involved

In this activity you will learn:

- to offer a variety of ways for parents to be involved in their child's life at child care; and

- to plan and implement a parent involvement strategy.

Most parents are interested in being part of their child's life at the center, but they may not know about all the different ways they can become involved. Sometimes parents can arrange their work schedules so they can go on field trips, eat lunch with the children occasionally, or work as a volunteer caregiver on a regular basis. It benefits both parent and child when the parent can visit the program during the day; however, many parents are not able to participate in this way. You and other staff need to work together to create a variety of options for parent involvement that match the interests, skills, and schedules of the parents.

You also need to let parents know how much their participation benefits the program. Parents who come on field trips may enjoy themselves so much that they don't need much encouragement to offer to do it again. The parent who sews new covers for the pillows in the library area, however, may never see the pillows in use. In such a case, be sure to send a note home thanking the parent. You could describe how the children are using the pillows or enclose a picture of children sitting among the pillows looking at books. Similarly, the parent who types the newsletter should be listed in every issue as the one who makes it possible for the news to get out to the other families.

Here are some suggestions for helping parents become more involved in your center:

- Have parents complete a brief **questionnaire** about ways they would like to be involved when they register their child at the center.

- Hold an **orientation** for new parents several times a year. Because a certain number of families come and go during the year, you need to provide more than one orientation.

- Hold a **family movie night** planned and hosted by parent volunteers. Parents could sell popcorn and juice to raise funds for extra materials or field trips.

- Organize a **family dinner** when parents can eat dinner at the center on their way home. Toddlers can help prepare part of the meal.

- Provide opportunities for parents to participate in **building or landscaping projects** that can be worked on over a period of time. When a project is completed, hold a celebration party.

- Schedule a **"fix-it"** night or a Saturday when families can work together to spruce up the center, paint walls, make a tire playground, or prepare a plot of ground for a garden.

- Keep a **job jar** in your room containing index cards listing center-related jobs you never get around to doing that a parent could do at home. Parents can select a job from the jar, then see you for additional instructions. Jobs could include repairing broken toys, gathering dress-up hats, or making matching boards or other materials for the room.

- Set up a **parent corner** at the center. Include books, magazines, brochures, and other resources of interest to parents. If possible, provide comfortable chairs and refreshments.

- Ask a parent to organize a **photo album** about the center. You can provide the pictures and the book; the parent can put it together. Display the photo album in the lobby. Include a cover page thanking the parent who organized the album.

- Use parents as **book reviewers**. Parents may read children's books or books on child development or parenting that they'd like to recommend to the center. Provide a book review form that they can complete, listing the title, author, publisher, and price. For children's books, leave space on the form for parents to record what ages the book is appropriate for, what the book is about, and why they and their child liked it. You can use these recommendations to select books for your room.

In this learning activity you will try out a parent involvement strategy. Select from those mentioned earlier, and discuss your selection with your supervisor and the other caregivers in your room. Ask for their ideas about implementing this strategy. If your supervisor or colleagues think this strategy is not appropriate for the parents at your center, then select another one. First read the example; then complete the chart that follows it to describe the strategy you chose and how it helped parents become involved.

Parent Involvement Strategy
(Example)

Strategy:

Parent volunteers will tape themselves singing songs. We have a tape player, but most of the tapes you can buy are too expensive or the stories are for older children.

Plans:

I will send a notice home with the children asking for volunteers. The center will supply blank tapes. The songs can be favorites from home. I'll try to make sure we tape a variety of songs in the different languages spoken by the families in our group.

Results:

Four parents volunteered to make tapes. Each parent taped several songs, so now we have a nice selection. The children really enjoy hearing their parent's voices on tape. All four parents said they would be happy to make more tapes whenever we need them.

Follow-up:

I will make this an ongoing parent involvement project. I asked Ms. Porter, one of the four parents who made tapes, to help me keep track of which songs we tape and which parents help. I think the children would like it if all the parents took a turn making a tape. This could be a good project for parents who aren't able to spend time at the center during the day.

Now select a parent involvement strategy to implement at your center. Discuss your selection with your supervisor and other caregivers in your room. Write your plans on the form below. After implementing your strategy, write the results and some plans for follow-up.

Parent Involvement Strategy

Strategy:

_____

_____

_____

_____

_____

Plans:

_____

_____

_____

_____

_____

Results:

_____

_____

_____

_____

_____

Follow-up:

_____

_____

_____

_____

_____

Discuss this activity with the other caregivers in your room and your trainer.

IV. Planning and Participating in Parent-Caregiver Conferences

In this activity you will learn:

- to prepare for a conference by reviewing information about a young child's development; and

- to participate in a parent conference.

At least twice a year, parents and their child's caregivers need to meet. Although much information about a child is shared daily, conferences are times when you and a child's parents can discuss a child in depth without distractions or interruptions. These conferences can reaffirm your partnership with parents.

Usually there is no single goal for the conference. Conferences can meet a number of different needs. Here's what other early childhood educators have said about their goals for parent conferences:[2]

> "To make the parents aware of how their child is developing, at what level she or he is functioning, and if she or he is in need of any special help." Janet Rogers, Lycoming Child Day Care, Williamsport, PA.

> "To project the importance of the child as a person and how necessary it is for parents and teachers to work together to develop in the child a good self-image." Louisa Pola, Guantanamo Bay Nursery School, U.S. Naval Station, Guantanamo Bay, Cuba.

> "To get to know the parents enough to feel comfortable with them and them with me; and to better understand the child through the parent." Lois Grigsby, Kendal Lab Child Care, Evanston, IL.

> "To give the parent confidence in the teacher; to establish a social relationship between parent and teacher." Margaret Frederickson, Northedge School, Sudbury, MA.

> "To discuss the child's development; to identify future goals." Shelly Brick, Kensington-Kingstowne Child Care Center, Philadelphia, PA.

> "To foster greater awareness of the importance the environment plays in a child's development—to educate the parents." Jan Lucas, Westend Day Care, Portage la Prairie, Manitoba, Canada.

---

[2]Reprinted with permission from "Ideas for Effective Parent Conferences," *Child Care Information Exchange* (Redmond, WA: Exchange Press, PO Box 2890, Redmond, Washington 98073 (206) 883-9394), November 1979), pp. 26-27.

"To provide support for working parents by supplying any information on child development, available social services, etc." Tracy Neri, The Day Care Center, Norwich, VT.

Parents also have goals for the conference. They may have a specific concern they would like to discuss or a suggestion for how they would like you to work with their child. They may have a concern about the program or a complaint about something you did or didn't do. Often parents want to be reassured that you like their child, that you are competent, and that you think they are doing a good job raising their child.

Planning for Conferences

To make the best use of the time set aside for the conference, it's important to do some planning. Talk to parents before the conference to let them know its purpose. Ask them to think of any questions they might have. Find out if there is any topic they want to cover. Tell them you hope to learn more about the child's life at home so you can better support the child's growth at the center. Ask parents about what is the best time to hold the conference, and agree on a time that will work for each of you.

You also need to think about what points you want to cover. Review your observation notes, anecdotal records, and any other written materials that provide objective information about the child. You can also collect samples of the child's art work or other creations. Organize your notes to make sure you have covered all areas of development—physical, cognitive, language, social, and emotional. If you have any concerns about the child's health, these should be documented. Ask the other caregivers in your room to provide any information they have about this child.

Parents often want to know what the child is like in a group situation. They would like to know as much as possible about what their child does all day, with whom he or she plays, what makes the child happy or sad, and what the child enjoys doing. Try to collect "stories" to share that will help parents picture and understand how their child spends his or her day.

Sometimes caregivers feel a little uneasy before a conference. It may help to role-play with your supervisor or a colleague. You can practice sharing your observations and answering the kinds of questions that the parents are likely to ask.

Participating in the Conference

At the start of the conference, try to establish a relaxed and comfortable tone. Anticipate at least five minutes of social conversation before beginning your more serious discussions. Before the conference, decide which of the center staff will take the lead in the conference. This person should begin by telling the parents how the conference will proceed: "I'm so glad you could both come today. Let's begin with your question about what Renee does all day. We have several observations to share with you. Then we'd like to know more about what she does at home."

During the conference, be sure there are many opportunities for parents to provide input and ask questions. To be successful, communication during a conference must be two-way.

Here are some other suggestions for conducting successful conferences.

- Begin and end the conference with a positive statement about your relationship with the child. "We really enjoy Timothy's playfulness. He makes us all smile."

- When parents seem reluctant to talk about their concerns, ask them an open-ended question. "What else about Rebecca or the program would you like to discuss?"

- Summarize your discussion at the end of the conference, emphasizing what actions you each have agreed to take. "I will spend more time looking at books with Laura now that I know she likes to do that at home. And you'll bring in her special blanket so she can have it during naps. That will make her feel more secure."

- When parents ask you for advice about handling a specific situation, respond in ways to help parents discover what will work best for their child and for them. You may sometimes share something you have learned from your experience or something you have observed other parents trying. Sometimes just by listening you can help parents see they already have an answer. "I think you are right. It is easier for Tenesha to get ready to go home when you are clear that it is time to go."

In this learning activity you will develop a plan for holding a conference with the parents of one of the children in your room. Include information from your own observations and those of other caregivers in the room. Conduct the conference, then answer the evaluation questions.

Planning a Conference
(Example)

Child _Richard_ **Age** _18 months_ **Age at last conference** _12 months_

Parent(s) _Mr. Lee_ **Caregiving team** _Ms. Little and Mr. Santana_

Conference date _January 15_ **Last conference date** _November 4_

What does this child like to do?

> _Richard loves to run and climb. He enjoys playing "peek-a-boo" as he opens and closes the door of our refrigerator box house._

What makes this child happy?

> _Playing in the park where there is lots of space to move and run. Spending time with Mr. Santana._

What makes this child sad?

> _His father leaving in the morning. Someone hitting him. Sometimes he gets sad when we tell him "no."_

What new skills is this child working on?

> _Richard is learning to climb up and down stairs._

Whom does this child play with, and in what ways?

> _Richard tries to get the caregivers to run with him in the park. He plays "peek-a-boo" with Reggie and Elizabeth._

Anecdotes to share:

> _Richard and Elizabeth laughed as they played "peek-a-boo" together. Looking at family pictures seemed to help Richard feel better after saying goodbye to his father._

Any concerns:

> _What else can we do to help make saying goodbye to his father easier for Richard?_

Conference Evaluation

After the conference, think about what happened and answer these questions.

How did you establish a relaxed tone?

I offered Mr. Lee a cup of coffee. We spent a few minutes talking about ourselves before beginning.

How did you start the conference?

I said I was glad for the chance to talk with him away from the hustle and bustle of the center. I said how much I enjoy the sparkle in Richard's eye and his joyfulness.

How did you provide for parent input?

I said we are a team and that while I had information to share, I wanted to know what Mr. Lee was seeing and thinking about Richard. I asked if there was anything else Mr. Lee wanted to talk about before we ended.

Were you asked for advice?

Yes. Mr. Lee asked me how to help Richard calm down after a period of running and climbing.

What stories or anecdotes did you tell about how the child spends the day?

I described Richard's joyfulness as he runs in the park.

I described how we sometimes sit together in the rocking chair and sing when I want to help Richard slow down a little.

What goals did you and the parents set for the child?

We decided to give Richard opportunities to practice climbing stairs.

We agreed to spend a little more quiet time with Richard singing or reading to give him another kind of experience.

How did you summarize the conference?

I reviewed our major points and asked Mr. Lee if he wanted to add anything.

How did you end the conference?

I said I was glad we had the opportunity to talk together and assured Mr. Lee I was available if he wanted to talk more before our next scheduled conference.

What would you do differently next time?

I was so nervous I ended up focusing on Mr. Lee's question about helping Richard calm down and forgot my concern about helping Richard with separation. Next time I will pause to look at my notes. I will be sure to talk about separation with him soon and not wait until our next conference.

Planning a Conference

Child _____ Age _____ Age at last conference _____

Parent(s) _____ Caregiving team _____

Conference date _____ Last conference date _____

What does this child like to do?

_____

_____

_____

What makes this child happy?

_____

_____

_____

What makes this child sad?

_____

_____

_____

What new skills is this child working on?

_____

_____

_____

Whom does this child play with, and in what ways?

_____

_____

_____

Anecdotes to share:

_____

_____

_____

Any concerns:

_____

_____

_____

Conference Evaluation

After the conference, think about what happened and answer these questions.

How did you establish a relaxed tone?

_____

_____

_____

_____

_____

How did you start the conference?

_____

_____

_____

_____

_____

How did you provide for parent input?

_____

_____

_____

_____

_____

Were you asked for advice?

_____

_____

_____

_____

_____

What stories or anecdotes did you tell about how the child spends the day?

_____

_____

_____

_____

What goals did you and the parents set for the child?

_____

_____

_____

_____

_____

How did you summarize the conference?

_____

_____

_____

_____

_____

How did you end the conference?

_____

_____

_____

_____

_____

What would you do differently next time?

_____

_____

_____

_____

_____

Discuss this learning activity with your trainer.

V. Resolving Differences

In this activity you will learn:

- to understand and appreciate differences in child rearing; and

- to develop strategies for resolving differences when they occur.

If parents of the same child disagree at times about what they think is best for their child, it is almost guaranteed that parents and caregivers will come up against differences in their work together. Infants and toddlers evoke deep feelings in their adults. Parents and caregivers each have their own family histories. They may come from different cultural backgrounds. Based on who they are, sometimes a child's parents and caregivers have conflicting views on child rearing. They may even have different ideas about a child's strengths, interests, and needs.

As a caregiver, your goal is not to prevent differences but to be sure they do not undermine your partnership with families and affect your ability to care for children. Sometimes this involves letting an issue go. You may be annoyed when Debbie's father forgets to bring in her sheet he took home to wash. But, you realize, there is a spare sheet she can use. It's no big deal.

At other times differences need to be addressed. Carol, a very experienced and skillful caregiver, got so upset at Jeff's parents, who were continually late at the end of the day, that she stopped communicating with them. Talking to her supervisor helped her see she wasn't getting all the information she needed to best meet Jeff's needs. She made an appointment to talk with them and explain the problem. They apologized and made arrangements for an aunt to pick up Jeff on days they were running late.

Differences can be experienced in almost any area, ranging from views on a child's eating, sleeping, or toileting patterns, to parents being late. When you find yourself feeling at odds with a parent, keep in mind that you have something in common—genuine concern for the well-being of the child.

Here are some suggestions to help you resolve differences in ways that can strengthen your partnership:

- Remember that some conflicts are to be expected. They are part of life, especially when infants and toddlers are concerned.

- Be aware of how your feelings about families and sharing care (discussed earlier in this module) can distort how you perceive and address a difference.

- Talk with someone outside the situation, such as your director or a colleague at another center, to help you step back and get a more objective picture of what is going on.

- Be willing to apologize when an apology is in order.

- Plan a meeting with parents when you need uninterrupted time to talk together and develop a strategy for solving a problem.

- Try to look at the situation through parents' eyes. Listen carefully to what they are saying.

- Help parents understand your perspective.

- Keep a child's best interests in the forefront as you address differences with parents.

A good working relationship is worth the time and effort it may take. Everyone benefits. Parents feel more confident in their parenting skills. Caregivers gain information that helps them take better care of children and feel a sense of achievement at helping not only children but families develop. Infants and toddlers feel more secure when they sense their adults working together. Their lives are enriched by knowing that both their parents and caregivers are people they can trust.

In this learning activity you will think about how you resolve differences with parents of the children you care for. Begin by reading three examples of case studies to see how one caregiver responded. Then describe how you would respond to the situations on the next page.

Differences Between Parents and Caregivers
(Example)

1. The Missing Mittens

"This is the second pair of mittens that have been lost this winter. Why can't you be more careful?" says Ms. Frank as she storms out of your room with her daughter Nancy. You are furious at her. You are careful. How can you be expected to keep track of everything? What will you do?

I would probably first blow off a little steam with my co-caregiver. I am careful. It's hard to keep track of little mittens. The next day, after I've cooled down, I would tell Ms. Frank I was sorry the mittens were missing. I'd assure her I work very hard to take good care of Nancy and the other children as well as their things and then listen to what she had to say.

2. The Party Dress

Again, Ms. Greene, Sandra's grandmother, has brought Sandra to child care wearing a frilly, light-blue party dress. She seems so proud as she tells Sandra to show you her party dress. You smile but you are thinking "this dress is asking for trouble" as you envision it smeared with paint or torn after getting caught in the climber. What will you do?

Ideally, I'd like Sandra's grandmother to dress her in playclothes. To me, dresses like this are a big bother. But I have a feeling it is very important for Ms. Greene to dress Sandra this way. I think it helps her feel like she is taking good care of Sandra. I would comment that the dress is very pretty. Then I'd explain to Ms. Greene I was concerned about what might happen to it during the day as Sandra painted, climbed, and helped prepare snacks. I'd suggest the idea of changing Sandra into playclothes after she arrives and hope Ms. Greene would agree.

3. Different Expectations

A few days ago you overheard Ms. Evans, Joannie's aunt, say to Joannie "You're being bad. I want you to share your blanket with Fred. He just wants to hold it for a while." Yesterday, she came to tell you that she is afraid Joannie is turning into a selfish child. You feel that Joannie, a 2-year-old, should not be expected to share—especially her special blanket. What will you do?

I think I'd arrange a time to talk with Ms. Evans. I'd ask her what she meant when she said, "Joannie is turning into a selfish child." I'd share some information about 2-year-olds with her. I'd observe some other toddlers in the room with her to try to help her see that Joannie is like other children her age.

Differences Between Parents and Caregivers

After reading each case study, write down how you think you would respond. Then plan a time to discuss your responses with your trainer and a group of colleagues. Remember that there can be many ways to achieve your goal of resolving differences and keeping the line of communication open between you and parents.

1. The Late Parent

It is the fourth day in a row that Kyle's father has come late at the end of the day to pick him up. The first few days you let it go. Things happen. But today he is already 15 minutes late, and you were planning to leave right at closing time to meet a friend for a movie and dinner. What will you do?

_____

_____

_____

_____

_____

_____

_____

2. Chocolate Cupcakes

Yesterday was Leon's first birthday. His parents brought in chocolate cupcakes for a snacktime celebration. Although you know the Jones don't like their daughter, Constance, to eat sweets, you thought one cupcake wouldn't hurt. Besides, Constance took a bite so quickly you couldn't have stopped her if you wanted to. You meant to tell Mr. Jones about the special snack, but things got so busy at pick-up time that you forgot. This morning Ms. Jones came in quite concerned. "I found chocolate on Connie's shirt when she got home last night. You know we don't want her to eat sweets. What is going on around here?" What will you do?

_____

_____

_____

_____

_____

_____

3. Reading and Writing

Mr. Gonzalez pulls you aside one morning and says, "Jorge will be 2 next week. When he was little, this baby stuff you do like taking walks and playing was great. But now it is time for him to begin working on letters and numbers." You know that 2 is too early to teach numbers and letters. You know toddlers learn as they play and participate in daily routines. Of course you talk about letters and numbers as you encounter them each day, but you have no intention of "teaching" them the way Mr. Gonzalez has in mind. What will you do?

_____

_____

_____

_____

_____

_____

_____

4. Bowling

You know it is important for parents to feel comfortable in your room. At first Roger's father seemed very shy. You went out of your way to make him feel welcome. Now, whenever he comes to visit, he sets up a bowling game in the middle of the room, and chaos erupts. What will you do?

_____

_____

_____

_____

_____

_____

_____

VI. Reaching Out to Families

In this activity you will learn:

- to recognize signs that families are under stress; and

- to provide support to families under stress.

Parents of infants and toddlers—especially first time parents—are often under stress. Lack of sleep, feeling unsure about sharing the care of their child, and not understanding children's behavior can all leave parents feeling in need of support. In your role of caregiver, you are in an excellent position to lend a helping hand. Some parents will feel comfortable sharing their worries and seeking advice. Others will not. Regardless of whether parents approach you or you approach them, remember that supporting parents means enhancing their sense of competence by helping parents discover their own answers.

You can support parents by helping them locate resources and giving them information and guidance on the growth and development of infants and toddlers.

You can reach out to parents by providing help, support, encouragement, and information. You can:

- recognize when parents are under stress;

- help parents locate resources; and

- give parents information and guidance on infant and toddler growth and development.

Recognizing When Parents Are Under Stress

When a family is under stress, the parents may seem disorganized, frequently forgetting important items such as diapers or bottles of formula. A parent might seem frustrated when a child is slow to get ready to go home, or the parent might state that he or she doesn't know how to handle the child's independent behavior. Parents under stress might be unwilling to accept help, or they might be more interested in talking about their own problems than their child's.

When you see signs of stress, it is important that you do not add to them. You can discuss their child's behavior or tell them about your upcoming vacation on another day. However, you will want to share information about their child's day that will help them get through a difficult evening. For example, letting a parent know that a teething infant has been cranky all day allows you to discuss ways to help ease the infant's pain. Because the parent knows why the infant is crying, he or she is less likely to be frustrated or angered by the crying and more likely to comfort the child. When parents feel less stress they are more likely to interact positively with their children and are less likely to become angry and lash out at them.

Here are some events that may cause stress:

- lack of sleep;

- serious illness or death of a family member;

- separation and divorce;

- an unplanned or unwanted pregnancy;

- failure to receive a promotion;

- extended travel; and

- geographic or social isolation.

Make an effort to really get to know the parents of the children in your group. Invite parents into the room when they bring their children to the center and pick them up. Place a suggestion box in a prominent place and draw attention to it. Invite parents to visit often, and make them welcome. Remember that you, the center, and the parents are part of a team working for the child's good.

Always notify your director when you think parents may need professional help. Your job is to help parents get the support they need, not to provide it yourself. Never make recommendations to parents without first clearing them with your supervisor.

Helping Parents Locate Resources

Parents often need information on where they can get help for themselves, their child, or the family. Your director can provide you with information about parent education opportunities. Here are some things you can do to help.

- Help parents connect with one another.

- Call parents' attention to resources, newspaper or magazine articles, workshops, and television or radio shows on stages of child development, positive guidance, and family life.

- Post notices of special programs offered by the center and in the community.

- Display books on topics of interest to parents—step-parenting, juggling home and work responsibilities, health and nutrition—and invite parents to borrow these resources.

- Tell them about services provided by the social services organizations in your community.

- Provide names, phone numbers, locations, and hours of operation when you suggest a program or event.

- Offer reluctant parents help in contacting other resources.

Giving Parents Information and Guidance on Infant-Toddler Growth and Development

Parents sometimes know very little about infant and toddler development. As a result, they may expect too much of a particular child at a particular age. Here are some things you can do to help.

- Observe a child together, asking yourselves "what is he or she experiencing?" to help parents see the world through the eyes of their infant or toddler.

- Tell parents about workshops on building self-esteem, adjusting to a new baby, independence, and other topics of interest.

- Be sure parents see information on growth and development in the center's newsletters.

- Invite parents to attend staff workshops.

- Lend books or videotapes from the center's library.

- Ask the director to schedule conferences to discuss particular problems.

- Introduce parents who are dealing with similar developmental issues.

Also, during drop-off and pick-up times and in longer visits during the day, without any extra effort or planning, you model for parents various developmentally appropriate ways to meet children's needs. For example, visiting parents might see the following interactions between a caregiver and the children in her care:

Ms. Danforth encourages Gina (28 months) to help put away the blocks, talks and laughs with Evan (6 months) as she diapers him, and asks Bart (32 months) a question about his painting—"Tell me how you made these long, squiggly lines?" These parents might comment, "I can't get her to put her things away at home." "He squirms around so much at home that I just want to get the diaper changed as quickly as possible." "All his paintings look the same to me." The caregiver can then use these comments to open conversations about ways to promote toddlers' self-help skills, take advantage of diapering routines to communicate with infants, and support creativity by asking about their children's paintings.

When you demonstrate positive ways of working with children, you do a lot to help parents improve their interactions with their children.

In this activity, you will keep records of times when you reached out to parents in response to their requests or because you noticed that they needed your support. Over the next few weeks, make a note of what you did. Write down the problem, what the parent asked for or what you saw was needed, how you responded, and what the outcome was. Begin by reading the example on the next page.

Reaching Out to Families
(Example)

Child *Larry*   **Age** *21 months*   **Date** *October 23*

Problem:

Larry is extremely jealous of his new baby sister, Elizabeth. His parents have stated that he hits and pinches her.

What parents asked for or what I saw was needed:

Help in stopping Larry from hitting and pinching her.

My response:

We talked about the problem. I suggested they talk with the Greenes, who also have a new baby. I asked how they think Larry might be feeling. I also gave them materials they could read to Larry about having a new baby in the family.

The outcome:

The parents say it was helpful to talk with someone in the same situation. They decided to spend extra time with Larry alone. Larry is not as upset, and he really likes story time with his Dad. He said, "Sissy can't read with Daddy, but I can."

Reaching Out to Families

Child _____ Age _____ Date _____

Problem:

_____

_____

_____

_____

What parents asked for or what I saw was needed:

_____

_____

_____

_____

My response:

_____

_____

_____

_____

The outcome:

_____

_____

_____

_____

Reaching Out to Families

Child _____   Age _____   Date _____

Problem:

_____
_____
_____
_____

What parents asked for or what I saw was needed:

_____
_____
_____
_____

My response:

_____
_____
_____
_____

The outcome:

_____
_____
_____
_____

Reaching Out to Families

Child _____   Age _____   Date _____

Problem:

_____

_____

_____

_____

What parents asked for or what I saw was needed:

_____

_____

_____

_____

My response:

_____

_____

_____

_____

The outcome:

_____

_____

_____

_____

Discuss your responses with your trainer.

Summarizing Your Progress

You have now completed all of the learning activities for this module. Whether you are an experienced caregiver or a new one, this module has probably helped you develop new skills in working with families. Before you go on, take a few minutes to summarize what you've learned. Review your responses to the pre-training assessment for this module. Write a summary of what you learned, and list the skills you developed or improved.

Your final step in this module is to complete the knowledge and competency assessments. Let your trainer know when you are ready to schedule the assessments. After you have successfully completed these assessments, you will be ready to start a new module. Congratulations on your progress so far, and good luck with your next module.

Answer Sheet: Working with Families

Communicating with Family Members Often to Exchange Information About Their Child at Home and at the Center

1. **Why did Ms. Lewis decide not to share the news about Janet's accomplishments?**

   a. She knew that Janet's parents were very excited and wanted to be there when Janet took her first step.

   b. She knew Janet would walk at home with her parents and they would enjoy the surprise.

2. **What kinds of information will Ms. Lewis and the Carters need to share now that Janet is beginning to walk?**

   a. How they can help her explore safely.

   b. Other tasks Janet tries to master, such as climbing stairs and running.

Offering a Variety of Ways for Family Members to Participate in Their Child's Life at the Center

1. **How did Ms. Bates help Mr. Bradley deal with his feelings about leaving Jerry at the child development center?**

   a. She asked him about his work and interests.

   b. She invited him to make something for the center.

2. **How did Ms. Bates help Mr. Bradley find a way to participate in Jerry's life at the center?**

   a. She invited him to stay at the center when he brought the new platform.

   b. She told him he was always welcome and it meant a lot to Jerry to have his dad around.

Providing Support for Families

1. **What did Mr. Jones do to help Ms. Thomas understand Marita's behavior?**

   a. He explained that Marita's behavior was typical of 1- and 2-year-olds.

   b. He explained that Marita was getting used to being separated from her parents.

2. **How did Mr. Jones help Marita and her mother cope with separation?**

   a. He scheduled a meeting with Ms. Thomas to tell her more about separation and what Marita did during the day.

   b. He held Marita for a clear farewell to Ms. Thomas.

   c. He suggested Ms. Thomas could call to check on Marita.

   d. He allowed Marita time to cry and calm herself.

   e. He had Marita pick out a story to read.

Module 12
Program Management

What Is Program Management and Why Is It Important?

Caregivers play many roles. The primary and most obvious role is to provide for children's health, safety, and developmental needs. But caring for infants and toddlers involves much more. It includes building children's self-esteem and responding to their explorations of the world around them. It involves supporting families and helping parents deal with working outside the home. And it also includes being a manager.

Picture yourself standing in the middle of a room wearing a shirt smeared with applesauce. You are rubbing the back of a crying infant while trying to convince a toddler to begin putting blocks back in the can rather than scattering them around the rug. In situations like this, which are not unusual when caring for infants and toddlers, you might find it difficult to think of yourself as a manager. But you are. Your management role, like that of executives in the business world, includes planning, conducting, and evaluating the program. As you perform these managerial tasks, you become more effective in promoting infants' and toddlers' development, setting up the environment, and handling other responsibilities.

Every day caregivers make countless decisions ranging from how best to respond to a crying child to what to make for snack. (During a one hour period, jot down all the choices you make. You'll be amazed!) To make decisions that add up to a good program for infants and toddlers, you must know every child in your group so you can meet their individual needs. By systematically observing children and recording what they do and say, you can gather the information you need to plan for each child.

As a manager, you also have to keep your group running. This means working as a team with the other caregivers to plan your program.

In addition to being responsible for what happens in your own room, you have a role to play in managing your center as a whole. As you complete your timesheets and required reports on time, you do your part to keep the center running smoothly.

Managing an early childhood program involves:

- observing and recording information about each child's growth and development;

- working as a member of a team to plan an individualized program; and

- following administrative policies and procedures.

Listed on the next page are examples of how caregivers demonstrate their competence in managing a program.

Observing and Recording Information About Each Child's Growth and Development

Here are some examples of what caregivers can do.

- Watch and listen to a child at play and write down what she or he does and says to help understand how the child experiences the world. "Mr. Jones, can you stay by the water table while I observe how Maria uses the nesting cups?"

- Use systematic observation to record information that is objective and accurate and avoids labeling. "Tawana (17 months) spent 10 minutes sitting in the sandbox shoveling sand into a bucket and then dumping it out."

- Communicate with parents to identify each child's strengths, needs, and interests. "Could you tell me how Henry comforts himself at home so that we can help him comfort himself when he misses you during the day?"

- Use all opportunities to gather information about children. "You closed your eyes when I began to pull the shirt over your head, Delante. I don't think you've done that before!"

Working as a Member of a Team to Plan an Individualized Program

Here are some examples of what caregivers can do.

- Find time to meet regularly with other caregivers. "Maybe we can ask our volunteer to keep her eye on the nap room so we can meet once a week while the children are sleeping."

- Use information gathered from observing to plan for each child. "Dexter has been easily upset lately. Maybe he needs some one-on-one time with his special caregiver."

- Communicate with parents about their child's growth and development. "What would you like Pam's experience in our program to be like?"

- Provide substitute caregivers with adequate information on the needs of individual children. "Kara likes to have her back rubbed as she is falling asleep."

Following Administrative Policies and Procedures

Here are some examples of what caregivers can do.

- Review center policies before starting a new task. "I need to find out how we arrange a walk to the park."

- Complete management tasks according to a schedule. "I'd like to review the parent evaluations, Ms. Snyder, so we can begin to make improvements."

- Use the center's system for recordkeeping. "Will you please keep an eye on the children while I fill out the accident report for Paul's skinned knee?"

- Keep informed about caregiver's job responsibilities. "I've heard that new child abuse reporting regulations are being developed. Will we have a staff meeting to discuss them?"

Being an Effective Manager

The following situations show caregivers managing a child development program. As you read, think about what the caregivers are doing and why. Then answer the questions following each episode.

Observing and Recording Information About Each Child's Growth and Development

As Will (33 months) picks up his spreading knife in his right hand, Mr. Jones scoots the serving bowl of peanut butter closer to the right side of Will's plate, "Ready to try some peanut butter on your bagel?" Mr. Jones says quietly. Will pokes the spreader into the peanut butter and the bowl slides on the table; Will's left hand comes up to hold the bowl steady. Mr. Jones observes as Will successfully scoops a lump of peanut butter from the bowl and then turns his attention to his bagel. "I'll pass the peanut butter to Emily now that you're done, Will," Mr. Jones says. He then gets his note cards out of his pocket and begins to record: "Without asking for help, Will used his spreader to get peanut butter from the serving dish. He stopped the bowl from sliding on the table by holding it with his left hand." Mr. Jones again glances at Will, who now holds the bagel in his left hand while happily eating the peanut butter directly off the spreader. "How about a bite of bagel with your peanut butter, Will?" Mr. Jones invites. Will looks at his bagel almost as if he had forgotten he had it in his hand.

1. **How did Mr. Jones use a daily routine to gather objective and accurate information about Will?**

   _____

   _____

   _____

2. **What are three things Mr. Jones learned about Will?**

   _____

   _____

   _____

Working as a Member of a Team to Plan an Individualized Program

Ms. Lewis asks each caregiver in her room to focus on infants' outdoor time during the week. "I'd like us to meet on Friday to talk about the kinds of things we currently do in the yard and develop plans for new activities," she says. She has copies made of weekly planning and evaluation forms to be filled in at the meeting. As she plays with the infants and toddlers outdoors, she thinks about the objectives set for each infant and notes skills they are using while they bat at soap bubbles wafting by, crawl after a rolling ball in the grass, and ride in the wagon pulled by an older toddler. On Friday the caregivers share their observations and develop plans for "wagon washing" and for play with child-sized cardboard boxes. Ms. Gonzalez offers to collect and bring out more balls—in a variety of sizes and colors.

1. How did Ms. Lewis use a team approach to planning?

_____

_____

_____

2. How did the caregivers use observation information for planning?

_____

_____

_____

Following Administrative Policies and Procedures

Ms. Bates reviews the staff handbook as she sits in the staff room. "Even though I've been a caregiver for a while," she tells Ms. Moore, "I need to review our policies now and then. I want to find out what the procedure is for scheduling my vacation. I'm sure that's in here. Also, do you know where I'll find information on preparing for a field trip?" Ms. Moore replies, "It's in the section on program activities. Samples of completed field trip forms are in the appendix. When my group recently went to the park, I used the sample forms to help me get the permission forms to the parents and back on time and to request petty cash to pay for a snack we stopped to buy along the way." Ms. Bates finds the program activities section and locates the sample forms. She later submits a request for annual leave, fills out the field trip request form, and sends permission slips home to the parents.

1. How did Ms. Bates stay informed about administrative policies and procedures?

_____

_____

_____

2. What tasks did Ms. Bates complete according to the center's policies?

_____

_____

_____

Compare your answers with those on the answer sheet at the end of the module. If your answers are different, discuss them with your trainer. There can be more than one good answer.

Managing Your Own Life

Many of the things you do at home contribute to your performance as a manager. You may be responsible for paying bills, buying food and clothing, deciding on major purchases such as a car or furniture, or planning a vacation or weekend outing. The same skills you use in managing the center program are used at home. When you make a grocery list, for example, you make decisions about what to buy based on what foods each member of your family likes, how many people will be eating each meal, and what ingredients you need for each recipe. You can do this because you observe each member of your family, include them in planning balanced meals, and follow recipes, the "policies and procedures" for food preparation.

Just as at the center, the more orderly and efficient you are in managing your home, the easier your life is. You have more time to spend on things other than chores. The more planning you do as a team, the more likely it is that you and your family will enjoy the time you spend together.

Think about times when careful management makes it easier to get chores done efficiently.

- You plan which errands need to be run and do them all at once rather than making several trips.

- You make sure you have all the tools and materials you need before starting a project such as painting the kitchen cupboards or baking a cake.

- You keep records of all bills and file receipts promptly.

- You keep emergency phone numbers posted beside the telephone.

- You talk with your family about what to do in case of fire and develop an evacuation plan.

- You plan outings or vacations that are of interest to everyone.

- You borrow a folding table and extra chairs from a neighbor when you are having a crowd over for a holiday meal.

Organizing your time and your environment to work *for* you rather than *against* you helps you manage more effectively. Use the chart on the following page to identify ways to manage your life more effectively.

Frustrating Situations in My Daily Life	What I Could Do to Improve the Situation?
I spend time practically every day searching for my keys.	*I will put a hook on the inside wall by the door where I will hang my keys every day when I get home.*

The skills you use in managing your life help you manage your role as a caregiver and help you enjoy that role and feel good about your performance.

When you have finished this overview section, you should complete the pre-training assessment. Refer to the glossary at the end of this module if you need definitions of the terms that are used.

Pre-Training Assessment

Listed below are the skills used by caregivers who are effective managers. Think about whether you do these things regularly, sometimes, or not enough. Place a check in one of the columns on the right for each skill listed. Then discuss your answers with your trainer.

SKILL	I DO THIS REGULARLY	I DO THIS SOMETIMES	I DON'T DO THIS ENOUGH
OBSERVING AND RECORDING INFORMATION ABOUT EACH CHILD'S GROWTH AND DEVELOPMENT 1. Watching and listening to young children and writing down what they do and say to learn more about their needs, skills, and interests.			
2. Recording infants' and toddlers' behavior in an objective, accurate way and avoiding the use of labels.			
3. Asking parents for information about what their child is like at home and using that information as you interpret observations.			
4. Observing each infant and toddler during different periods of the day: arrival, indoor and outdoor play, meal, naps, and departure.			
5. Recording many instances of a young child's play before drawing conclusions about that child's abilities, interests, and needs.			

SKILL	I DO THIS REGULARLY	I DO THIS SOMETIMES	I DON'T DO THIS ENOUGH
WORKING AS A MEMBER OF A TEAM TO PLAN AN INDIVIDUALIZED PROGRAM			
6. Meeting regularly with other caregivers to plan developmentally and culturally appropriate activities for the group.			
7. Using information gained through observing to get to know children as individuals.			
8. Using information from parents to learn more about who children are.			
9. Planning the environment, daily activities, and special activities to meet the needs of individual children.			
10. Evaluating the program constantly to help plan for the future.			
11. Working with other center staff to provide input on program issues.			
12. Acknowledging the strengths of other team members: other caregivers, aides, parents, and volunteers.			
13. Knowing social services, health, and education resources in the community or region and using them as needed.			

SKILL	I DO THIS REGULARLY	I DO THIS SOMETIMES	I DON'T DO THIS ENOUGH
FOLLOWING ADMINISTRATIVE POLICIES AND PROCEDURES 14. Knowing and understanding responsibilities as outlined in staff and parent handbooks.			
15. Reviewing center policies before starting a new task.			
16. Completing management tasks according to a schedule.			
17. Following the center's system for recordkeeping.			
18. Reviewing memorandums and other documents to keep informed about caregivers' job responsibilities.			

Review your responses, then list three to five skills you would like to improve or topics you would like to learn more about. When you finish this module, you will list examples of your new or improved knowledge and skills.

_____

_____

_____

_____

_____

_____

_____

_____

Now begin the learning activities for Module 12, Program Management.

I. Using a Systematic Approach to Observing and Recording

In this activity you will learn:

- to identify reasons for making observations; and

- to develop a system for regularly observing and recording infants' and toddlers' behavior.

Observation in a child development program is used to provide high-quality care for all children. High-quality care is based on knowledge of each child and the use of accurate information to meet each child's needs. When caregivers know how each child is growing and developing and plan a program based on this knowledge, the care they provide is more likely to be developmentally appropriate.

Observing is an ongoing process. It involves systematically watching what a child is doing and saying in order to better understand what that child is experiencing.

Only by observing a child regularly over a period of time can you begin to understand a child's special strengths, abilities and needs. Although young children can't tell us who they are in words, we can see them thinking, learning, and feeling as they move, play, and take part in daily routines. Observing can help you learn about a child's temperament as well as issues and skills they are working on, such as limit-setting and eye-hand coordination.

A single observation cannot provide a complete picture of a child. Children, like adults, do not behave in the same ways all the time. Illness, reactions to events at home or at the center, and other things affect what a child does and says. Children's abilities, interests, and needs change over time; therefore, observation needs to be an ongoing process. When caregivers have collected several recordings on a child, they can see patterns and make comments such as the following:

- "Carlos (6 months) seems to be an easy-going baby."

- "Sarah (18 months) is going through a time when saying goodbye to her parents is particularly difficult."

- "Leo (31 months) is learning the names of colors."

In addition to observing to get to know children as individuals, caregivers observe infants and toddlers for these reasons:

- **To plan a program** based on the interests, strengths, and needs of each child. "Bobby gets distracted and upset when there is too much noise and confusion. Let's plan to divide up for walks so he has time each day in a small group."

- **To measure each child's progress.** "I've recorded Sarah's new skills in gross motor development."

- **To develop a strategy for dealing with a challenging behavior.** "I've been keeping notes, and I think Jim seems to hit other children when things get confusing and he feels closed in. I think we should guide him to avoid the refrigerator box house when it gets crowded."

- **To collect information about children to share** with parents, colleagues, and specialists. "I'd like to set up a meeting with you, Ms. White, to talk about Jared's progress."

- **To evaluate a program's environment and activities**. "Please bring your observations of snacktime to Friday's meeting so we can discuss how things are going."

To manage good programs for infants and toddlers, caregivers must observe carefully and systematically. This involves watching, listening to, and writing down or recording what children do and say as it happens according to a particular method. It involves planning with the other caregivers in your room to make a series of brief observations (three to five minutes) of each child in the group during different times of the day over time.

Some caregivers feel that making observations and recording them will take away from their time with children. Sometimes caregivers resent a colleague's taking a few minutes to step back and observe. This leads to caregivers trying to jot down things that happened at the end of the day or not observing at all. Because observing provides such essential information, it is worth the time and effort to figure out strategies to observe and record what you see as soon as possible. For example, you may want to jot down notes during naptime or ask a colleague to take your place so you can step back for a few minutes to write.

Developing a system can help you and the caregivers you work with integrate observing and recording into your day. Here are some suggestions for observing children systematically.

- Write what you see, not what you think is happening.

- Jot notes frequently. Carry a pad or index cards and pencil with you.

- Write in short phrases rather than complete sentences to save time.

- Try to abbreviate and shorten what a child said—don't try to write all the words, but get the gist of what is said.

- Describe *how* a child is doing or saying something.

- Make diagrams of the environment showing the child in relation to the setting, other children in the room, and adults.

- Date each note you make on a child.

- Plan time in your daily schedule to observe a child, if only for three minutes.

- Work out a schedule to regularly observe all children in your group.

- Use your observations to change activities or to meet a child's needs.

- Share your observations with fellow staff members in a confidential and professional manner.

- Use your observations as you communicate to parents about their children's interests, needs, and progress in your program.

To be complete, recordings must include several facts. These are:

- the observer's name;

- the child's name and age;

- the date of the observation;

- the setting (where the activity is taking place and who is involved—for example, "Debby and Ron sit on the floor in the book area looking at books"); and

- the behavior (what the child you are observing does and says).

It may be useful to develop a format for observing that includes spaces for the needed information on a notepad or on index cards. Your format may look like the sample below.

SAMPLE OBSERVATION FORM

Child _____ Age _____ Date _____

Setting _____ Observer _____

Behavior: _____

_____

_____

_____

Throughout the year, observations should be made in all areas of each child's development. You can organize your observations into the following categories:

- fine and gross motor development;

- cognitive development;

- language development;

- creativity;

- self-discipline;

- self-help skills;

- self-esteem; and

- social development.

No matter how good your system is or how well you organize observations, gathering useful observations depends on you, the observer. You are the camera. You must be sure that you observe and record objectively and accurately. Objective and accurate recordings include only the full facts about what is seen and heard. They do not include labels or judgments. Compare the following excerpts from an observation of a child at the water play table.

Example 1
Objective and Accurate

Behavior: *Tony (30 months) poured the water quickly with the pitcher. The water splashed inside and outside the basin. Some fell on other children's shoes. Tony began to giggle.*

Example 1 is an objective recording. It includes only the facts of what Tony did ("quickly poured the water"), what happened ("the water splashed inside and outside the basin"), and his reaction ("Tony began to giggle"). Accurate recordings include *all* the facts about what a child does and says in the order they happen. Information is not omitted or recorded out of order. Read the following two examples about the same observation.

Example 2
Not Objective

Behavior: *Tony (30 months) was bad today. He angrily splashed water on the floor and on other children at the water basin. Then he laughed at them.*

Example 2 is not an objective recording. A label ("bad") is used and a judgment is made ("he angrily splashed the water"). Given what the caregiver saw, she or he could not know what Tony was laughing at. A recording that he was "bad" does not tell anything useful about his behavior, since "bad" is a word that means different things to different people.

Example 3
Not Accurate

Behavior: *Tony (30 months) stood at the water basin, looking to see if a caregiver was watching him. He giggled and began to splash water on other children.*

In Example 3, a fact is added that has not been observed ("looking to see if a caregiver was watching him"). A fact is omitted ("Tony poured the water quickly with the pitcher"). And a fact is written out of order ("He giggled and began to splash water...").

Making an objective and accurate recording such as Example 1 requires practice. No matter how good an observer you are, you can always sharpen your skills. With time and practice you can get even better at observing and recording children's behavior as you play with and care for them throughout the day.

On the next page you will see several examples of observations recorded by caregivers of infants and toddlers.

Child _Nicholas_ **Age** _4 months_ **Date** _May 12_

Setting _On the patio, with other children_ **Observer** _Ms. Jackson_

Behavior: Nicholas is on his belly on a blanket. Ms. Jackson walks onto the patio singing a song: "I'll be coming to the patio, Nicholas, Nicholas...." She's coming up from behind him, but Nicholas doesn't respond to the sound of her singing. She walks around in front of Nicholas and crouches down. When he sees her, he squeals and waves his arms and legs in delight.

Child _Lionell_ **Age** _6 months_ **Date** _February 14_

Setting _Crib, awakening from morning nap_ **Observer** _Ms. Benson_

Behavior: Lionell lifts his stockinged feet in the air and stretches out his hands. He grabs his right toe. When he flexes his knee, the sock slips and he's holding onto a sock without toes in it. A few vigorous kicks and the baggy sock falls off. Feet in the air again, he grabs his naked toes.

Child _Natalia_ **Age** _18 months_ **Date** _February 4_

Setting _Near the entrance, in cubby area, at morning arrival time_ **Observer** _Mr. Gleese_

Behavior: Natalia enters, holding her grandfather's hand. Grandfather unzips her parka and pulls it off. Natalia smiles at her grandfather as she sits on the floor and silently lifts her foot up. Grandfather kneels down and takes her boots off. Then Grandfather leaves, and Natalia begins crying as the door closes behind him.

Child _Luke_ **Age** _33 months_ **Date** _March 10_

Setting _Table, Luke sits with 4 children and Mr. Jones, lunchtime_ **Observer** _Mr. Jones_

Behavior: Mr. Jones passes the plate of meatloaf and beans to Luke. Luke looks at him. "What's that?" "It's meatloaf and beans. Help yourself." When Luke has a piece of meatloaf on his plate, Mr. Jones says, "Take a piece of bread, Luke." Luke takes bread from the plate. "Apple, too," Mr. Jones says as he passes the bowl. Luke takes two apple slices, puts one slice in his mouth, holds the other in his left hand. He puts the slice down, picks up his fork with his left hand. Holding his fork upside down he stabs several times at the meat. He moves the meat around on the plate.

286

Making valid observations also requires being aware of yourself as an observer. People often perceive the same situation differently. Eyewitness accounts of an accident demonstrate how several people, seeing the same event, have different stories to tell. This may happen to caregivers as well.

One caregiver may see Todd (9 months) dumping a can of blocks on the rug and Linda (20 months) feeding her baby doll dirt. Another, watching the same children, may observe Todd messing up the room and Linda smearing mud on a doll. Knowledge of what a child has done in the past, your feelings about a certain type of behavior, tone of voice, and many other factors influence what you observe and record.

It is useful to compare your recordings about a child with another caregiver's observation information. If they are similar, an accurate record of a child's growth and development is being maintained. If they are very different, the information collected may not be useful. Two caregivers with different perceptions of a child's behavior should observe the child together over a short period of time. After each observation they can compare their recordings and discuss what they have seen. This method helps ensure accurate recordings. If the recordings still differ greatly, the center director can assist them in solving the problem.

In this learning activity you will practice observing and recording. Select a child to observe for a two-week period and observe the child for three to five minutes, once per day. Ask your center director, another caregiver, or trainer to observe the same child at the same time as you are observing, on at least four occasions. Compare your recordings after each co-observation and at the end of the two-week period.

Make several copies of this form before recording your observations.

OBSERVATION FORM

Child _____   Age _____   Date _____

Setting _____   Observer _____

Behavior: _____

_____

_____

_____

_____

_____

_____

_____

_____

_____

_____

If your recordings are objective, accurate, and similar to those of your co-observer, begin the next learning activity. If your recordings differ and are not objective and accurate, select another child to observe, and repeat this learning activity. Ask your trainer to observe with you again and record information about the same child. Then discuss your recordings with your trainer and begin the next learning activity.

You may also want to review other types of observation and ways to record them. These can be found in the books included in the Bibliography.

II. Individualizing Your Program

In this activity you will learn:

- to use information you gain from observing and working with young children to better understand each child's interests, strengths, and needs; and

- to plan individualized activities for each infant and toddler in your group.

In your role as manager, you have very important responsibilities to meet for each child you care for. It is up to you to build upon a child's sense of trust in the world and self that begins at home. As a "home base" in child care, it is up to you to help children feel safe and secure so they will be free to explore and take advantage of the rich experiences your program has to offer. To meet these responsibilities, you must individualize your program.

Individualizing a program means setting up an environment and offering daily activities that reflect and respond to children as individuals. In an individualized program, the foundation for everything that happens is based on a knowledge of each child. Caregivers know infants' eating and sleeping schedules and adapt the daily schedules accordingly. They know what individual children are working on and offer activities such as jumping on pillows or eating with a spoon to encourage children to develop their skills. They help children feel competent by including them as partners in daily routines according to their abilities.

Creating an individualized program requires knowing children as individuals. As you live each day with children, you learn a lot about who they are. You see their style of dealing with the world, what skills they are working on, what they like to do. Systematically observing and recording can help you confirm your impressions and fill in your pictures of each child. You can also learn about children by talking with their parents. As discussed in Module 11, parents know their children best of all. By developing a partnership with parents, you will have their help in getting to know their child.

Although your program may look like other infant/toddler child care programs because you do many of the same things, such as taking walks around the neighborhood, preparing and eating snack, and making playdough, your program is unique because the children are. You can show respect for the unique individuals in your room by hanging pictures of children's families on the wall, organizing naptime so Jake's special caregiver is available to help him fall asleep by rocking him, and listening to the jazz that Dennis and his father brought in to share.

In this activity you have the opportunity to practice your observation skills again. You will observe two children in your group over a period of two weeks.

First decide how you will record your observations. You can use a notepad, index cards, or copies of the observation form in Learning Activity I. Your recordings should include at least the information asked for on the observation form.

Then select two children to observe. Observe each child for a three- to five-minute period at least once each day. After you have collected all your observations, re-read them to see what you have learned about these children. (Although you will be observing only two children to complete this activity, we suggest you duplicate the Guide to Individualizing Your Program form and complete it for all the children in your group to help you individualize your program.)

On the next page you will find an example of a Guide to Individualizing Your Program. It shows you how one caregiver summarized what she learned from her observations of two children and used her information to individualize her program. After you have read this example, you will be ready to complete the guide provided for you, using your own recently collected observations.

Guide for Individualizing Your Program
(Example)

	Child _Valikia (2 years)_	Child _Carlos (11 months)_
How would you describe this child's temperament?	_Valikia is easily upset by the slightest change._	_Carlos is rather quiet in a new situation. Once he is comfortable he smiles and is more active._
Is there anything new happening at home or in child care that might be affecting him or her?	_Valikia's grandparents are visiting for the week._	_Not that I know of._
What skills is this child working on?	_Valikia is learning to put on her coat using the "flip-flop" method._	_Carlos cruises holding onto furniture. We think he is on the edge of taking his first steps._
What new experiences can you provide for this child to build on these skills?	_We can write a book about Valikia putting on her own coat._	_We can walk with Carlos, holding his arms. We can offer Carlos a chair to push across the floor._
How can your physical environment reflect this child's needs and interests?	_We can ask Valikia's mother to bring in a picture of her grandparents._	_We can keep the floor clear of small objects Carlos might trip on. We can check to be sure table corners are padded in case he slips and falls._
Choose a daily routine (dressing, nap, snack, toileting). Describe how you include this child in ways that respond to his or her needs.	_We allow Valikia plenty of time to put on her own coat when we go outside._	_We allow a little extra time to help Carlos fall asleep at naptime, and we don't get upset if he can't sleep. It is often hard for an "almost-walker" to sleep._

Guide for Individualizing Your Program

	Child _____ ( )	Child _____ ( )
How would you describe this child's temperament?		
Is there anything new happening at home or in child care that might be affecting him or her?		
What skills is this child working on?		

Guide for Individualizing Your Program		
	Child _____ ( )	Child _____ ( )
What new experiences can you provide for this child to build on these skills?		
How can your physical environment reflect this child's needs and interests?		
Choose a daily routine (dressing, nap, snack, toileting). Describe how you include this child in ways that respond to his or her needs.		

Discuss your observation recordings and your plans for these two children with your trainer. If you found it difficult to complete your recordings, talk with your trainer about why that was so, and try to find ways to make it possible to record observations on a regular basis.

Plan to observe all the children in your group on a regular basis to provide an individualized program.

III. Working as a Team to Plan the Program

In this activity you will learn:

- to recognize planning as an effective management tool; and

- to develop weekly plans.

Planning forces you to think about what activities you want to do and how you will do them. Caregivers who plan are better prepared. They have the materials they need ready and can focus on the children rather than searching for a wooden spoon or another paintbrush. Their daily program runs more smoothly.

Planning provides you with a sense of order that can be elusive in an infant or toddler child care setting. Having plans gives you the flexibility you need to meet children's individual needs. Even when you end up changing your plans—a common occurrence—you have an overall picture that allows you to make a decision rather than surrender to a sense of confusion.

When a walk to the park stops just outside the center door where toddlers discover their reflections in the glass and begin dancing, you can make a decision about how best to respond. You may decide to let them dance as long as they wish. If, on the other hand, the dancing turns into a tumbling match, you may insist on gathering everyone together and continuing on your way.

Planning also allows caregivers the satisfaction of evaluating their own growth. Having a clear idea of their goals for children gives caregivers the freedom to experiment with activities and materials. Knowing what they want to accomplish means caregivers can judge for themselves how they are doing and make necessary adjustments in how they are managing their program.

As a caregiver, you are also a member of a team. It is very important that all the team members —caregivers, aides, parents, and volunteers—be included in the planning process. Each member has valuable observations, ideas, or concerns to contribute. An attitude of trust and respect toward other team members enables each one of you to communicate problems and to recognize and appreciate successes. The more involved each of you are in making the plans, the more likely you will feel a sense of commitment to your program.

What Kind of Planning Is Needed

Three types of planning are useful for caregivers: long-range planning, weekly planning, and daily planning. Long-range planning involves thinking ahead, perhaps a month or more, about your goals for the program and children in your care. For example, if you know that you want to work on individualizing your program, you can come up with a plan. Someone can take responsibility for duplicating the forms in Activity II. You can decide who is going to observe which children and set a date to share your observations. The next step would be implementing changes in your environment and activities. Looking ahead at the broad picture can help ensure that you will reach your goals.

Weekly plans are more detailed than long-range plans. Programs often design their own formats for weekly planning. What works well for one caregiving team may not work for another. A good place to start is to ask yourself, "What do I need to plan that will help me be a better manager?"

Many caregivers find it useful to plan in the following categories:

- **Changes in the environment**—the addition of new props or materials, or changes in the arrangement of indoor or outdoor space. For example, new books can be rotated into the library center, several key rings might be added to the dramatic play area, and a blanket "tent" could be set up over a table outside.

- **Special activity**—an activity planned for a small group of children or the whole group. Caregivers might plan a bubble activity or a city bus ride, for example.

- **Target children**—those children who may have special needs or interests that caregivers want to address during a given week. Target children may include a child whose mother is going on a trip. This child may need extra time with a caregiver, special attention waking up from nap, "peek-a-boo" games, and other play about people leaving and returning.

- **Caregiver responsibilities**—the assignment of specific tasks to each caregiver to ensure that they get done. For example, if the plan is to have children wash the wagons, someone must be responsible for collecting rags or sponges and wash tubs, and setting up wash water.

What Guides the Planning Process

Caregivers have many tools and strategies they can use to help them plan. First, they know what infants and toddlers can and should be doing at a given age and stage of development. The child development charts at the beginning of Modules 1 through 10 in this training program define the skills and abilities of young children at each stage of development.

Second, caregivers have specific knowledge about each child. Information gathered through observations and recordings, and from home visits with parents, is invaluable in the planning process. Knowing, for example, that one child is going on a trip may lead caregivers to add suitcases and books about trips to the play area. Caregivers sometimes find it helpful to identify specific children who have a particular interest or strength, a special need, or a particular skill they are struggling to master. By targeting these children during the planning process, caregivers can design activities and materials to meet their needs.

Caregivers use yet another strategy that guides the planning process: they carefully observe how infants and toddlers are using the environment each day. Daily observations give caregivers important clues as to what changes are needed in the environment. For example, if the same toys have been on a low shelf in the room for several weeks, caregivers may note that there is little interest in the area. Putting some toys away, adding new ones, or even changing the location of some toys can renew young children's interest. Daily observations also let caregivers know when something planned is not working. For example, if children are unable to complete the puzzles and often leave them out unfinished, the puzzles may be too difficult for them. This tells caregivers that they should try puzzles with fewer pieces and less complex shapes.

Finally, caregivers consider what special activities they want to offer in a given week. Special activities are usually planned on the basis of the children's interests. For example, if a group of toddlers particularly likes seeing the fish in the pet store, caregivers may arrange a trip. Special activities may coincide with the time of year—in the Fall, a walk to collect pine cones or leaves—or they may simply be activities that caregivers think the children will enjoy— making applesauce or planting a garden. The special interests or talents of the teaching team are valuable here. An adult's enthusiasm for music or books is quickly communicated to the children and can extend the children's interests.

How Planning Is Done

Weekly planning does not need to be a lengthy process. Finding time for planning can be difficult; however, in many centers, caregivers conduct planning meetings before children arrive, after they leave, or during rest time. Caregivers who work together should plan together. In many centers, parents are regularly invited to participate in both the planning and the doing of activities.

A planning form can be very helpful. In your center there may be a planning form that everyone uses. You can also use the form provided in this module. Whatever format you use for planning, it should include the categories discussed:

- your goal;

- changes in the environment;

- special activities;

- individual children to focus on; and

- caregiver responsibilities.

Evaluating the Program

Evaluation of the experiences you provide for infants and toddlers is an integral part of the planning process. After you have prepared for and conducted activities, it is helpful to think about the following:

- **What happened during each day?** What types of activities did infants and toddlers engage in? What did caregivers do to respond to children's actions? What activities did caregivers initiate?

- **How was each child's learning and development facilitated?** What worked well? What did not work well? Did each infant and toddler have many opportunities to explore, experiment, and learn by doing?

- **In light of each day's experiences, what changes should be made in the environment?** Should furniture and equipment be rearranged? Should new toys or props be added to the room? Should a different style of interaction be tried with certain children? What activities should be repeated?

It is important for caregiving teams to go through an evaluation such as this one during each planning meeting.

In this learning activity you will review a sample planning form that includes all the categories discussed. Begin by reviewing the sample weekly planning form for your age group. Then agree on a time to meet with a colleague to plan together. Develop a weekly plan using the blank form provided after the examples on the following pages. Finally, implement the plan and evaluate how it worked.

Weekly Plan
(Example)

Goal *Doing more cooking with children*   **Week** *February 17-21*

Changes in the Environment

Hang pictures of people cooking in the housekeeping corner. Add a few more pans and spoons.

Organize the kitchen drawers and shelves. (Maybe one reason we don't cook is that we can never find what we need.)

Special Activities

Monday	*Take children shopping. Write a list with them including potatoes, bananas, and ingredients for English muffin pizzas. Get graham crackers and juice from the kitchen in case our plans fall through one day.*
Tuesday	*Invite children to scrub and mash potatoes.*
Wednesday	*Children will peel and cut banana halves.*
Thursday	*Make English muffin pizzas.*

Target Children

Jerry is having a tough time with his new baby sister at home. Invite him to cook to help him feel competent, and give him special time in a small group.

Andrea needs practice on fine motor skills. Encourage her to join in scrubbing, mashing, cutting, and pouring.

Caregivers' Responsibilities

Ms. Hernandez will look through our cookbooks for some simple recipes and bring in her toaster oven on Friday.

Mr. Kaminski will talk with parents about what they cook with children at home.

Meet with your planning team (aide, other caregivers, volunteer, parent) in your room to develop a weekly plan using the form below.

Weekly Plan

Goal _____   Week _____

Changes in the Environment

_____

_____

_____

Special Activities

_____

_____

_____

_____

_____

_____

Target Children

_____

_____

_____

_____

Caregivers' Responsibilities

_____

_____

_____

_____

_____

_____

For one week, use the plan you developed as a guide. Then answer the following questions.

How did infants and toddlers react to changes in the environment?

_____

_____

_____

_____

How did children react to special activities?

_____

_____

_____

_____

What did you accomplish with target children?

_____

_____

_____

_____

What changes did you make in the plan?

_____

_____

_____

_____

What would you do differently next time?

_____

_____

_____

_____

Discuss your plan and your experiences in using it with your trainer and other caregivers.

IV. Following Administrative Policies and Procedures

In this activity you will learn:

- to identify your center's administrative policies and procedures; and

- to complete management tasks according to a schedule.

As a caregiver in a child development program, you are a part of a large system. Your role in this system includes coordinating with other caregivers, with all center staff, with parents, and possibly with other offices or agencies in the community.

A center runs smoothly when administrative policies and procedures are understood and followed by center staff. These policies and procedures are outlined in the center handbooks. They usually address the following topics:

- hours of operation;

- acceptance/registration procedures;

- fees and service charges;

- safety requirements;

- medical and health requirements;

- fire prevention and evacuation procedures;

- policy on closing for bad weather;

- contingency plans for use in emergencies;

- reporting accidents;

- use of consumable supplies and reporting needs for new supplies;

- reporting suspected child abuse and neglect;

- reporting maintenance needs for furniture and equipment; and

- discipline.

Caregivers should be aware of these policies and procedures so that all staff follow the same regulations during the center's day-to-day operations. In addition, parents may seek answers to questions about discipline, accidents, or other issues. Caregivers should know the procedures regarding such issues so they can provide parents with information or direct them to discuss an issue with a supervisor, when appropriate.

Types of Records

The center's policies and procedures also address the kinds of records and forms that clerical/administrative staff are required to collect or keep on file and the role caregivers play in this management task. These records may include:

- physical examination reports;
- height/weight charts;
- observation and assessment reports;
- daily attendance reports;
- parent contact forms;
- contagious disease exposure forms;
- medical emergency consent forms;
- weekly plan outlines;
- field trip permission forms;
- food service reports;
- inventory records;
- supply request forms;
- staff time sheets; and
- staff leave request forms.

To follow the center's procedures for reporting and recordkeeping, you may find it helpful to keep a list of necessary reports and the date each is due. Some reports may be due daily or weekly. Others are completed when an incident occurs, such as an accident. Others, such as inventory reports, are used once a year. Your role will vary according to the reporting task. Some information, such as observation and assessment reports for children, may be collected and periodically reviewed by caregivers. Other reports, such as a summary of a parent conference led by another staff member, may be completed by others but kept on file in case others need to review the information.

Finally, your role includes not sharing with anyone, other than those who also care for your group, any confidential information. Maintaining confidentiality is a basic part of being a professional caregiver.

In this learning activity you will review your center's administrative policies and procedures for completing various kinds of reports. Then you will complete a report schedule indicating when these reports are due and what caregivers' responsibilities are with regard to completing these forms. First read the example of a report schedule on the next page.

Report Schedule
(Example)

REPORT	CAREGIVER'S RESPONSIBILITY	DATE DUE
Observation and assessment	*Complete daily recordings, record assessment information on observation and assessment report*	*Review with supervisor on last Friday of each month*
Attendance	*Record arrival and departure times each day*	*Every Friday*
Timesheet	*Fill in hours worked each day*	*Every Friday*
Supply requisition	*Request consumable supplies when inventory is low*	*15th of each month*
Annual leave request	*Request leave*	*Two weeks prior to date for which leave is requested*
Contagious disease exposure	*Complete form when parent notifies caregiver of child's illness*	*By 6:00 p. m. on the day parent notifies me of illness*
Inventory	*Record quantities of equipment, toys, and consumable supplies*	*May 30*

Now complete the schedule below for reports you must complete in your program and note your responsibilities for completing them.

Report Schedule

REPORT	CAREGIVER'S RESPONSIBILITY	DATE DUE

Discuss this schedule with your trainer. Review and follow your center's administrative policies and procedures throughout the year.

Summarizing Your Progress

You have now completed all of the learning activities for this module. Whether you are an experienced caregiver or a new one, this module has probably helped you develop new managerial skills. Before you go on, take a few minutes to summarize what you've learned.

- Turn back to Learning Activity II, Individualizing Your Program. Review the recordings completed for the children in your group. Why are they examples of objective and accurate recordings? How did you use this information to individualize your program for these children? Was this information included in your weekly plans for your group?

- Next, review your responses to the pre-training assessment for this module. Write a summary of what you learned, and list the skills you developed or improved.

_____

_____

_____

_____

_____

_____

_____

_____

_____

Your final step in this module is to complete the knowledge and competency assessments. Let your trainer know when you are ready to schedule the assessments. After you have successfully completed these assessments, you will be ready to start a new module. Congratulations on your progress so far, and good luck with your next module.

Answer Sheet: Being an Effective Manager

Observing and Recording Information About Each Child's Growth and Development

1. **How did Mr. Jones use a daily routine to gather objective and accurate information about Will?**

   He recorded what Will did and didn't do (ask for help) during snack time.

2. **What are three things Mr. Jones learned about Will?**

   a. Will is confident about serving himself peanut butter.

   b. He can hold a spreader.

   c. He can serve peanut butter.

   d. He can use two hands to complete a task.

   e. He is developing an awareness of cause and effect (hold the bowl, it won't slide).

   f. He can solve a problem without assistance.

Working as a Member of a Team to Plan an Individualized Program

1. **How did Ms. Lewis use a team approach to planning?**

   She asked each caregiver to prepare for a meeting by gathering information, to bring prepared copies of the planning and evaluation forms to the meeting, and to participate actively.

2. **How did the caregivers use observation information for planning?**

   On the basis of what the infants did during the week, the caregivers developed plans to conduct activities and bring new materials outdoors to build on infants' and toddlers' interests.

Following Administrative Policies, Practices, and Procedures

1. How did Ms. Bates stay informed about administrative policies and procedures?

She reviewed the staff handbook and discussed certain procedures with a colleague.

2. What tasks did Ms. Bates complete according to the center's policies?

She submitted a request for annual leave, filled out the field trip request form, and sent permission slips home to parents.

Glossary

Administrative policies and procedures
The systems outlined by the center's staff handbook and parent handbooks that ensure the smooth operation of the center.

Individualized program
A program in which the environment and caregivers' interactions with children are suited to each child's interests, strengths, and needs.

Objective recordings
Written information that includes only the facts about behaviors that are seen and heard.

Planning
The establishment of specific steps to accomplish program objectives.

Systematic observation
Consistent watching, listening to, and recording of what children say and do, according to a particular method.

Module 13
Professionalism

What Is a Professional and Why Is a Commitment to Professionalism Important?

A professional is a person who uses specialized knowledge and skills to do a job or provide a service. As an infant or toddler caregiver, you are a member of an important profession. You work with young children during a time when they are developing more quickly than they will at any other period in their lives. You help shape children's views about learning and the world around them. The care you provide influences how children feel about themselves. If you build infants' and toddlers' self-esteem during these early years, they will be more likely to succeed in life.

Professionalism for caregivers means providing care based on your knowledge of what infants and toddlers do and how they need to grow and develop. It also means taking advantage of opportunities to learn more about children and yourself and to develop new skills that will make you more competent.

Your professional skills also support families. By being aware of the roles you play in a child's life and building a partnership, you help parents feel competent and good about themselves. When parents have confidence in the reliable, high-quality care you and your colleagues provide, their own job performance is improved because they know their children are well cared for at the center.

When you need a service (such as medical or legal advice, or electrical repair), you look for a professional business or individual who can meet your needs. You choose professionals because you want:

- the needed service;

- specialized knowledge;

- a commitment to quality;

- dependability; and

- effectiveness.

In all these areas, caregivers make unique professional contributions. They provide:

- the needed service—a high-quality infant and toddler development program;

- specialized knowledge—an understanding of how infants and toddlers grow and develop and of how to meet their needs appropriately;

- a commitment to quality—providing a developmentally appropriate program in a safe and healthy environment;

- dependability—providing a service on a regular basis; and

- effectiveness—providing a program that helps infants and toddlers begin to build cognitive and creative skills and develop self-discipline and self-esteem.

Lilian Katz, an early childhood educator, has studied how teachers of older children grow professionally. She suggests that they pass through four different stages of professional development. These stages apply to caregivers as well.

Stage One: Survival

Teachers are new and often insecure. They devote most of their attention to learning routines and performing tasks as assigned. If you are at this stage, orientation, training, and experience will help you move to stage two, consolidation.

Stage Two: Consolidation

Teachers become more confident and begin to look beyond simply completing the daily routines. They seek new ways to accomplish routine tasks and to handle problems. If you are at this stage, you will find it useful to spend time with other caregivers exchanging ideas and feelings. Conversations, group meetings, training sessions, and open discussions will help you grow and move to stage three, renewal.

Stage Three: Renewal

After a year or two on the job, teachers begin to be bored with the day's routines. Often their interest drops and enthusiasm falls. Teachers in this stage need a renewal—new challenges. If you are at this stage, you should try to attend conferences and workshops, join professional organizations, or pursue a special interest. These professional activities will provide needed stimulation and help you move to stage four, maturity.

Stage Four: Maturity

Teachers at this stage are committed professionals. They understand the need to seek new ideas and skills. They continue to grow professionally. If you are a mature caregiver, you can be a model for new caregivers. You might also seek new challenges as a supervisor, trainer, or center administrator.

Caregiving is a profession that requires many different kinds of skills. In your work you fulfill the roles of educator, child development specialist, health care advisor, and nutritionist. Your work is important to the children you care for, their families, and the community.

Maintaining a commitment to professionalism has several positive results. First, it builds your self-esteem. You feel proud when you learn new skills, acquire knowledge, and become more competent. The sense of success you experience as you become a competent caregiver is rewarding and fulfilling.

Second, when you provide professional care, you are helping children grow, learn, and develop to their full potential. And third, your professional behavior helps the field of early childhood education. As you and others provide high-quality programs for children, you build respect for the profession, which can result in more recognition for the important service you provide.

Caregiving is not just a job—it's a profession. While you help children grow and develop, you can enjoy your work, do the best job you can, and continue to grow and advance as a caregiver and as a person.

Maintaining a commitment to professionalism means:

- continually assessing one's own performance;

- continuing to learn about caring for infants and toddlers; and

- applying professional ethics at all times.

Listed below are examples of how caregivers maintain a commitment to professionalism.

Continually Assessing One's Own Performance

Here are some examples of what caregivers can do.

- Identify areas where performance could be improved. "I can't figure out how to help Johnnie learn to use his words instead of hitting other children. Perhaps this article will help me."

- Know how to judge their own competence in a certain area. "I'm not really providing enough sensory experiences for the infants. I'll talk with one of the other caregivers to get some ideas."

- Compare their own performance against professional standards and guidelines. "I know that I should never leave a group of toddlers unsupervised. I'll wait until Ms. Lann returns before I go to the supply room."

- Participate in professional organizations and/or professional activities. "I think I will attend this conference to learn more about advocacy."

Continuing to Learn About Caring for Infants and Toddlers

Here are some examples of what caregivers can do.

- Keep current about procedures and guidelines concerning child development. "I have a few free moments. I'll review this new policy on reporting suspected incidents of child abuse."

- Keep informed of the latest early childhood practices. "I'd like to attend that workshop on curriculum next weekend. I can share the information at the next staff meeting."

- Apply knowledge and skills on the job. "Helping Sara learn to use the potty was much easier after I read *Toilet Learning* by Alison Mack. The ideas in the book really worked."

- Talk with colleagues about child development and child care. "I think I'll try to take my break with Ms. Williams today. Maybe she has some suggestions on how we can rearrange our room."

Applying Professional Ethics at All Times

Here are some examples of what caregivers can do.

- Maintain respect and confidentiality for each child. "The files that we keep on each child are confidential, Ms. Robinson. Arnisha's file will be kept in our locked cabinet. Only the caregivers, the center director, and you and her father are allowed to read your child's file."

- Be dependable and reliable in performing their duties and responsibilities. "Boy, I'm tired this morning, but I won't call in sick, because I know those infants need me."

- Show no personal bias against children because of culture, background, or gender. "Let's be sure we encourage both boys and girls to express their feelings."

- Speak out against practices that are not developmentally appropriate. "We don't want to force Tanya to learn to use the toilet before she's ready, Mr. Grisson. Very few children are ready at 17 months."

- Stand up for parts of the program that you believe are appropriate for the children. "Dramatic play helps toddlers make sense of the world, Ms. Grundy. They will still learn the difference between make-believe and fibbing."

- Support the center director and other administrative staff by avoiding gossip. "I know you're upset, Ms. Frilles, but if you don't agree with your performance appraisal, you really should discuss it with the center director. Why don't you make an appointment to talk with her next week?"

- Show support for other caregivers when they need assistance. "I'd be happy to help you rearrange your room, Mr. Jones. Just let me know when you're ready."

Maintaining a Commitment to Professionalism

In the following situations, caregivers are maintaining a commitment to professionalism as they care for infants and toddlers. As you read each one, think about what the caregivers are doing and why. Then answer the questions that follow.

Continually Assessing One's Own Performance

Ms. Lewis sinks down into her chair to think at the end of a long day. The morning started out smoothly, but by late afternoon everything was crazy. Clean and dirty clothes were mixed together. Parents had complained earlier in the week that their infants had on someone else's clothes. Today she spent 10 minutes finding Joseph's hat and gloves. The gloves were found with Matthew's coat. The hat was near the block corner where she had left it when they came in from outdoors. "This cannot go on," she said to herself. "I have to get more organized. Ms. Jackson always seems so organized. Maybe she can give me some pointers. My supervisor can give me some suggestions, too."

1. **How did Ms. Lewis assess her own performance?**

   _____

   _____

   _____

2. **What did she decide to do with the results of her self-assessment?**

   _____

   _____

   _____

Continuing to Learn About Caring for Infants and Toddlers

Ms. Jackson completed a self-assessment for infant and toddler caregivers and worked with her supervisor, Ms. Lee, to identify three areas where she could improve her skills. They discussed what might be reasonable goals. Ms. Jackson decided that she would review a module on learning environments (one of the three areas) during the following month and attend the in-service training session on the same topic. Ms. Lee also scheduled a visit to Ms. Jackson's room so that she could observe and offer suggestions on how the environment could be improved. They planned to meet again in a month to discuss how their plan is working and what Ms. Jackson is learning.

1. How did Ms. Jackson decide what knowledge and skills she should work to improve?

_____

_____

_____

2. How did Ms. Jackson plan to expand her existing knowledge and skills?

_____

_____

_____

Applying Professional Ethics at All Times

Ms. Johnson, a parent, arrived to pick up her child, Dora, from the center. When she walked in, Dora was building with the unit blocks. A second child, Joshua, was about to jump from the bookshelf. Mr. Jones said, "Hello, Ms. Johnson. Excuse me a moment," and turned immediately to Joshua. "Joshua," he said, "I know you like to climb and jump, but it is not safe for you to jump from this shelf. Let me help you down. You can jump near the pillows where it is safe." When he came back, Ms. Johnson said: "Boy, he's wild, isn't he?" Mr. Jones responded, "Joshua really enjoys climbing, he's busy learning about his body in space. Now, let me tell you about Dora's day."

1. How did Mr. Jones maintain professional ethics in talking to Ms. Johnson?

_____

_____

_____

2. How did Mr. Jones interact with Joshua in a professional manner?

_____

_____

_____

Compare your answers with those on the answer sheet at the end of this module. If your answers are different, discuss them with your trainer. There may be more than one good answer. As you complete the other modules in this training program, you will become more competent in caring for young children. Enhanced knowledge and skills will increase your level of professionalism. This module addresses other areas that can help you stay committed to being a professional caregiver.

The Early Childhood Profession and You

Many of us feel that an early childhood program is "a great place to work." We feel our work is important to the young children and families we work with each day.

As professionals we are continually reflecting on our feelings about working with young children, expanding our knowledge base, and developing positive relations with parents and each other. Despite the importance of our work, the early childhood profession does not always receive the status and recognition it deserves.

All these factors may contribute to how you feel about your career in the early childhood field. Consider the following questions:

1. How do you feel about being an infant and toddler caregiver?

_____

_____

_____

_____

2. Why did you choose this profession?

_____

_____

_____

_____

3. What do you like best?

_____

_____

_____

_____

4. What would you like to change?

_____

_____

_____

_____

5. What can you begin to do to bring about these changes?

_____

_____

_____

_____

Answer these questions and discuss them with your trainer and a group of other staff members.

When you have finished this overview section, you should complete the pre-training assessment. Refer to the glossary at the end of this module if you need definitions for the terms that are used.

Pre-Training Assessment

Listed below are the skills that caregivers use to maintain their commitment to professionalism. Think about whether you do these things regularly, sometimes, or not enough. Place a check in one of the columns on the right for each skill listed. Then discuss your answers with your trainer.

SKILL	I DO THIS REGULARLY	I DO THIS SOMETIMES	I DON'T DO THIS ENOUGH
CONTINUALLY ASSESSING ONE'S OWN PERFORMANCE 1. Knowing how to judge my competence in a certain area.			
2. Comparing my performance against the center's procedures and guidelines.			
3. Comparing my performance against the recognized standards of the early childhood profession.			
4. Applying my unique skills and experiences to my work as a caregiver.			
CONTINUING TO LEARN ABOUT CARING FOR INFANTS AND TODDLERS 5. Participating in professional early childhood education organizations.			
6. Reading books or articles about infant/toddler development and early childhood education practices.			

SKILL	I DO THIS REGULARLY	I DO THIS SOMETIMES	I DON'T DO THIS ENOUGH
7. Talking with or observing other caregivers to learn more about managing a group of children.			
8. Participating in training offered by the center or other groups.			
APPLYING PROFESSIONAL ETHICS AT ALL TIMES 9. Keeping information about children and their families confidential.			
10. Carrying out my duties in a dependable and reliable way.			
11. Speaking out when child care practices are not appropriate.			
12. Supporting early childhood education practices that are developmentally appropriate.			
13. Showing no personal bias against any child in my care.			

Review your responses, then list three to five skills you would like to improve or topics you would like to learn more about. When you finish this module, you will list examples of your new or improved knowledge and skills.

_____

_____

_____

_____

Now begin the learning activities for Module 13, Professionalism.

I. Assessing Yourself

In this activity you will learn:

- to recognize your unique skills and abilities; and

- to use the profession's standards to assess your own competence.

Each caregiver, just like each child, is a unique person with special interests and strengths. You bring your own interests and skills to your profession, and you share them with the infants and toddlers you care for. One caregiver may share a love for music with children; another may share a love for the outdoors. In this way everyone benefits. The children pick up on a caregiver's enthusiasm and learn to appreciate something new. In turn, the caregivers are able to use their special interests on the job, which makes working more satisfying and fun.

What are you really good at? What do you most enjoy? What do you like best about your job? What would you like to change? These are all questions that caregivers can ask themselves. They will help you focus on what makes you unique and what special qualities you bring to your profession.

Begin this learning activity by reading "Being Curious About Yourself" and "Carol Hillman: Gardener, Naturalist, Teacher" on the following pages. The first reading will help you think about yourself; the second tells how one early childhood professional brought her special interests and abilities to the classroom.

Next, use the form that follows the readings to record your responses to questions about how you feel about being a caregiver. Take time to think about what you really want to say.

Being Curious About Yourself[1]

Who are you? What do you care about? Why are you here? What interests you about children? What gives you pleasure in being with them? Which of your interests do you enjoy sharing with them? What are your goals for them?

Does all this seem obvious—of course you know about yourself? In fact, most of us keep growing in self-understanding, and we learn in the same way we learn about other people—by observing and reflecting on our observations. Why did I get so mad when Marta dropped a cup yesterday? It was an accident. Did it trigger something from my own past that had very little to do with the present situation? Why do I find it so hard to like Jorge? I catch myself being almost mean to him—sarcastic, in a way that just isn't appropriate with little kids. Why do I do that?

Sometimes a friend or colleague can help us think through our self-observations if we're willing to share them. It can be uncomfortable, learning more about ourselves, especially about the parts of ourselves we really don't like. Some people go to therapists to get help with this process, to have someone who can listen thoughtfully to their questions about themselves.

What do you like to do with children? Sing, cook, go on walks, pet animals, have conversations, watch them playing, snuggle, comb hair, and wash faces? Do you get to do what you like to do on your job? If not, could you? If you're a caregiver spending every day with children, it's important that you have many opportunities to be a decision maker, to say, "This is what I want to do next." Not at the children's expense, but in response to both your needs and theirs. If caregivers are contented and growing, children are more likely to be contented and growing too.

Which describes you better: You like parenting children; you like teaching children; you like playing with children? Competence in child care may be based on any of these enjoyments. Parenting is being responsible, taking good care of children, appreciating their growth; if you're experienced as a parent, that may be the role you fall into naturally in child care. Teaching implies particular interest in children's thinking and problem solving, in what they know and understand—and in helping them learn. Playing with children implies being in touch with the child in yourself.

What kind of learner are you? How do you learn best? Different people learn by reading, by taking classes, by observing children's behavior, by discussing their experiences with colleagues and friends, by going to conferences and workshops, by trying things for themselves and seeing what happens. Which of these things work for you? Does your center encourage you to keep learning and give you credit for what you do? A child care center is a *living place* for children and adults. It should be a good place to live together and learn together about the world. What are you learning at your work? What risks are you taking?

---

[1]Reprinted with permission from Elizabeth Jones, "The Elephant's Child as Caregiver," *Beginnings* (Redmond, WA: Exchange Press, PO Box 2890, Redmond, Washington 98073, (206) 883-9394), 1986), p. 10.

Carol Hillman: Gardener, Naturalist, Teacher[2]

I believe deeply that what you are outside of school affects what you are in school. I have a farm in Massachusetts that has for many years been a resource to me and to the children in my classroom.

There I grow things, looking after the whole process myself. I like having the knowledge that I can grow vegetables or flowers without relying on chemicals. The flowers are just as important as the edible things. I pick and dry many of them, making everlasting bouquets from them. The whole process gives me a feeling of self-sufficiency and a kind of calmness.

Those feelings translate to the classroom in ways that you might not suspect. I come to the classroom with a keen sense of the pleasure it can be to do with what you have, without having to go out and buy things. I try to show the children those same pleasures. We make bird feeders from cups and chenille-wrapped wire. They take the feeders home and have a season's worth of birds coming and going. For me, that is much better than robots, superheroes, or transformers.

Growing things takes attention—you are constantly watching what needs water, what needs thinning, what can be picked. I want to communicate that awareness to children. Every morning we have a meeting, and I ask them what they notice that is different. Almost every day we go outdoors, not just to a playground, but to the woods that surround us on practically all sides. I want the children to become investigators in the natural world: I want them to be curious about the stream, the trees, and the leaves on the ground.

Something else is fed by growing things—my aesthetic sense, a love for beautiful arrangements, shapes, and colors. Many years ago, on my first job after college, I worked at an art gallery in New York City and learned, among other things, how to hang an exhibition. Since then, I have carried with me the importance of placement, whether I am placing blocks on a shelf or plants in a garden.

That, too, carries over to the classroom. The blocks, the baskets of parquetry blocks, the puzzles and pegboards must each stand apart to command their own space and importance. What I am after is a sense of order, not a strict cleanliness—children need messiness, too.

But beyond that sense of order, my experiences in gardens and the wider outdoors have given me a taste for naturally beautiful things. Rather than stickers or predrawn forms, the children in my classes make collages from shells and sand, sweetgum pods, the bright orange berries of bittersweet vines, acorns, and pine cones.

Outside my garden, the most important part of my life as a part-time naturalist is raising monarch butterflies. For a number of years, I've worked with Dr. Fred Urquart of Toronto,

---

[2]Reprinted with permission from Carol Hillman, "Teachers and Then Some: Profiles of Three Teachers," *Beginnings* (Redmond, WA: Exchange Press, PO Box 2890, Redmond, Washington 98073, (206) 883-9394), 1986), pp. 21-22.

who was trying to locate the hidden spot where monarchs migrate during the winter months. I've been a part of that search by raising, tagging, and releasing butterflies. Only a few years ago, after a lifetime of tracking the butterflies marked by many people such as myself, Urquart was able to locate the monarch's wintering spot high in the mountains near Mexico City.

I have a whole portion of my garden devoted to milkweed, which is the sole food source for monarchs. I find the small caterpillars on the plants and take them into school. During the first few weeks of school each year, the children and I watch the whole metamorphosis—from caterpillar, through chrysalis, to full butterfly. We keep the monarchs in a huge butterfly case for a few days after they emerge. Then, on warm, blue sky days, children take turns holding and releasing the monarchs into the air. It is probably a moment they won't forget.

Taking a Look at Yourself

I think I'm really good at:

_____
_____
_____
_____

I really enjoy:

_____
_____
_____
_____

I can share my interests and skills with infants and toddlers in the following ways:

_____
_____
_____
_____

I would like to be better at:

_____
_____
_____
_____

I would like to know more about:

_____
_____
_____
_____

Discuss your responses with two colleagues. Have they learned anything new about you? Do they see things that you did not see? Use the space below to write what you learned from doing this exercise.

_____
_____
_____
_____

Standards of the Child Care Profession

Every profession sets standards for performance. Your center has defined administrative policies and procedures. In addition, the child care profession has several statements of standards. You should become familiar with all of them. These standards are not intended to restrict you. Effective caregivers are always prepared to adjust daily routines to meet individual children's needs and interests. These standards act as guides. In using them, you, other early childhood professionals, and parents can confirm that you are providing high-quality care.

Several documents are accepted by the early childhood profession as indicators of professional work. Reviewing these documents can help you evaluate your performance.

- The *Child Development Associate (CDA) Competency Standards* define 13 skill areas needed by early childhood staff. Caregivers who master the skill areas can earn a credential that is based on performance with infants and toddlers rather than on formal training. The competency standards also serve as guidelines for caregivers who are not seeking a CDA credential but want to improve their child care skills.

- *Accreditation Criteria and Procedures of the National Association for the Education of Young Children* is NAEYC's accreditation position statement. The program, administered by the National Academy of Early Childhood Programs, is the largest and most widely recognized voluntary accreditation system for early childhood programs. This position statement offers criteria for high-quality early childhood programs in ten categories. Centers are accredited through a three-step process that includes self-study, a validation visit, and a commission review and decison.

- The publication *Developmentally Appropriate Practice in Early Childhood Programs,* Rev. ed., developed by NAEYC, gives guidelines for the kinds of practices that are suitable for children at particular ages and stages of development. Appropriate activities and teaching practices are outlined for children from infancy through age 8.

Reviewing these documents and completing the self-assessments for each of the self-instructional modules in *Caring for Infants and Toddlers* should give you a comprehensive picture of your skills and capabilities. This review will also identify areas you need to know more about and skills you need to develop or improve.

Obtain a copy of NAEYC's *Developmentally Appropriate Practice* statement and review the section on programs for infants and toddlers. (NAEYC has a toll-free number you can call: 1-800-424-2460.) Write a paragraph about one aspect that is particularly meaningful to you. Discuss how this statement relates to what you do in your classroom.

_____

_____

_____

_____

_____

_____

_____

_____

_____

_____

_____

_____

_____

_____

_____

_____

_____

_____

Discuss your statement with your trainer.

II. Continuing to Learn About Caring for Infants and Toddlers

In this activity you will learn:

- to continue to expand your knowledge and skills; and

- to make short- and long-range professional development plans.

No matter how many years you have been working with young children or how much you already know, it is important to continue to learn more about your profession. This is true for a number of reasons.

- **There is always new information to be learned.** Professionals need to keep up with the latest developments in the field. New research often leads to new, more effective strategies for working with children. Learning and growth are ongoing for the child care professional.

- **Continual learning makes you an active, thinking person.** Caregivers who also are always learning new things are more interesting people and are more likely to inspire the children in their care. If you enjoy learning, you are more likely to help others enjoy it, too. Caregivers who keep learning always have new ideas to bring to the center.

- **You care about children.** Each article or book you read and every discussion or conference you participate in may give you new insights or help you resolve nagging problems. Suppose, for example, that an infant or toddler with special needs joins your group. You may have to learn new ways to meet this child's needs. Because you care about all young children, you are always alert for new and helpful information relating to their development.

- **You want to grow professionally.** A commitment to continue learning can lead to improved performance. Learning can not only result in an increased feeling of confidence but may also lead to more responsibility, a higher position, and more pay.

How can caregivers continue growing and learning? In addition to participating in this self-instructional training program, there are many other ways you can continue learning. You might:

- join professional organizations;

- read books and articles;

- network with other professionals in the field;

Joining Professional Organizations

Professional organizations help you keep up to date on the latest information and current issues in the profession. These organizations offer newsletters, books, brochures, and other publications with useful information and helpful tips. Their conferences provide a way to meet others with similar interests and concerns. Many organizations have local affiliates that meet regularly. The following are descriptions of some of the major professional organizations in the child care profession.

Association for Childhood Education International (ACEI)
17904 Georgia Avenue, Suite 215
Olney, MD 20832
(301) 570-2111
(800) 423-3563
www.udel.edu/bateman/acei

ACEI, established in 1892, is dedicated to the dual mission of promoting the inherent rights, education, and well-being of children from infancy through early adolescence, and the professional development of educators and others working on behalf of these children. ACEI publishes the professional journals *Childhood Education* and *The Journal of Research in Childhood Education*, plus books, newsletters, and audio and videotapes. ACEI also sponsors annual international conferences.

Center for the Child Care Workforce (CCW)
A Project of the AFT Educational Foundation
555 New Jersey Avenue, NW
Washington, DC 20001
202-662-8005
www.ccw.org

CCW, founded in 1978 as the Child Care Employee Project, focuses on issues important to child care workers. Since November 2002, CCW has been a project of the American Federation of Teachers Educational Foundation (ATEF). As an ATEF project, CCW will continue to advocate for and assemble resources for improving early childhood worker wages, workplace environments, and staff development. The programs that CCW developed in leadership and management training will continue to be offered by other cooperating organizations; for details, visit the CCW web site. CCW publications (free and for-fee) on issues in the child care workplace also remain available from its web site. Historical note: between 1994 and 1997, CCW was known as the National Center for the Early Childhood Work Force.

Council for Early Childhood Professional Recognition
2460 16th Street, NW
Washington, DC 20009-3575
(202) 265-9090
(800) 424-4310
www.cdacouncil.org

The Council—established in 1985 as The Council for Early Childhood Professional Recognition—is the national credentialing program in early child care. Its goal is to professionalize the early child care field by assessing, improving, and recognizing the skills of educators and caregivers. To this end, the Council offers training and workshops and awards two credentials: the Child Development Associate (CDA) credential to professionals who care for children from birth through 5 years of age, and the Army School-Age Credential (ASA) to Army school-age child care providers. Council publications include the newsletter *Council News & Views*, training and study guides, and the *National Directory of Early Childhood Teacher Preparation Institutions*, Fourth Edition.

National Association for the Education of Young Children (NAEYC)
1509 16th Street, NW
Washington, DC 20036-1426
(202) 232-8777
(800) 424-2460
www.naeyc.org

NAEYC, established in 1926, is the nation's largest and most influential organization of early childhood educators and others dedicated to improving the quality of programs for children from birth through third grade. Together with its local affiliates, NAEYC does public policy/outreach on behalf of young children and offers professional development to their educators and caregivers. Publications include *Young Children*—a journal for early childhood professionals, *Early Years Are Learning Years*—a collection of one-page articles on current topics of interest, books, reports, and other materials. The NAEYC annual conference combines a broad variety of workshops with the opportunity for professional networking and socializing. NAEYC's Professional Development Institute offers more in-depth study of issues in early childhood.

National Association of Child Care Resource and Referral Agencies (NACCRRA)
1319 F. Street, NW, Suite 500
Washington, DC 20004-1106
(202) 393-5501
www.naccrra.org

NACCRRA is a non-profit association of community-based child care resource and referral (CCR&R) agencies and child care advocates. NACCRRA services include an annual conference, regional staff development institutes, and coverage on its web site of events, research, and employment opportunities in the early childhood field. NACCRRA also administers the Child Care Aware® Consumer Education Quality Assurance Program, which provides voluntary accreditation for child care providers and information resources for families seeking child care.

National Black Child Development Institute (NBCDI)
1101 15th St NW Suite 900
Washington, DC 20005
(202) 833-2220
www.nbcdi.org

The mission of NBCDI, founded in 1970, is to improve and protect the quality of life of African-American children and families. Programs include early childhood advocacy, legislative monitoring, and outreach within the African-American and Latino communities. NBCDI affiliate programs support local communities with advocacy, training, and other information. For the list of affiliates (26 cities/18 states as of January 2003) and their contact information, visit the NBCDI web site. NBCDI publishes the quarterly newsletter *Child Health Talk (CHT),* and the biannual newsmagazine *Black Child Advocate (BCA). CHT* discusses parenting and child development issues, with a focus on African-American experiences. *BCA* covers current Congressional legislative activity and voting records, recently published books, and public health data affecting African-American children.

ZERO TO THREE: The National Center for Infants, Toddlers and Families
2000 M Street, NW Suite 200
Washington, DC 20036-3307
(202) 638-1144
(800) 899-4301 for publications
www.zerotothree.org

This nonprofit organization offers high-level advocacy and support to the professionals serving infants and toddlers and their families. From its establishment in 1977, Zero to Three has taken a multidisciplinary approach, drawing on knowledge in child development, medicine, mental health, and scientific research to gather and disseminate information on very young children. Zero to Three also supports community projects and public policy outreach. The annual National Training Institute promotes professional networking and sharing the latest developments in the field. Zero to Three publications include its highly-regarded bimonthly newsletter *Zero to Three*, plus books, studies, and policy reports. Zero to Three is not a membership organization in the traditional sense (having a national group plus local affiliates), but as a resource/research organization it offers many opportunities for professional growth.

Reading Books and Articles

Books and articles help you expand your knowledge and skills. You can review articles or chapters in a book during lunch or at home. A Bibliography of helpful resources can be found in the Orientation in Volume I. You can also borrow materials from the public library in your community.

Networking

Networking is spending time with people who perform similar tasks to share ideas, information, and experiences. It is a good way to find solutions to problems, gain new knowledge, or help colleagues cope with difficult situations. You can network with one other person or with a group. Group networks can include other child care professionals in the local community or in the state. Meetings can be very informal, perhaps after work or on a Saturday. They can also be formal, with speakers and an agenda. What is important is that caregivers meet, share ideas, and get support in coping with the demands of their jobs.

Observing Other Caregivers

You can learn a lot by visiting the room of another caregiver, either in your center or at another child care program. Because each caregiver is unique, you can observe others and learn new approaches to solving discipline problems, managing a transition time, or coping with feeding three hungry children at one time.

Participating in Training

Training is another way to keep up to date in the child care field and develop new skills. You can attend courses offered by community groups. County extension agencies offer nutrition courses, and public school adult-education programs offer courses on a wide range of topics. College or university courses may also be an option. Your participation in this 1 self-instructional training program will enhance your knowledge of child development and your child care skills. It is an example of your professionalism.

Begin this learning activity by reviewing your answers on page 325, "Taking a Look at Yourself." Pick one item from your responses to "I would like to be better at" or "I would like to know more about." Consider the sources of assistance available to you: the public library, workshops, professional organizations, your supervisor, and other colleagues. Identify what specific resources can help you with the task or topic you have selected. Use the form on the next page to list what you find.

I want to improve or learn more about:

_____

_____

_____

_____

_____

_____

_____

_____

Resources I can use:

SOURCE	CONTACT PERSON
Public library	
Workshops	
Professional organizations	
Supervisor/colleagues	

Making Plans for Continued Learning

Now that you have identified resources to help you in an area you want to work on, you need to plan how and when to use those resources. When you develop a plan, you clarify what you want to achieve—your goal—and how you will go about achieving it. With a written plan in front of you, you feel like you're already making progress. And you are! Knowing where you're going and how you're going to get there makes it easier to take each step and to recognize your goal when you reach it. As you take each step and check it off on your plan, you can visualize your movement toward your goal.

You can improve your skills in the following ways:

- Take advantage of opportunities that come your way. Attend workshops and training offered by your center or other groups.

- Use other caregivers as resources, and offer yourself to them as a resource. Consult your supervisor about theoretical issues and practical concerns. Share your ideas with other caregivers.

- Review how you manage your time. If you look closely at how you spend each day, you may find some time-wasting activities. Finding ways to do things faster or better may leave extra time for reading, studying, and reassessing how you are doing in your work.

- Set specific goals for yourself. Try to do something on a regular basis to fulfill them.

In Learning Activity I, Assessing Yourself, you identified skills you would like to improve. You also identified skills that you're good at. The chart you just completed helped you think about resources that are readily available to you. Use the results of these two activities to make plans for your professional development. For the short term you may want to focus on skills you think most need improving. For the long term you may want to build on an area you are strong in and become even more skilled—so that you can share your competence with others while you increase your self-confidence.

In this learning activity you will make some short- and long-range plans for yourself. Then you will identify possible barriers and decide how to overcome them. Read the example on the following page and fill out the chart that follows.

Plans for Professional Development
(Example)

Short-Range Plans

What would I like to do right away to improve my skills?

- *Take a course on how to guide mobile infants' and toddlers' behavior.*
- *Learn more activities for infants to do outside.*
- *Complete Module 8, Self.*

What barriers might hinder me from completing these plans?

- *It's hard to find time to complete the module activities and still care for children.*
- *I can't find any resources on the reasons for mobile infants' behavior.*

What can I do to overcome these barriers?

- *I can talk with other caregivers about trading some responsibilities so we can all have more time to work on the modules.*
- *I'll send away to NAEYC for two brochures: "Helping Children Learn Self-Control" and "Love and Learn: Discipline for Young Children."*

Long-Range Plans

What would I like to be doing a year from now?

- *Begin working on a degree in early childhood education.*
- *Join one professional association.*
- *Complete the self-instructional modules.*
- *Advance one grade on the pay scale.*

What barriers might hinder me from completing these plans?

- *I have no money to attend school.*
- *My spouse may be transferred to a new place before I finish.*

What can I do to overcome these barriers?

- *I can take one or two courses at a time rather than a full load.*
- *I can find out about loans that might be available for going to school.*
- *I can find names of colleges and universities where I might transfer credits if I relocate.*

On the form below, make some short- and long-range plans. Think about barriers that might keep you from completing those plans and ways to overcome them.

Plans for Professional Development

Short-Range Plans

What would I like to do right away to improve my skills?

_____

_____

_____

_____

What barriers might hinder me from completing these plans?

_____

_____

_____

_____

What can I do to overcome these barriers?

_____

_____

_____

_____

Long-Range Plans

What would I like to be doing a year from now?

_____

_____

_____

What barriers might hinder me from completing these plans?

_____

_____

_____

_____

What can I do to overcome these barriers?

_____

_____

_____

_____

Discuss your plans with your trainer. What barriers can you overcome? Agree on an overall plan to achieve your goals, both short and long term.

III. Applying Professional Ethics at All Times

In this activity you will learn:

- what it means to act in a professional manner; and

- to identify professional behavior.

As discussed in Learning Activities I and II, being a professional involves assessing one's knowledge and skills and continually building on them. But professionalism is more than having expertise. It has to do with how you apply your knowledge and skills daily as you work with parents, children, and staff. It means doing your job to the best of your ability. And it involves your actions in the child care setting and in the community.

Professionals need to do what is right rather than what is easy. Practicing professionals are committed to doing what is best for all children in their care, on every occasion. Here are some examples.

ETHICS OF CAREGIVING	PROFESSIONAL BEHAVIOR	UNPROFESSIONAL BEHAVIOR
Maintaining confidentality about children and their families. Avoiding talking to other parents about a particular child, especially in front of that child.	Discussing a child's problem confidentially with another caregiver or the supervisor and trying to identify ways to help the child. "Ms. Kim, sometimes Ms. Gabriel brings Tommy to the center in dirty clothes. We need to discuss the situation with our supervisor."	Talking about a child in front of the child or with a parent other than the child's. "Did you see what that child was wearing? I'm glad you don't dress your child in rags."
Being honest, dependable, and reliable in performing duties. Being regular in attendance and performance. Coming to work on time, returning from breaks on time, and performing duties on schedule.	Arriving at work every day on time and performing assigned duties. "I'll be ready to go home just as soon as I finish wiping down these tables."	Calling in sick unnecessarily, arriving late, or not doing assigned duties. Paying more attention to adults in the center than to children. "You'll have to watch these babies yourself. I have to go call my girlfriend."

ETHICS OF CAREGIVING	PROFESSIONAL BEHAVIOR	UNPROFESSIONAL BEHAVIOR
Treating parents with respect even during difficult situations.	Talking to a parent who always comes late about the problem this causes and discussing possible solutions. "Ms. Lowell, our center closes at 6:30. If you can't get here by then, who is authorized to pick up Jennifer?"	Getting angry at a parent who is late and demanding that he or she do better. Talking to other parents or acquaintances outside the center about parents. "This is the third time you've been late this week. Don't you know I need to go home, too?"
Treating each child with respect regardless of gender, culture, or background. Treating each child as an individual; avoiding comparisons.	Comforting a child who is hurt or upset. Including activities and materials that reflect the cultures and backgrounds of all children.	Teasing children if they cry. Asking one child to behave just like another child. "Why can't you go potty like Timothy does?"
Making sure activities, practices, and routines are developmentally appropriate.	Talking with parents about appropriate activities for their child's stage of development.	Making all children do the same activities or meeting all children's needs on a strict schedule. "Wake up, Damian, it's time for everyone to eat. You've been sleeping long enough."
Providing a good model for learning and for language and communication skills. Using good grammar and sentence structure. Never using profanities in front of children.	Pronouncing words correctly. Using complete sentences when talking with children. "Free play is over now. It's time for everyone to pick up the toys."	Using poor grammar, slang, or profanity with children. "No more time to mess around. Pick up the toys now."

ETHICS OF CAREGIVING	PROFESSIONAL BEHAVIOR	UNPROFESSIONAL BEHAVIOR
Dressing to do the job. Being conscious of dress, grooming, and hygiene.	Wearing comfortable clean clothes so that you can play with and care for children: clothes you can sit on the floor in, bend and lift in, and move quickly in when necessary. "I like your new outfit, Ms. Carter. It looks comfortable and it's very flattering."	Wearing clothes that hinder movement and that you have to worry about. "You'll have to ask Ms. Peterson to help you. I can't walk on the grass in these heels."
Recording information appropriately.	Keeping good records to aid in making accurate reports to parents and the supervisor. "Lori's mother said she really likes our recordkeeping center. She can look on the chart and see what Lori's day was like."	Not taking the time to record needed information because it's too much trouble. "No one ever reads these accident reports. I'm not wasting my time filling one out."
Advocating on behalf of children, families, and others. Letting others know the importance of child care work.	Joining a professional organization. "I'm really glad I joined NAEYC. Their materials really help me be a better caregiver."	Belittling child care work as "only babysitting." "As soon as I can, I'm going to get myself a real job."

In this activity you will list examples of how your behavior conforms to the ethics of caregiving. Then you will read several case studies and identify what a professional early childhood educator should do in each situation.

ETHICS OF CAREGIVING	EXAMPLES OF YOUR OWN PROFESSIONAL BEHAVIOR
Maintaining confidentality about children and their families. Avoiding talking to other parents about a particular child, especially in front of that child.	
Being honest, dependable, and reliable in performing duties. Being regular in attendance and performance. Coming to work on time, returning from breaks on time, and performing duties on schedule.	
Treating parents with respect even during difficult situations.	
Treating each child with respect regardless of gender, culture, or background. Treating each child as an individual; avoiding comparisons.	

ETHICS OF CAREGIVING	EXAMPLES OF YOUR OWN PROFESSIONAL BEHAVIOR
Making sure activities, practices, and routines are developmentally appropriate.	
Providing a good model for learning and for language and communication skills. Using good grammar and sentence structure. Never using profanities in front of children.	
Dressing to do the job. Being conscious of dress, grooming, and hygiene.	
Recording information appropriately.	
Advocating on behalf of children, families, and others. Letting others know the importance of child care work.	

Ethical Case Studies[3]

The following situations were published by the National Association for the Education of Young Children. After reading each one, write down what you think a good early childhood educator would do. Then plan a time to discuss your responses with your trainer and a group of colleagues.

1. Case Study: The Abused Child

Mary Lou, a 2-year-old in your room, is showing the classic signs of abuse: multiple bruises, frequent black eyes, and psychological withdrawal. Her mother, a high-strung woman, says she falls a lot, but nobody at the center has noticed this. Her father twice seemed to be drunk when he picked up Mary Lou. The law says you must report suspicions of abuse to Child Protective Services. But in your experience, when the authorities get involved, they are usually unable to remove the child from the home or improve the family's behavior. Sometimes the families simply disappear, or things become worse for the children.

What should a good early childhood educator do?

_____

_____

_____

_____

2. Case Study: The Working Mother

Timothy's mother has asked you not to allow her almost 3-year-old son to nap past 1:30 in the afternoon. She says, "Whenever he naps past 1:30 he stays up until 10:00 at night. I have to get up at 5:00 in the morning to go to work. I am not getting enough sleep." Along with the rest of the toddlers, Timothy takes a 2- or 2 1/2-hour nap almost every day. He seems to need it in order to stay in good spirits in the afternoon.

What should a good early childhood educator do?

_____

_____

_____

_____

[3]Adapted with permission from Stephanie Feeney, "Ethical Case Studies for NAEYC Reader Response," _Young Children_ (Washington, DC: NAEYC, May 1987), pp. 24-25.

3. Case Study: The Aggressive Child

Eric is a large and extremely active 18-month-old who often frightens and hurts mobile infants and even older toddlers. You have discussed this repeatedly with the director, who is sympathetic but unable to help. The parents listen but feel that the behavior is typical for boys his age. A specialist from the Department of Mental Health has observed the child, but her recommendations have not helped either. Meanwhile, Eric terrorizes other children, and parents are starting to complain. You are becoming stressed and tired, and your patience is wearing thin. You and your co-caregiver are spending so much time dealing with Eric that you are worried that the other children are not getting the attention they need.

What should a good early childhood educator do?

_____

_____

_____

_____

4. Case Study: The "Academic" Preschool

Heather has just gone back to school to prepare for her Infant-Toddler Child Development Associate credential: she has been assigned as your trainee. She has taught in the 2-year-old class at a preschool for several years, is happy there, and receives a good salary. When you have observed her, you have seen 2-year-olds using coloring books. The daily program includes repetitive drill on shapes and colors. Children are regularly being "taught" the alphabet and rote counting to 10. You have also noticed that most interactions are initiated by adults and that children have few opportunities to interact with materials.

You mention to Heather that you do not think the school's curriculum is appropriate for toddlers. She replies that she had a similar reaction when she began working there but that the director and other caregivers assured her there was no problem with the curriculum. They told her that this is the way they have always taught at the school. The parents are very satisfied with it.

What should a good early childhood educator do?

_____

_____

_____

_____

When you have completed these case studies, plan a time to discuss your responses with your trainer and other caregivers. These are difficult situations to handle, and it will help you to discuss your ideas with others.

IV. Becoming an Advocate for Children and Families

In this activity you will learn:

- to recognize the importance of being involved in advocacy for children and families; and

- to become involved in advocacy efforts.

Early childhood educators are directly affected by local and national policies and programs for children and families. Therefore, becoming an advocate on behalf of high-quality programs for children and families is part of being a professional.

Advocacy is working for change. This often means taking the opportunity to speak out on issues that may be affecting the children and families in your program or on issues that affect your own working conditions.

How You Can Become an Advocate[4]

A first step in becoming an early childhood advocate is to understand the importance of advocacy. This means recognizing how public and private policies affect children's lives and accepting that children need a strong voice to ensure that the programs they attend support their development. Advocates must ask themselves: "What can I do to ensure adequate attention to children's needs by policymakers, elected officials, administrators, schools, businesses, and other groups?" Answering this question, however, requires making a commitment to act.

Advocacy efforts try to improve the circumstances of children's lives so they get what they need to grow to their full potential. Early childhood educators are especially well informed on this issue from both theory and practice. Early childhood advocates commit themselves to sharing this knowledge with others. They act on what they know; they move beyond good intentions and take action. Advocates overcome the fear of becoming involved. They realize that children's problems are a collective responsibility. They take the crucial, transforming step from concern to action.

As early childhood educators, we expand our commitment to children, families, and our profession when we act on our beliefs and share our knowledge with others. Early childhood educators can contribute to advocacy in six ways.

---

[4]Adapted with permission from Stacie G. Goffin and Joan Lombardi, *Speaking Out: Early Childhood Advocacy* (Washington, DC: National Association for the Education of Young Children, 1988), pp. 2-5.

Contribution 1: Sharing Our Knowledge

Our beliefs and knowledge are based on an understanding of child development, the practice of early childhood education, and relationships with parents. Therefore, we can make important contributions to policy debates about the developmental needs of children and the characteristics of safe and nurturing early childhood environments. This is our professional knowledge base. We need to assume responsibility for sharing these understandings with parents, policymakers, and other decisionmakers. We can help decisionmakers focus on the role of policy in enhancing children's development. In these ways our advocacy efforts can become a catalyst for change.

Contribution 2: Sharing Our Professional Experiences

We work with children and their families daily. We experience firsthand the impact of changing circumstances—such as unemployment, lack of child care, inappropriate curricula, and conflicts between work and family—before decisionmakers are informed that these issues are "new trends." When children and families in our programs receive services from public and private agencies, we are firsthand observers and monitors of whether children's needs are being met. As a result, we have the opportunity—and a professional responsibility—to share the personal stories that give meaning to group statistics. Without sharing confidential information, we can describe how policies affect children and families.

Personal experiences help us become more persuasive. We live these stories in our day-to-day work with children and families.

Contribution 3: Redefining the "Bottom Line" for Children

The debate about programs for young children is often tied to other policy issues such as welfare, job training, and teenage pregnancy. Funding for children's programs is often seen as an investment directed toward children's future productivity. Joining children's issues with broader political issues and social concerns is an effective political technique. These strategies can expand our base of support and help frame children's issues in ways consistent with many of society's accepted values.

Our unique perspectives on children, however, also enable us to speak out for children's inherent "worth." We know that childhood is a meaningful time for development in its own right. If policies for children and families are made solely on the basis of "return on investment," children will suffer when investors seek a higher return or decide to pull out of the "market." Early childhood educators must remember that these investment strategies are means to achieve a desired end. They must not become so effective that they undermine the "bottom line" of early childhood advocacy—encouraging policies that promote children's development.

Contribution 4: Standing Up for Our Profession

Early childhood is growing as a profession. We know how important our jobs are to children and their families. Therefore, we must speak out on behalf of caregiving and early childhood education as a profession and for the special expertise needed to be a professional.

Many people are unaware that early childhood education has a distinctive, professional knowledge base. We know that the quality of early childhood programs depends on the training and compensation of the staff providing the care and education. Early educators know firsthand about the impact of low wages, high staff turnover, burnout, and inadequately trained staff and administrators. We are obligated to share these stories, too.

Advocacy efforts on behalf of our profession are most effective when we emphasize the benefits of our work for children and families. We must begin to exercise our power to speak out on issues that affect our profession.

Contribution 5: Involving Parents

Our daily interactions with parents provide many opportunities for us to share our common concerns and goals for children's well-being. We have a unique opportunity to help parents recognize their power as children's primary advocates—for both their own and other people's children.

Parents can be especially effective advocates on behalf of their children. Parents represent a critical consumer voice. By involving parents, we can dramatically expand the constituency speaking out for children.

Contribution 6: Expanding the Constituency for Children

Early childhood educators have important linkages with public school administrators and teachers, health care providers, religious organizations, and many other professional and volunteer groups. These interactions provide natural opportunities to inform others about the developmental needs of children, appropriate teaching practices, and the supports families need to strengthen themselves. We can act as catalysts to help others understand children's needs as our collective responsibility and our shared future.

In this activity you will identify advocacy steps that you feel you can take and develop a plan to become involved. First read "Actions Early Childhood Educators Can Take"; then answer the questions that follow the reading.

Actions Early Childhood Educators Can Take[5]

You can choose from many courses of action once you make a commitment to become an advocate for children, their families, and your profession. Here are a few of the choices:

- Share ideas for appropriate practice with other caregivers and parents (instead of just observing disapprovingly).

- Explain to administrators why dittos are inappropriate learning tools for young children (rather than using them and feeling resentful that you have to practice your profession in ways inconsistent with its knowledge base).

- Explain to parents why children learn best through play (instead of bemoaning that parents are pushing their children or giving in and teaching with inappropriate methods and materials).

- Write a letter to the editor of a newspaper or magazine to respond to an article or letter (instead of just complaining about how other people don't understand the needs of children, their families, or their caregivers).

- Write to your state or federal legislators about a pending issue and share your experiences as a way to point out needs (rather than just assuming someone else will write).

- Meet someone new who is interested in early childhood education and ask her or him to join a professional group such as NAEYC, NBCDI, SECA, or ACEI (instead of just wondering why the person isn't involved).

- Ask a friend to go with you to a legislator's town meeting (instead of staying home because you don't want to go alone).

- Volunteer to represent your professional group in a coalition to speak out on the educational needs of young children (instead of waiting to be asked or declining because you've never done it before).

- Agree to serve on a legislative telephone tree (rather than refusing because "my phone call won't matter anyway").

- Work and learn with others to develop a position statement on a critical issue (instead of saying "I don't really know much about this topic").

- Volunteer to speak at a school board meeting about NAEYC's Position Statement *Developmentally Appropriate Practice in Early Childhood Programs, Revised Edition* (instead of resigning yourself to the fact that your school system doesn't understand much about early childhood education).

---

[5]Reprinted with permission from Stacie G. Goffin and Joan Lombardi, *Speaking Out: Early Childhood Advocacy* (Washington, DC: National Association for the Education of Young Children, 1988), pp. 14-15.

kids

- Conduct a local or state survey of salaries in early childhood programs (instead of ignoring the issue because no one has the facts).

- Persuade colleagues that it is important to work toward accreditation from the National Academy of Early Childhood Programs (rather than assuming no one wants to improve the program).

A Plan to Become an Advocate

1. Which activity listed in the reading is of most interest to you?

_____

_____

_____

_____

_____

2. Why is it often difficult to speak out on these issues?

_____

_____

_____

_____

_____

3. How do you think you could become more involved in speaking out for young children, families, and the profession?

_____

_____

_____

_____

_____

Discuss your responses with your trainer.

V. Taking Care of Yourself

In this activity you will learn:

- to recognize the importance of taking care of yourself; and

- to take care of yourself physically, emotionally, socially, and intellectually.

Although your first responsibility as a caregiver is to take care of the needs of children, you also have a responsibility to take care of yourself. The most important resource you have to give children is yourself—your caring, your energy, and your commitment. You cannot do this when you are not at your best. To teach young children, you need to be in good physical and emotional health. You also need to feel that you are appreciated, meaningfully connected to others, intellectually stimulated, and performing a job worth doing.

Taking care of yourself means considering your needs and well-being in four areas: physical, emotional, social, and intellectual.

Your Physical Well-Being

Health is very important to a person who cares for infants and toddlers. Without physical stamina, good health, and a good diet, a caregiver is not adequately prepared to work with young children for long hours every day. Physical well-being is influenced by three key factors: good diet, adequate rest, and regular exercise. Taking care of your physical well-being means being sure you eat foods that are good for you, get enough rest, and exercise several times a week.

Your Emotional Well-Being

The way you feel about yourself, your work, and the world affects how you interact with the children and adults around you. The more positive you feel about yourself, the better you will be able to care for young children. When you start to feel worried or depressed, it is good to talk with family and friends about your concerns.

Your Social Well-Being

Having people to talk to is essential for survival. A trusted person with whom to share your joys, frustrations, and ideas can be very important in determining how you feel about yourself as a person and as a caregiver. The person may be a colleague, spouse, relative, or friend. What is important is that you have someone (at least one, but preferably several people) with whom you can exchange ideas, feelings, resources, and moral support.

Your Intellectual Well-Being

Most adults enjoy learning something new and being challenged. Like children, adults need to continue to explore, experiment, and learn. Your learning can be about job-related issues such as child development and about other topics as well.

In this learning activity you will assess how well you are taking care of yourself. Record your activities for two days. For Day 1 record your activities for today. Review your answers, note areas where you could take better care of yourself, and try to improve your schedule tomorrow. Record that schedule under Day 2.

	DAY 1	DAY 2
Physical Well-Being		
Did I eat three balanced meals?	_____	_____
How much sleep did I get? (Is that average?)	_____	_____
Did I get any exercise?	_____	_____
Emotional Well-Being		
Did I have a generally positive outlook?	_____	_____
Did I take a few moments to relax after a stressful situation?	_____	_____
Social Well-Being		
Did I spend time with someone I care about?	_____	_____
Did I talk through a day's problem with a friend or colleague?	_____	_____
Intellectual Well-Being		
Did I read anything for information or interest—a book, an article, the newspaper?	_____	_____
Did I learn something new?	_____	_____

Discuss this activity with your trainer and make a commitment to take good care of yourself. Use the space below to note what actions you will take.

I will do the following things to take care of myself:

_____

_____

_____

_____

_____

_____

_____

_____

_____

_____

Summarizing Your Progress

You have now completed all of the learning activities for this module. Whether you are an experienced caregiver or a new one, this module has probably helped you maintain a commitment to professionalism. Before you go on, review your responses to the pre-training assessment for this module. Write a summary of what you learned, and list the skills you developed or improved.

Your final step in this module is to complete the knowledge and competency assessments. Let your trainer know when you are ready to schedule the assessments. After you have successfully completed these assessments, you will be ready to start a new module. Congratulations on your progress so far, and good luck with your next module.

Answer Sheet: Maintaining a Commitment to Professionalism

Continually Assessing Your Own Performance

1. **How did Ms. Lewis assess her own performance?**

   a. She thought about how the day had progressed.

   b. She considered feedback from parents.

   c. She thought about how she felt about the day's events.

2. **What did she decide to do with the results of her self-assessment?**

   a. She decided to become more organized.

   b. She decided to talk to Ms. Jackson, another caregiver, to get some pointers.

   c. She decided to talk to her supervisor to get some suggestions.

Continuing to Learn About Caring for Infants and Toddlers

1. **How did Ms. Jackson decide what knowledge and skills she should work to improve?**

   a. She completed a self-assessment.

   b. She talked with Ms. Bates, her supervisor, to identify areas for improvement.

   c. She set specific goals.

2. **How did Ms. Jackson plan to expand her existing knowledge and skills?**

   a. She selected a module to review.

   b. She planned to attend in-service training.

   c. She planned an observation and feedback visit from Ms. Bates.

   d. She scheduled a follow-up meeting with Ms. Bates.

Applying Professional Ethics at All Times

1. **How did Mr. Jones maintain professional ethics in talking to Ms. Johnson?**

   a. He greeted the parent politely when she arrived.

   b. He responded to Ms. Johnson's comments in a positive way.

   c. He maintained confidentiality by not discussing Joshua's behavior with another parent.

2. **How did Mr. Jones interact with Joshua in a professional manner?**

   a. He acted quickly to ensure Joshua's safety.

   b. He used positive guidance techniques to redirect Joshua to a safe place for jumping.

Glossary

Competence	A skill or ability to do something well.
Ethics	A set of principles, standards, or guidelines that direct acceptable behavior—what is right or good rather than quickest or easiest.
Job description	The official written statement describing a caregiver's job.
Maintaining confidentiality	Sharing information only with people who have a right to know.
Networking	Spending time with people who perform similar tasks to share ideas, information, and experiences.
Professionalism	A commitment to gaining and maintaining knowledge and skills in a particular field, and to using that knowledge and those skills to provide the highest-quality services possible.
Professional behavior	The consistent, thorough application of knowledge and skills.